FOR ORGANS, PIANOS & ELECTRONIC KEYBOARDS

E-Z PLAY TODAY

303

THE BEST CONTEMPORARY CHRISTIAN SONGS EVER

ISBN 0-634-06849-0

HAL•LEONARD®
CORPORATION
7777 W. BLUEMOUND RD. P.O. BOX 13819 MILWAUKEE, WI 53213

Visit Hal Leonard Online at
www.halleonard.com

CONTENTS

Abba
(Father)

Registration 1
Rhythm: Rock or 8 Beat

Words and Music by Rebecca St. James,
Tedd Tjornhom and Otto Price

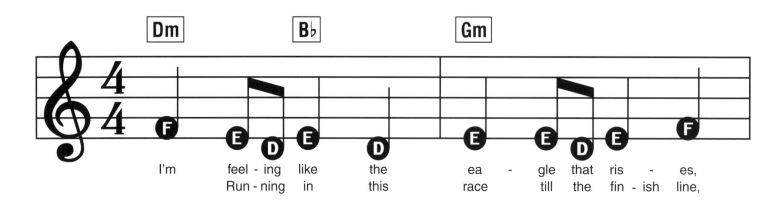

I'm feel-ing like the ea - gle that ris - es,
Run - ning in this race till the fin - ish line,

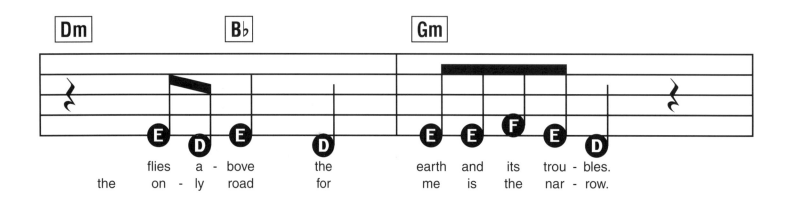

flies a - bove the earth and its trou - bles.
the on - ly road for me is the nar - row.

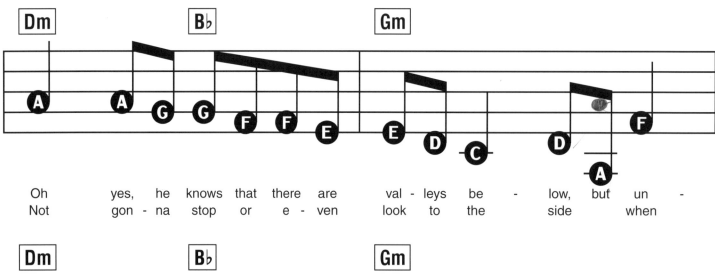

Oh yes, he knows that there are val - leys be - low, but un -
Not gon - na stop or e - ven look to the side when

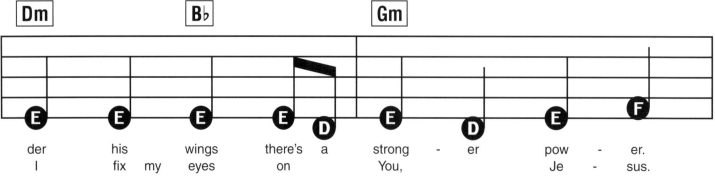

der his wings there's a strong - er pow - er.
I fix my eyes on You, Je - sus.

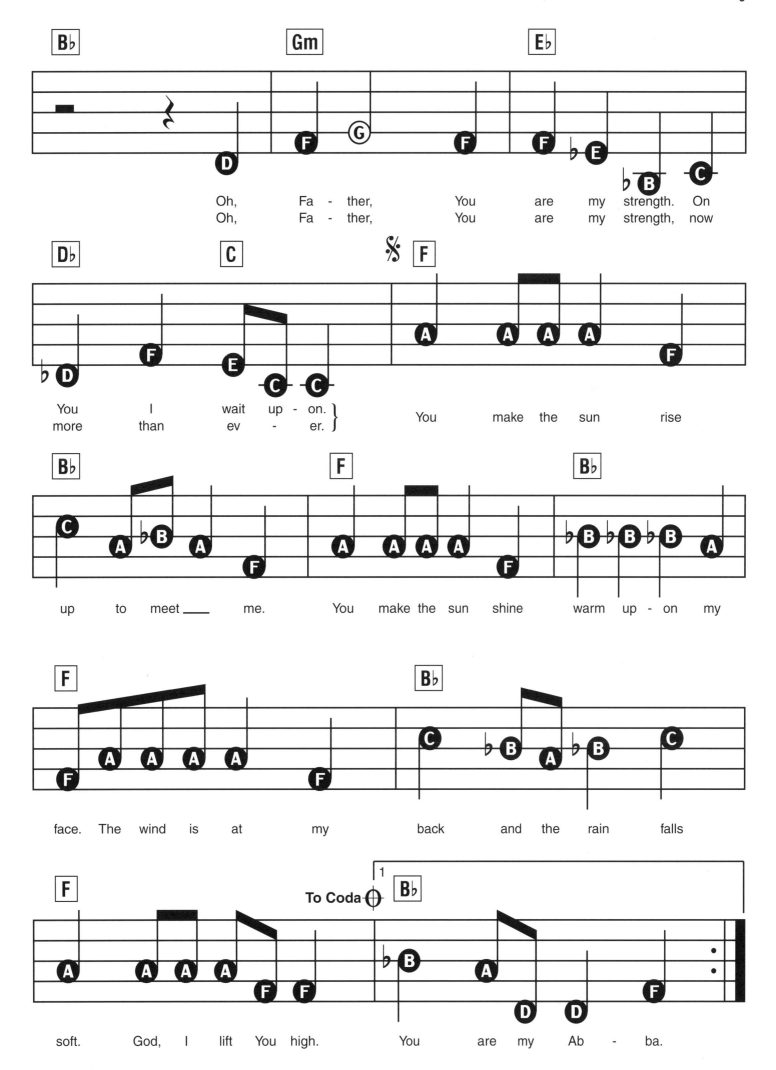

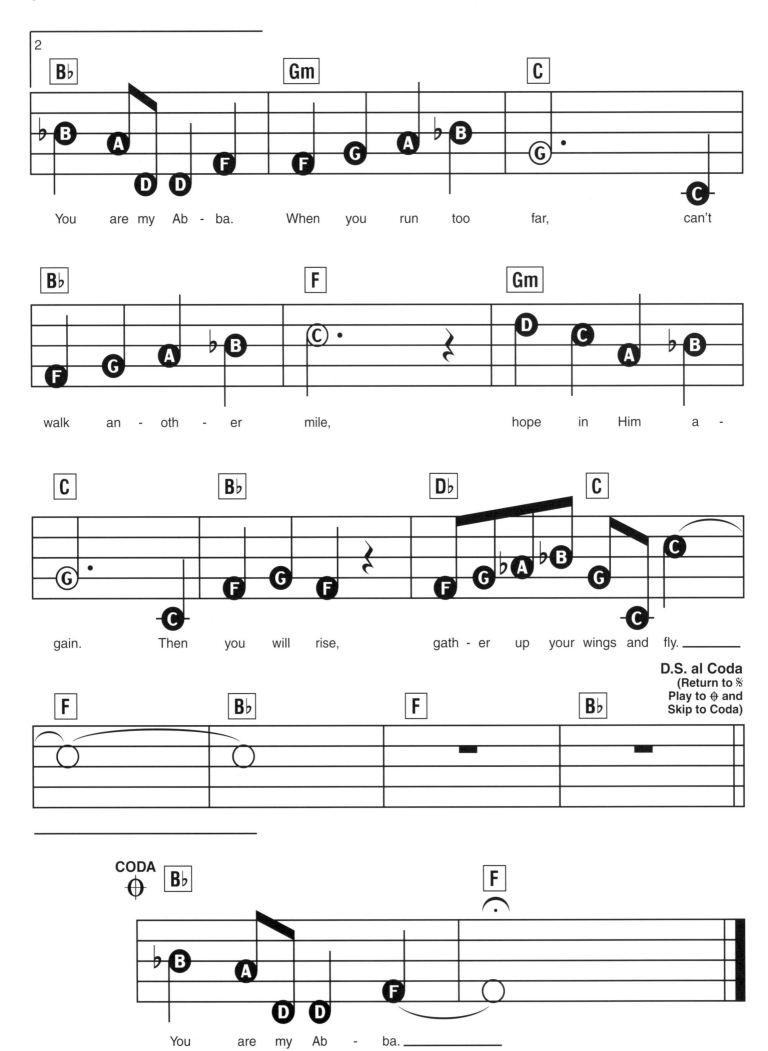

Always Have, Always Will

Registration 8
Rhythm: Pop or 8 Beat

Words and Music by Grant Cunningham,
Nick Gonzales and Toby McKeehan

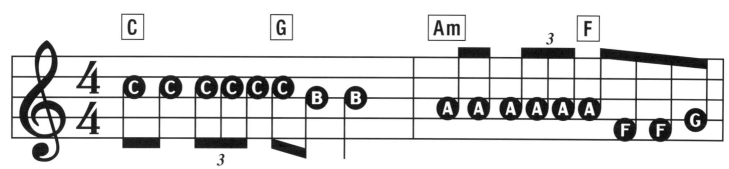

Part of me is the prod - i - gal,   part of me is the oth - er broth - er.
I   was born with a way - ward heart,   still I   live with a rest - less spir - it.

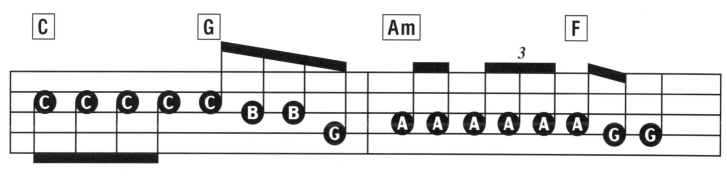

But I think the heart of me is   real - ly some - where be - tween ___ them.
My soul is so well - worn, you'd   think I'd have   ar - rived by now.

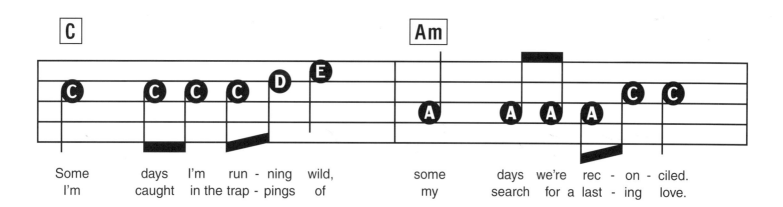

Some   days I'm run - ning wild,   some   days we're rec - on - ciled.
I'm   caught in the trap - pings of   my   search for a last - ing love.

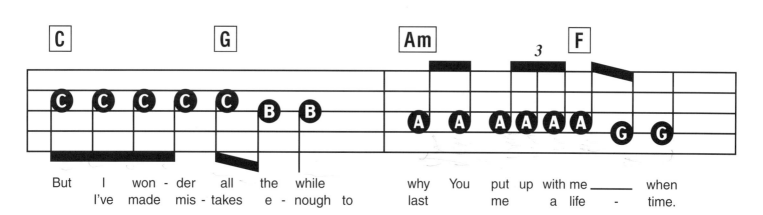

But   I won - der all the while   why You put up with me _____ when
I've made mis - takes e - nough to   last   me   a life - time.

8

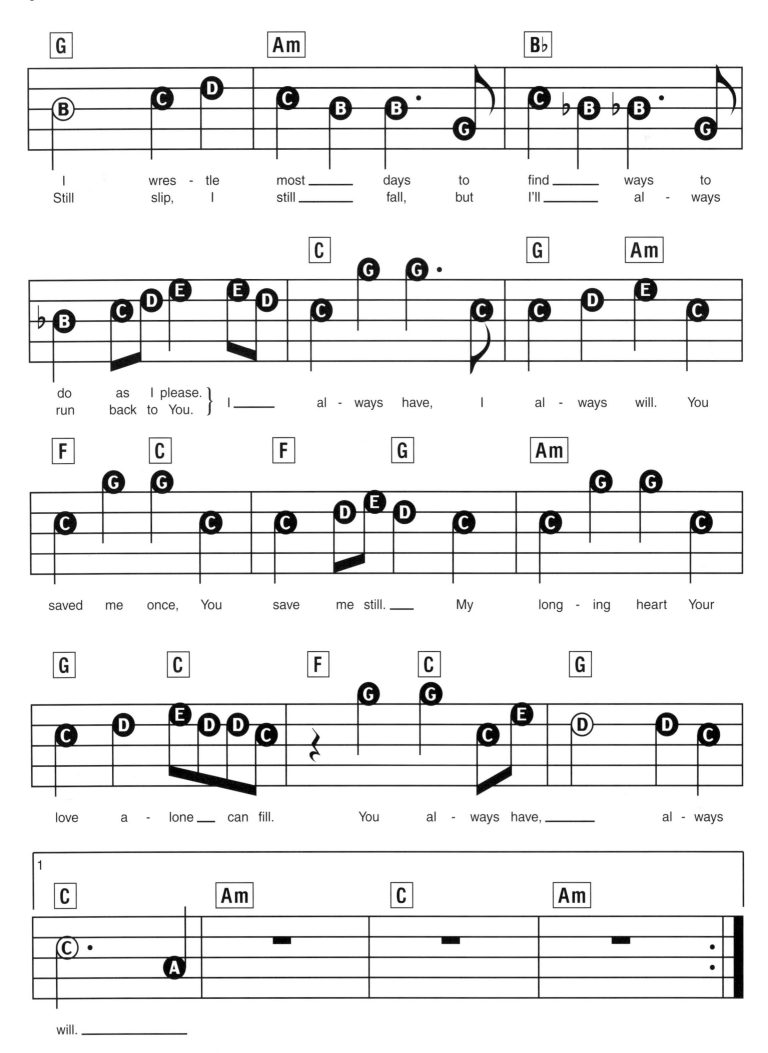

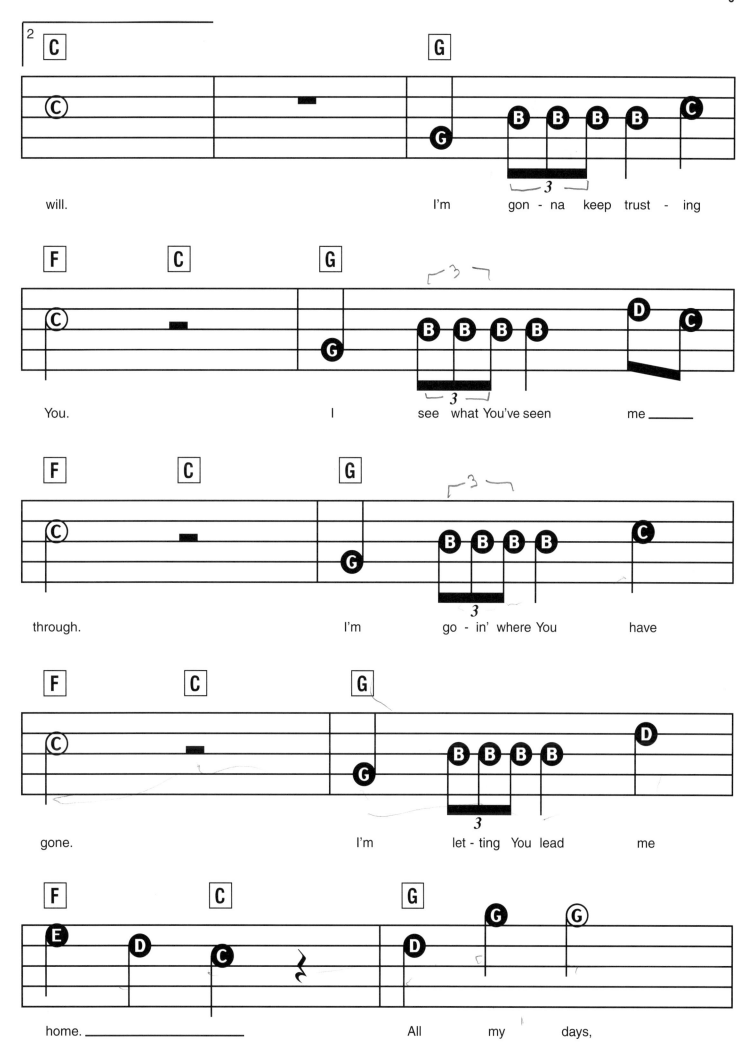

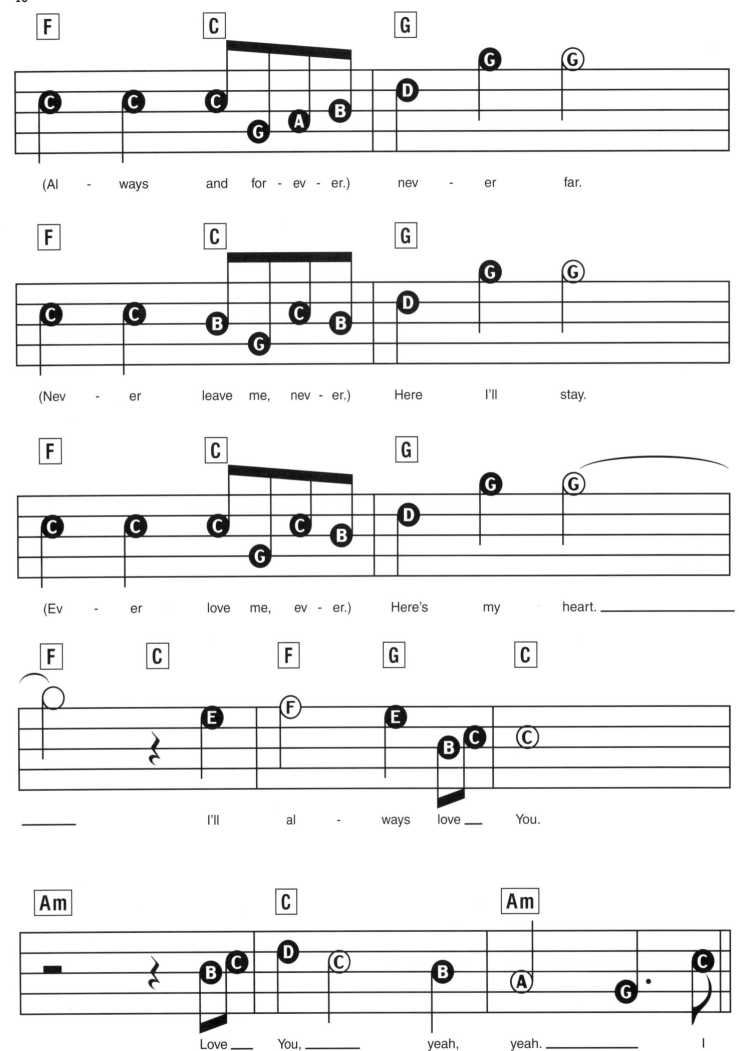

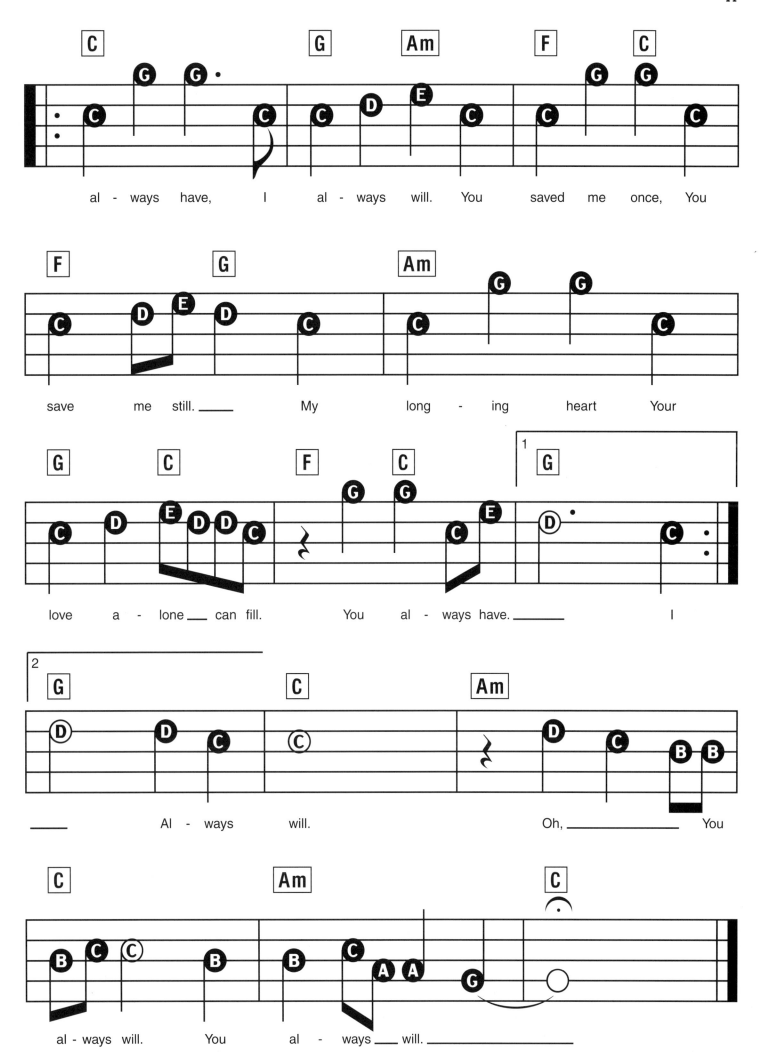

Arms of Love

Registration 8
Rhythm: Ballad

Words and Music by Amy Grant,
Michael W. Smith and Gary Chapman

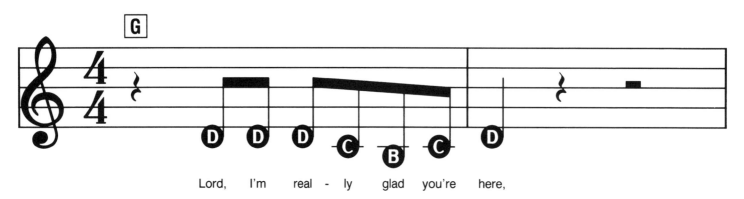

Lord, I'm real - ly glad you're here,

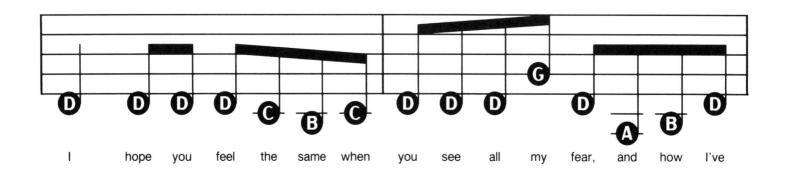

I hope you feel the same when you see all my fear, and how I've

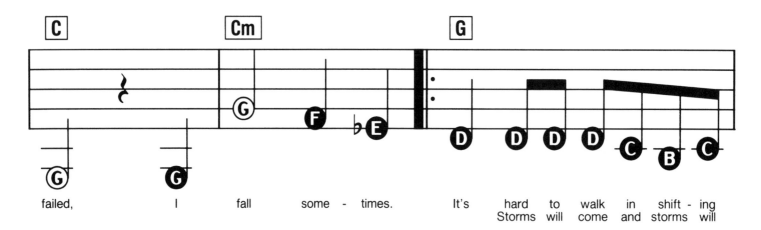

failed, I fall some - times. It's hard to walk in shift - ing
                                Storms will come and storms will

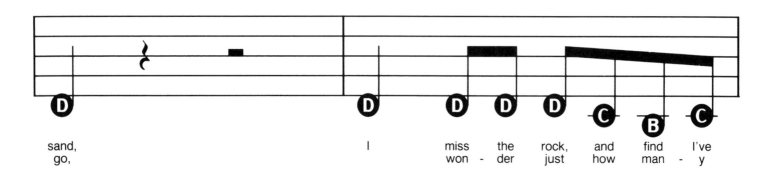

sand,   I miss the rock, and find I've
go,   won - der just how man - y

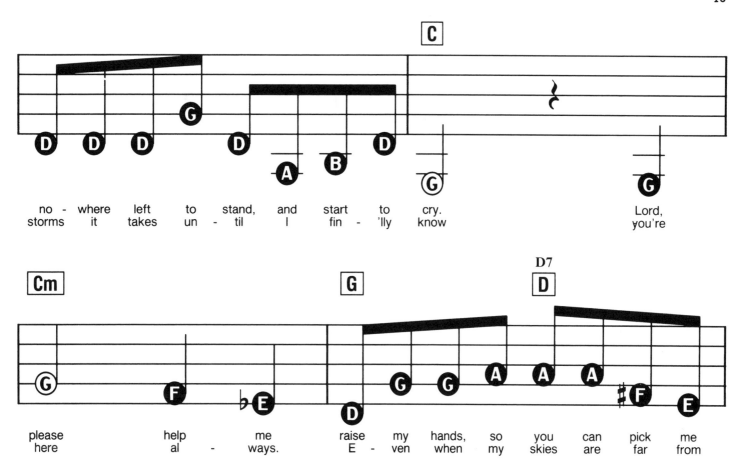

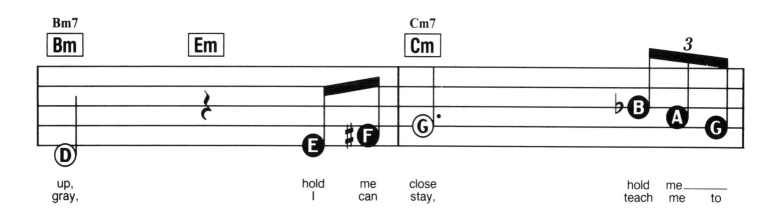

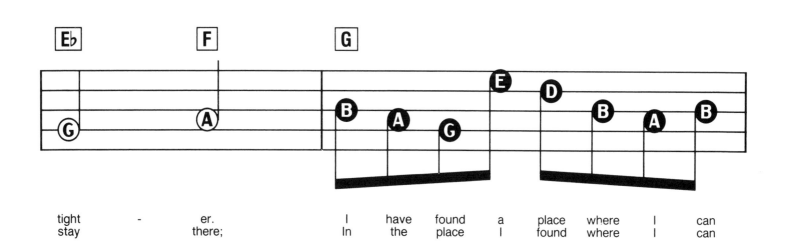

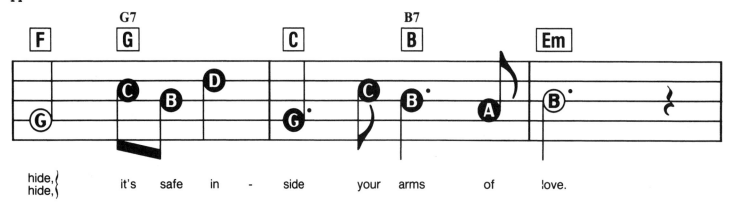

hide,
hide, it's safe in - side your arms of love.

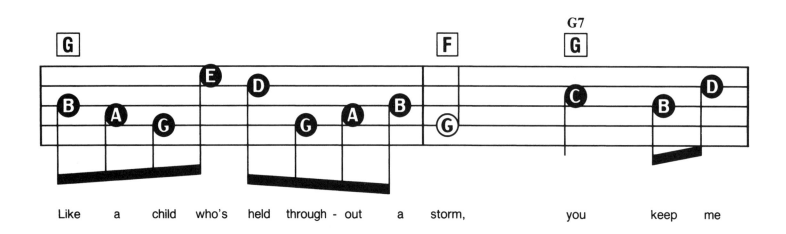

Like a child who's held through - out a storm, you keep me

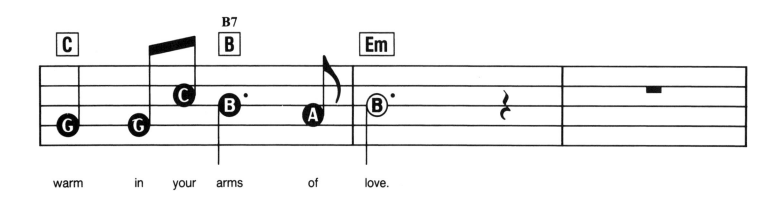

warm in your arms of love.

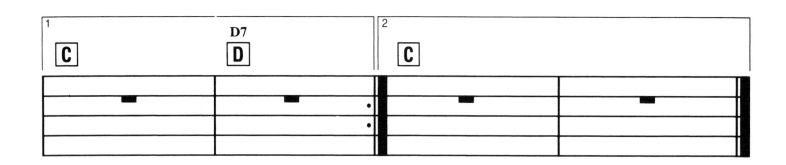

Awesome God

Registration 2
Rhythm: 8 Beat or Rock

Words and Music by
Rich Mullins

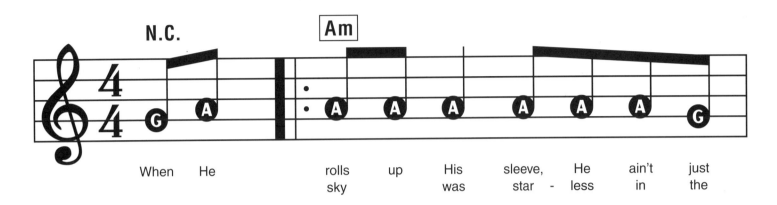

When He rolls up His sleeve, He ain't just
sky was star - less in the

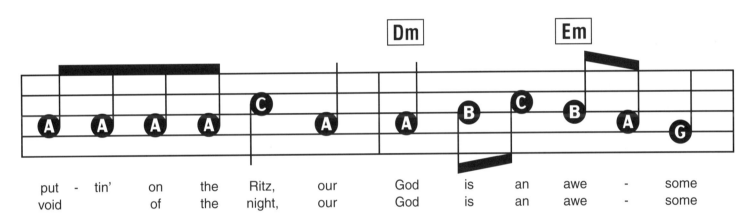

put - tin' on the Ritz, our God is an awe - some
void of the night, our God is an awe - some

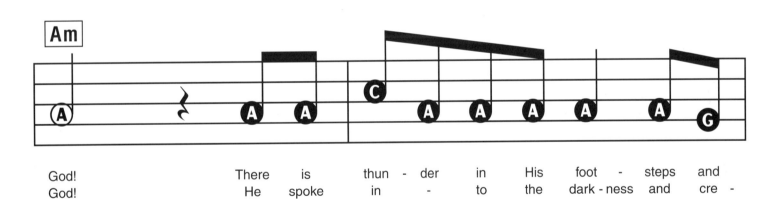

God! There is thun - der in His foot - steps and
God! He spoke in - to the dark - ness and cre -

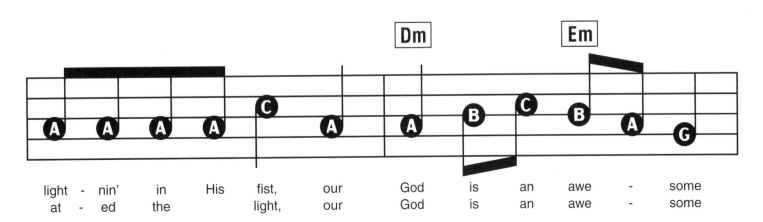

light - nin' in His fist, our God is an awe - some
at - ed the light, our God is an awe - some

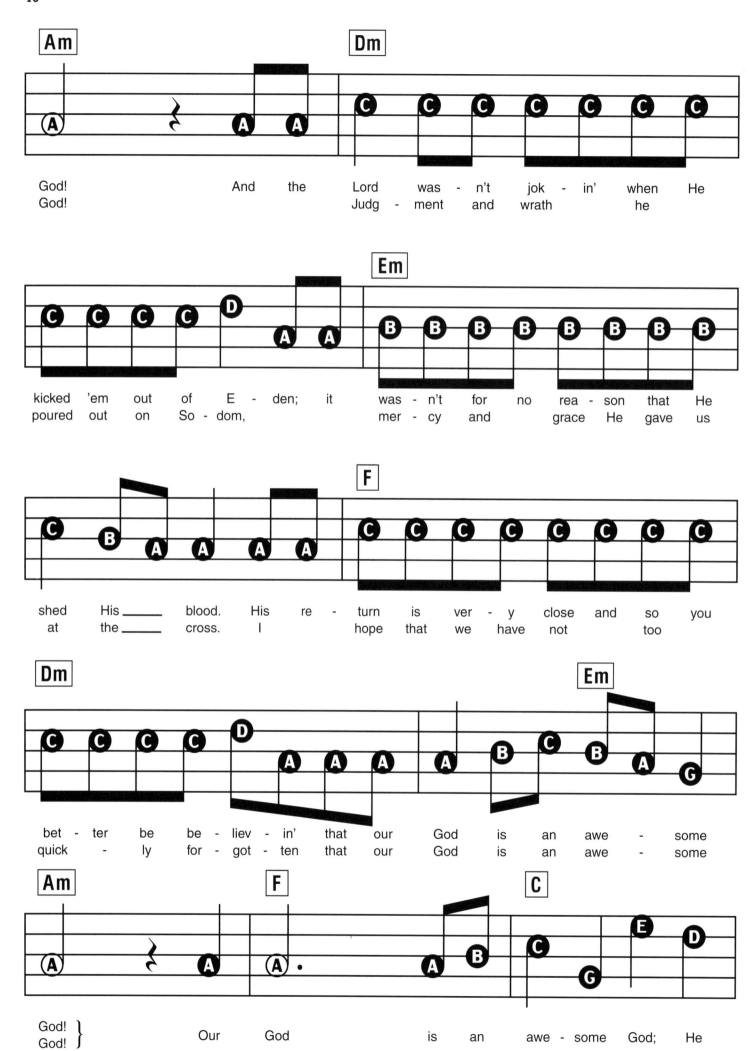

17

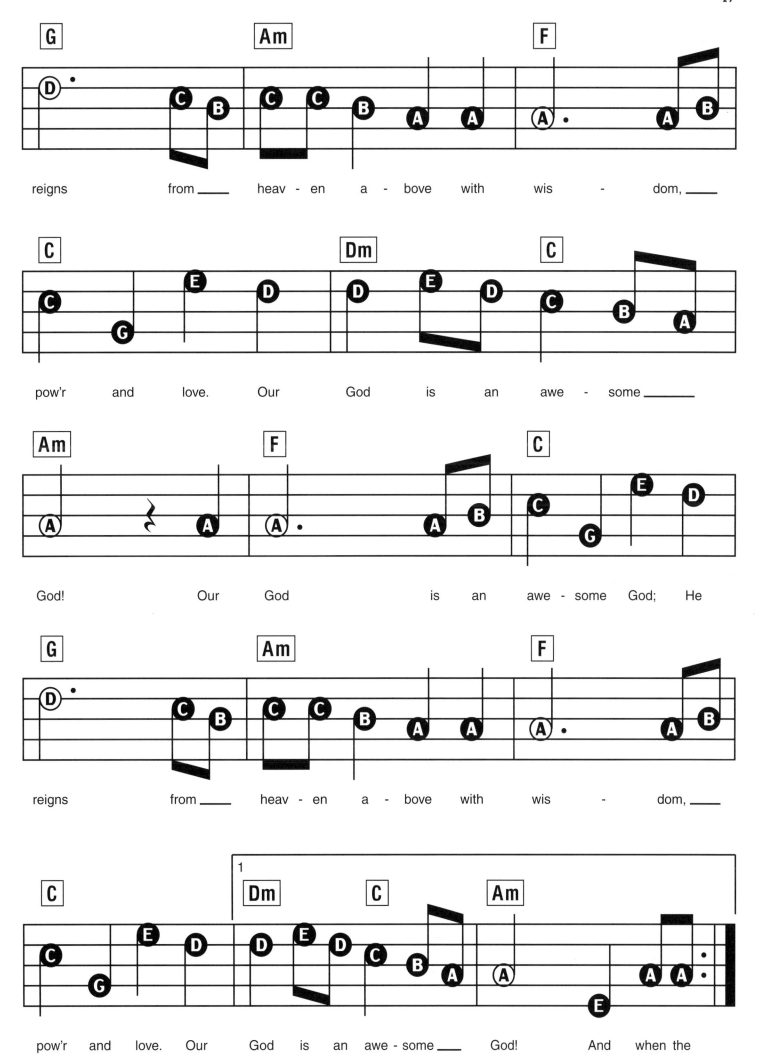

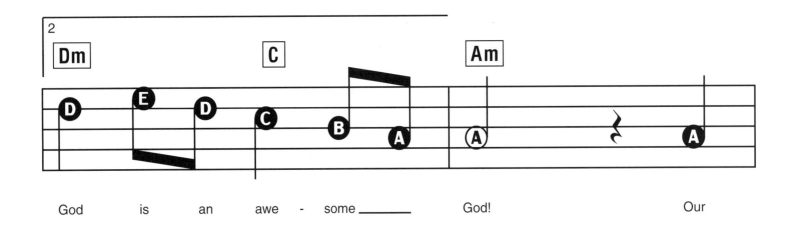

God   is   an   awe - some _____ God!   Our

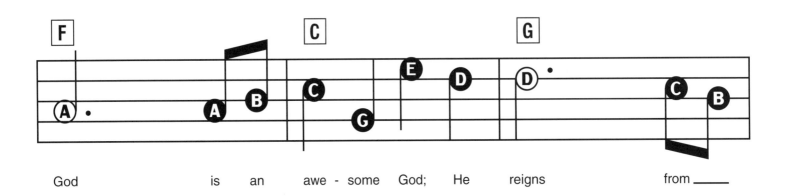

God   is   an   awe - some   God;   He   reigns   from _____

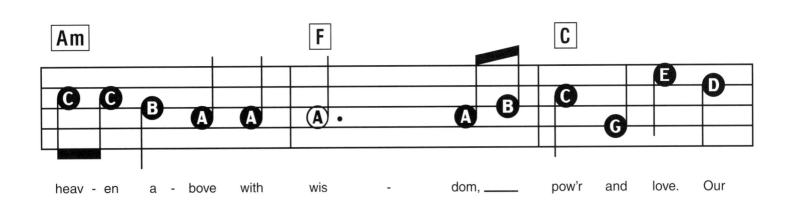

heav - en   a - bove   with   wis   -   dom, _____   pow'r   and   love.   Our

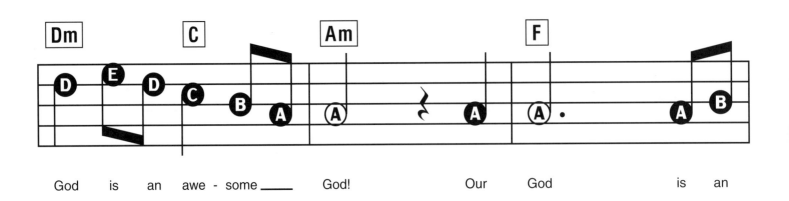

God   is   an   awe - some ____ God!   Our   God   is   an

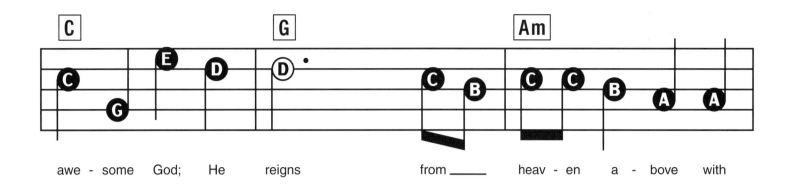

awe - some God; He reigns from ____ heav - en a - bove with

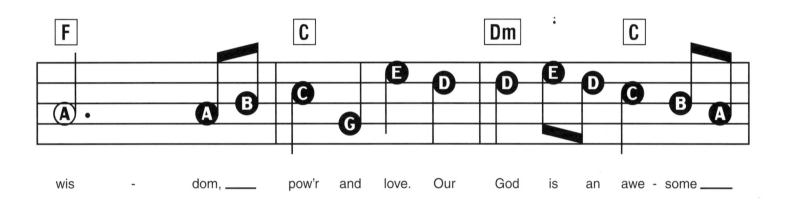

wis - dom, ____ pow'r and love. Our God is an awe - some ____

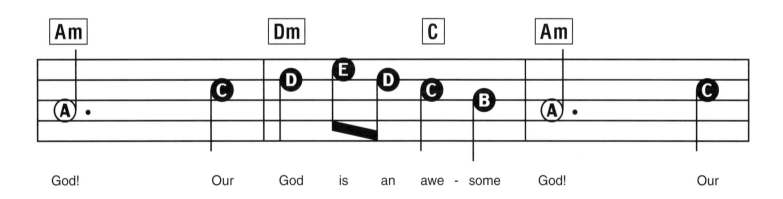

God! Our God is an awe - some God! Our

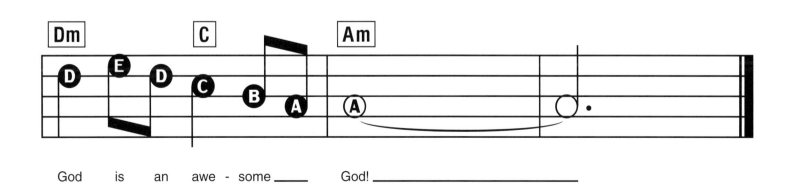

God is an awe - some ____ God! ____

The Basics of Life

Registration 7
Rhythm: Swing Waltz

Words and Music by Don Koch
and Mark Harris

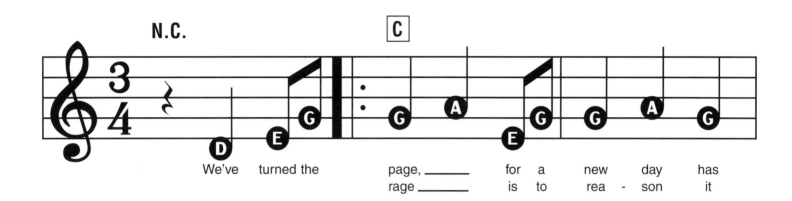

We've turned the page, _____ for a new day has
rage _____ is to rea - son it

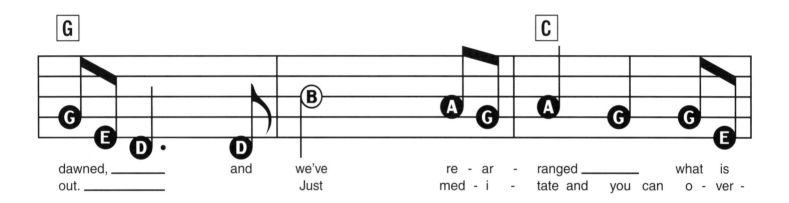

dawned, _____ and we've re - ar - ranged _____ what is
out. _____ Just med - i - tate and you can o - ver -

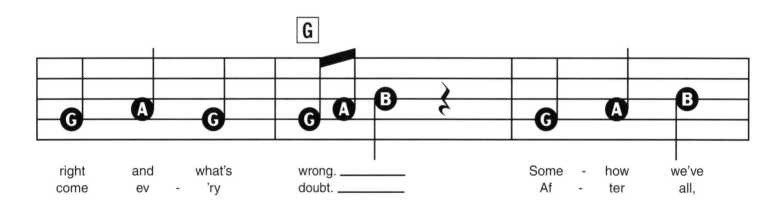

right and what's wrong. _____ Some - how we've
come ev - 'ry doubt. _____ Af - ter all,

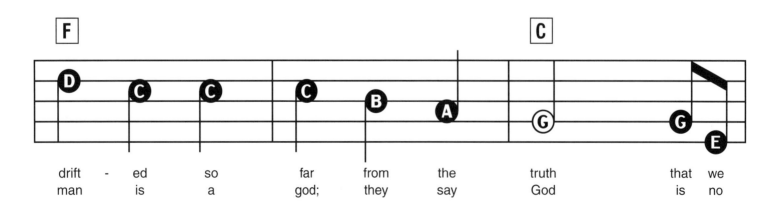

drift - ed so far from the truth that we
man is a god; they say God is no

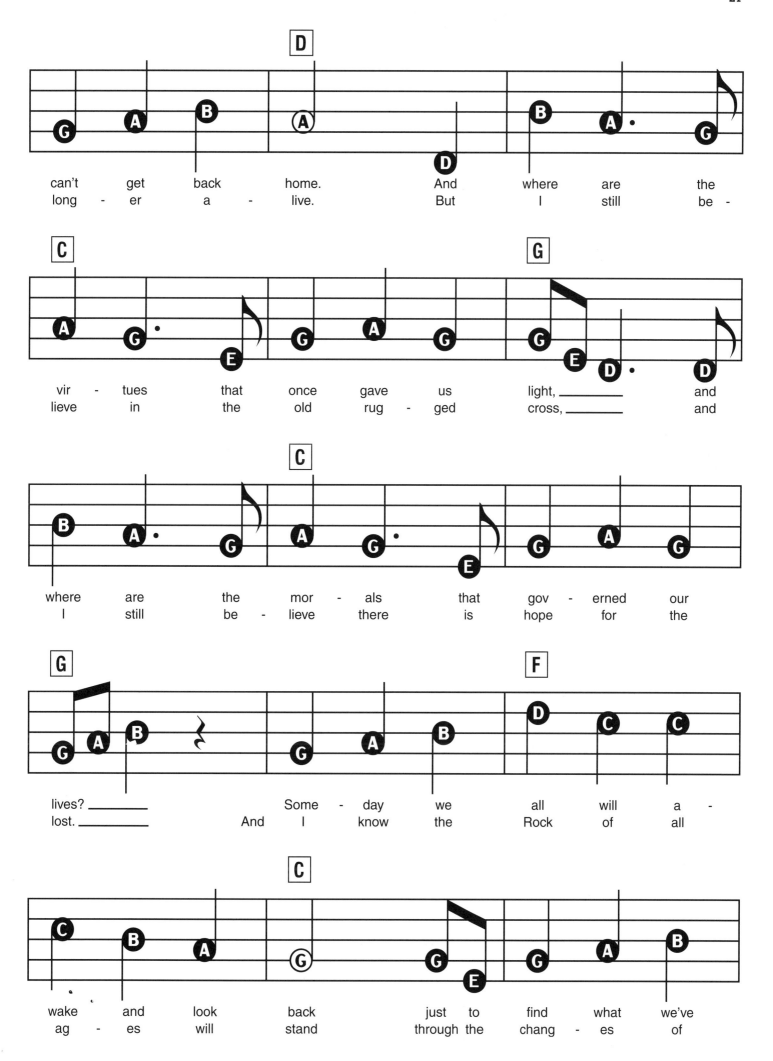

21

22

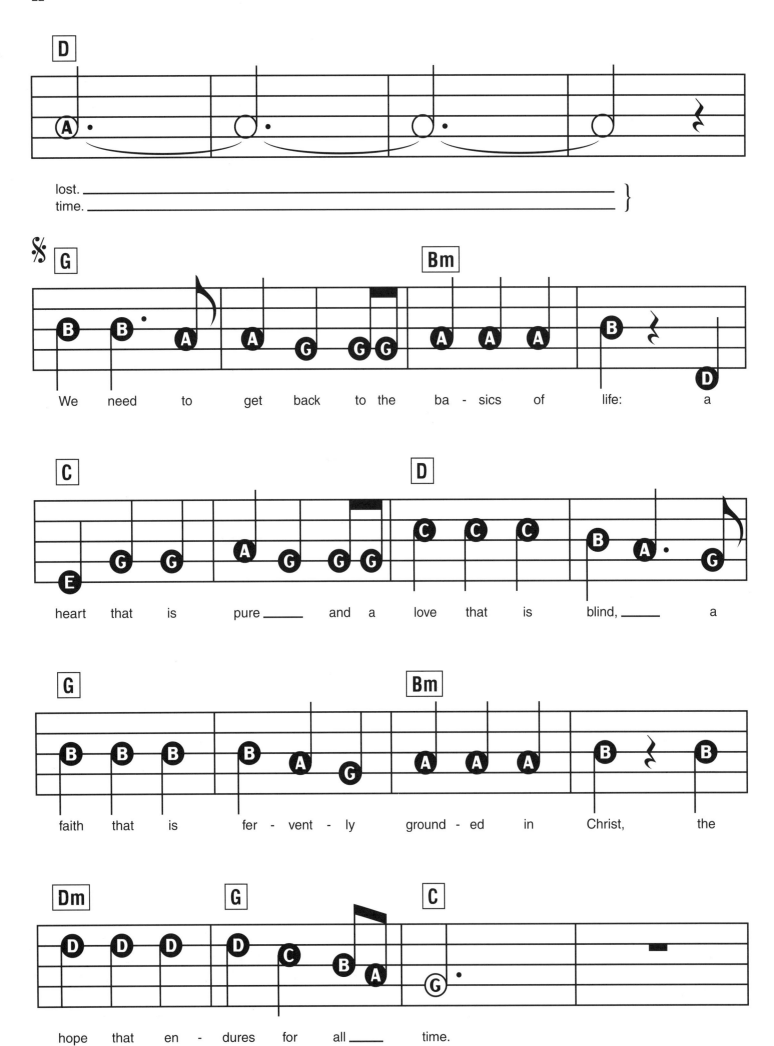

23

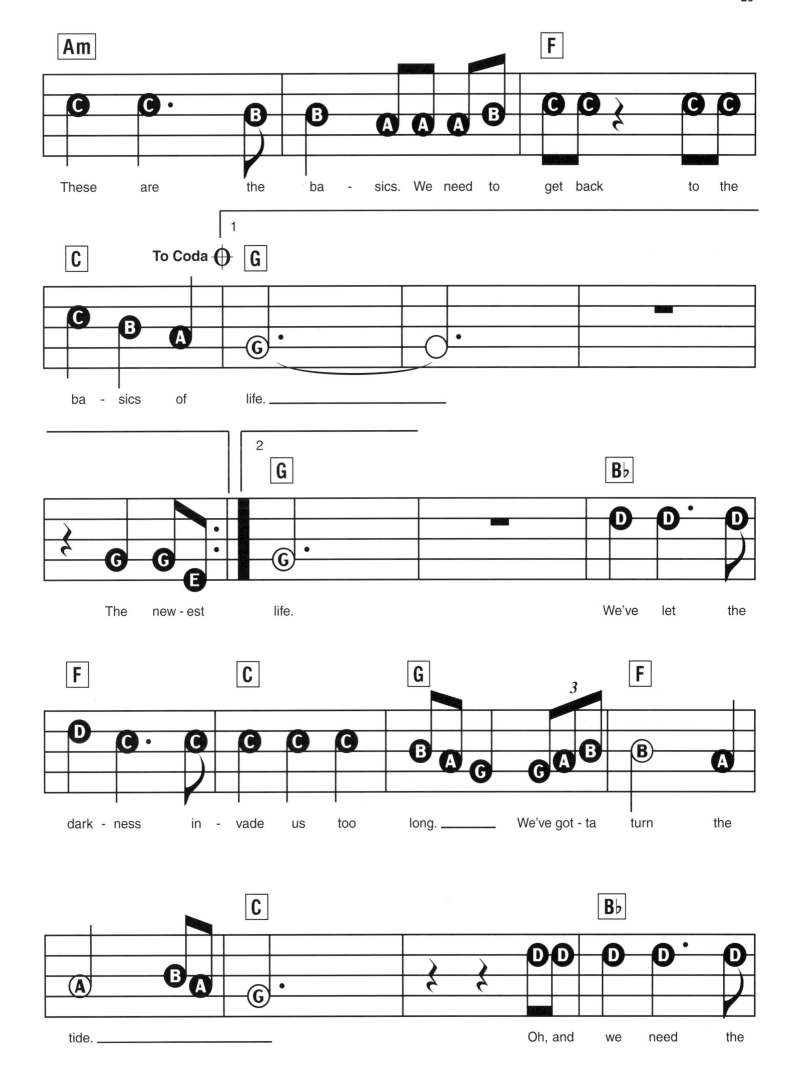

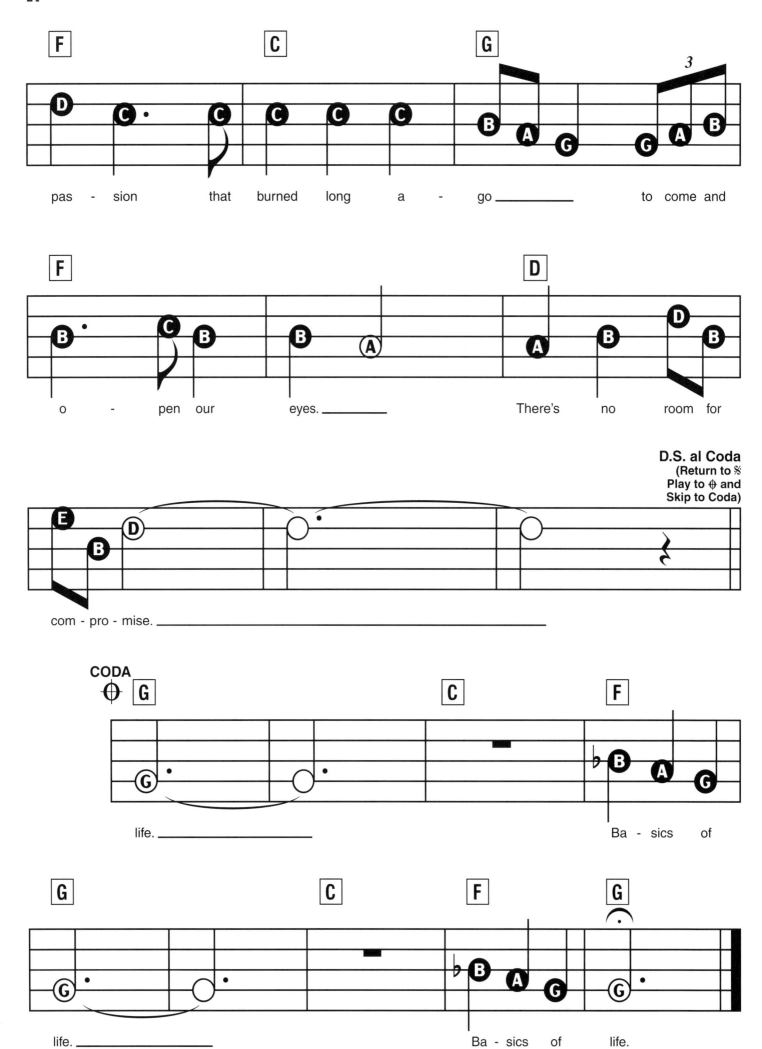

24

Crucified with Christ

Registration 1
Rhythm: Ballad or 8 Beat

Words and Music by Randy Phillips, Denise Phillips,
Dave Clark and Don Koch

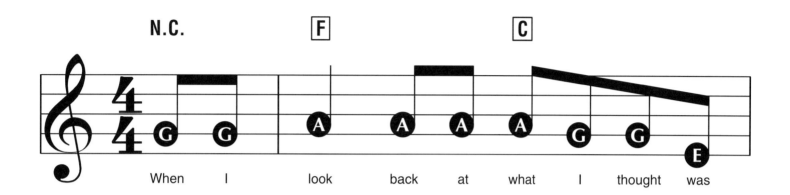

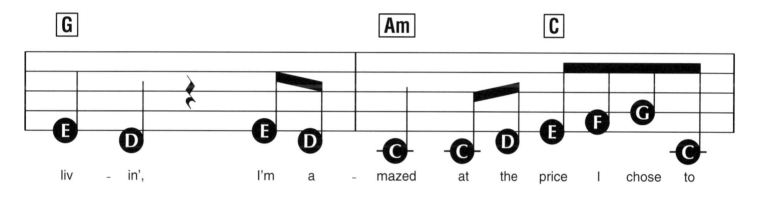

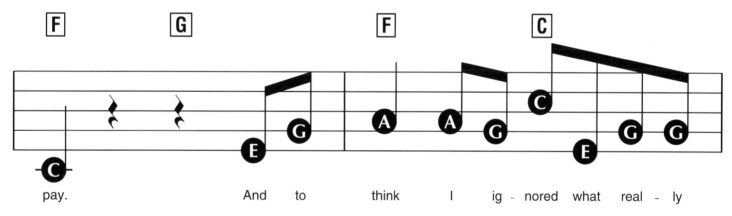

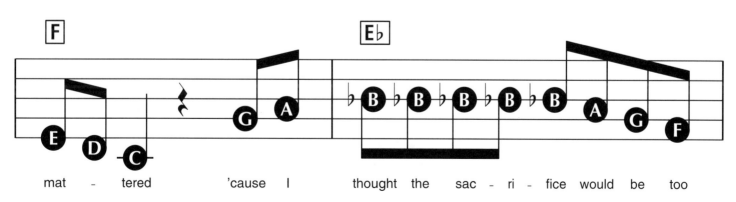

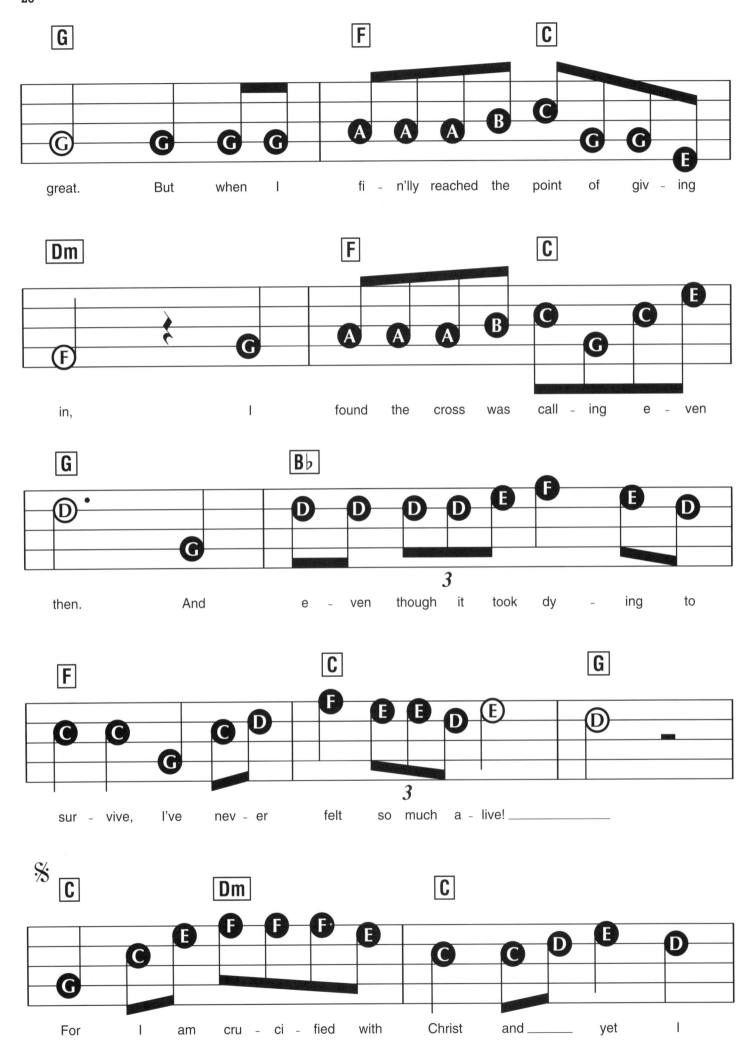

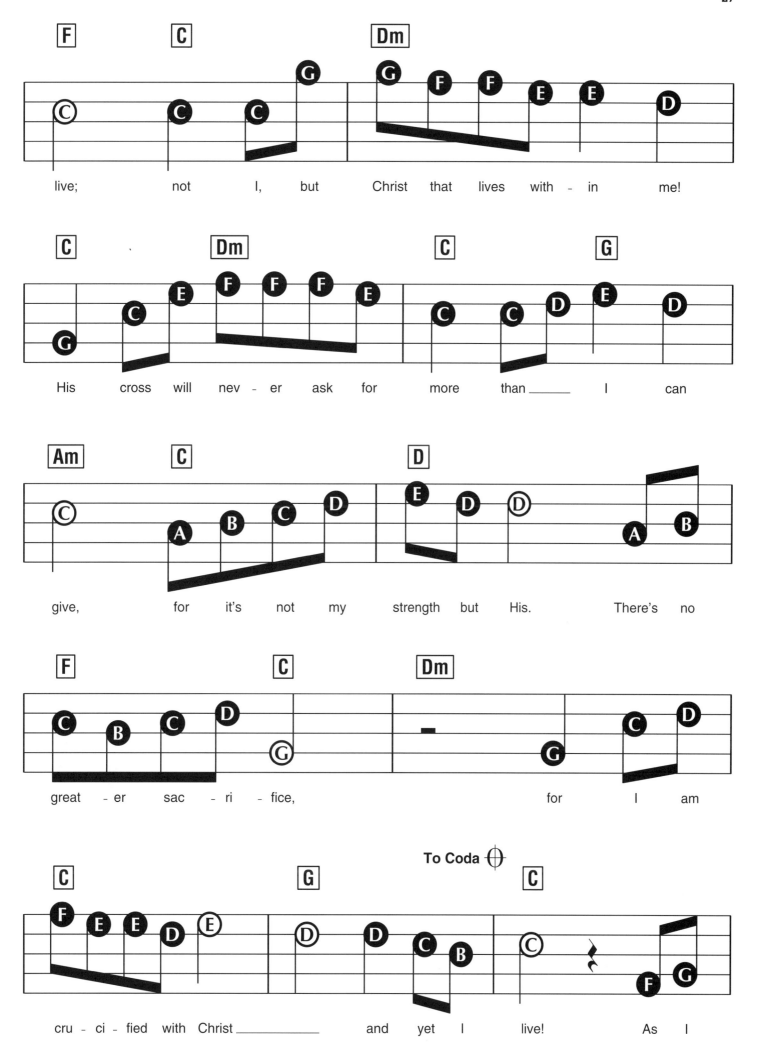

28

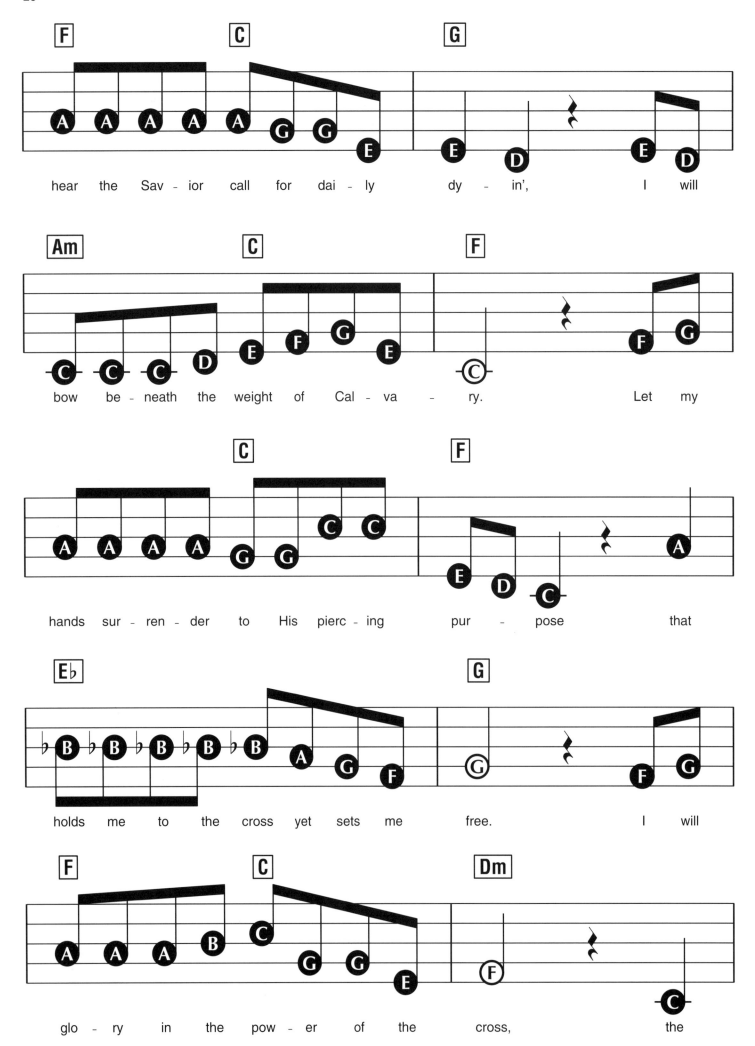

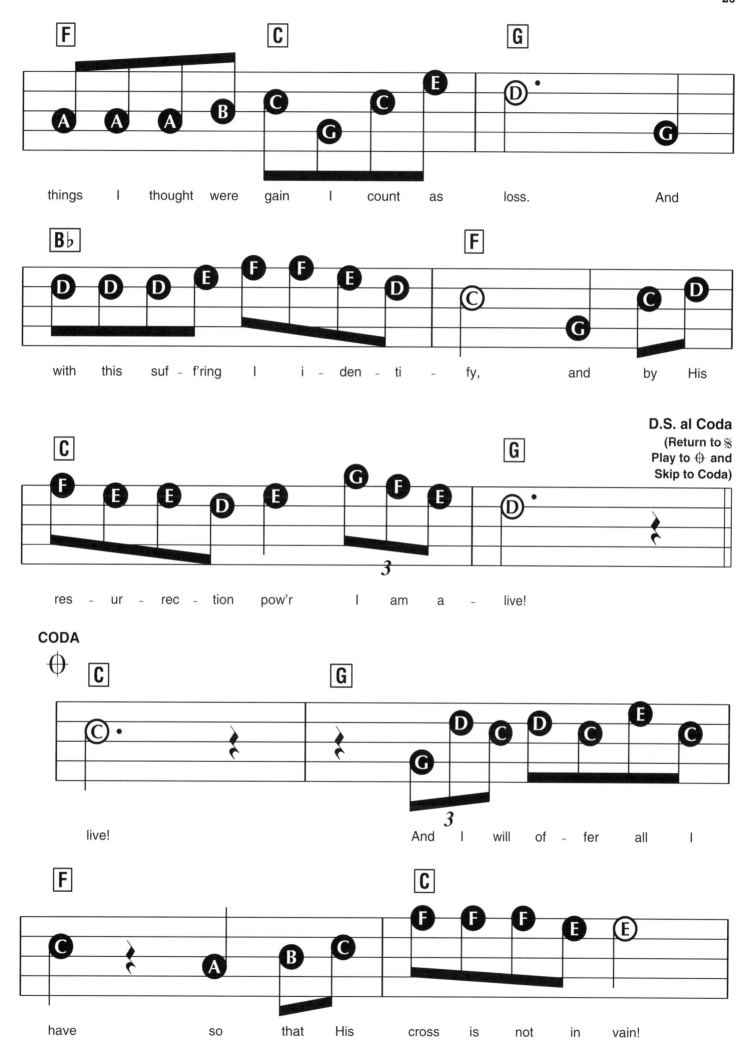

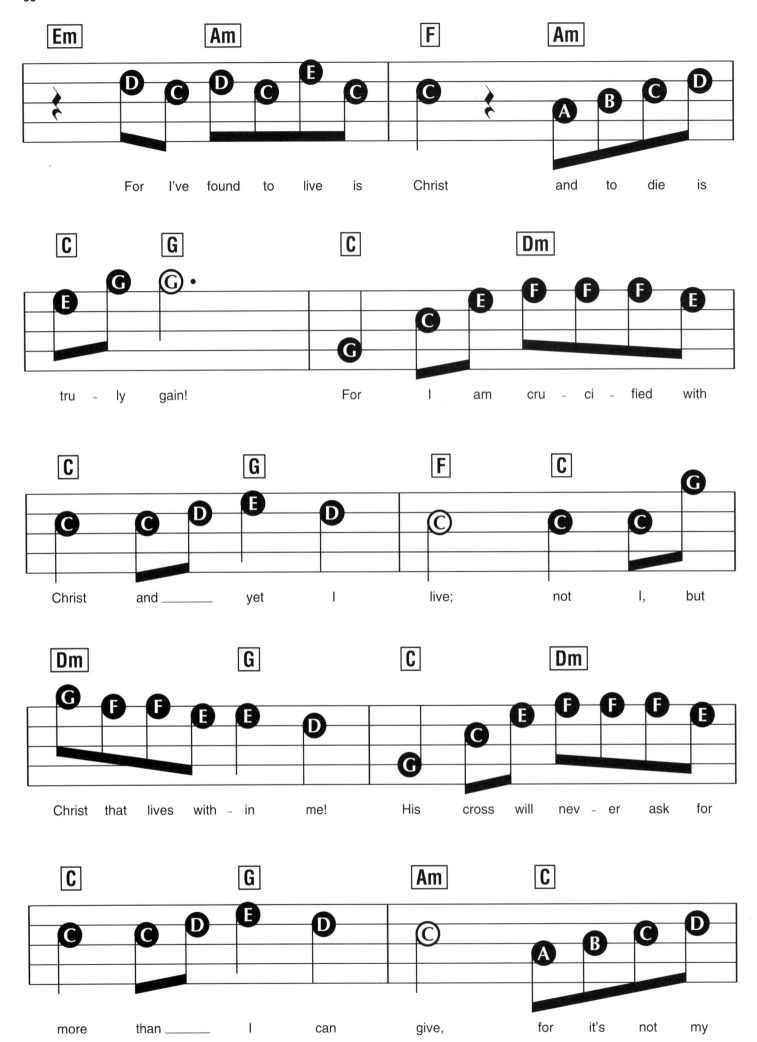

31

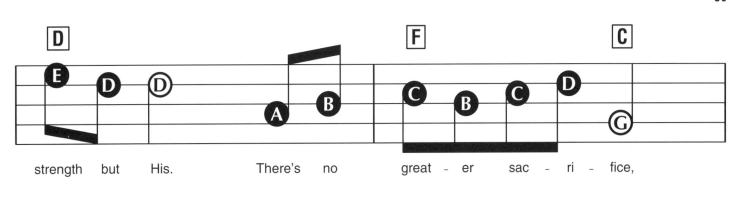

strength but His.   There's no   great - er   sac - ri - fice,

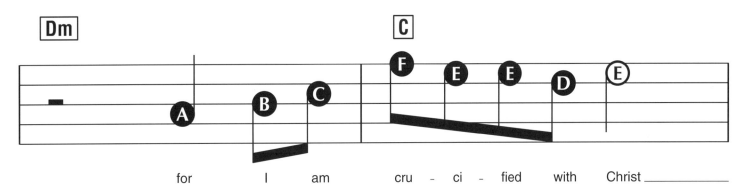

for   I   am   cru - ci - fied   with   Christ _____

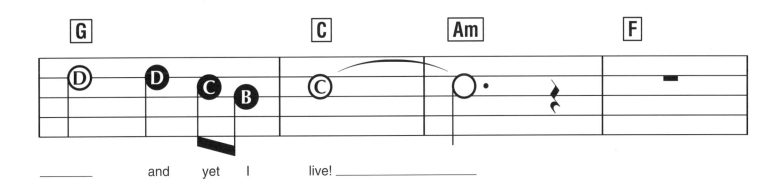

_____   and   yet   I   live! _____

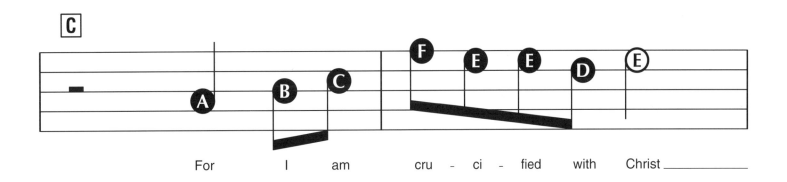

For   I   am   cru - ci - fied   with   Christ _____

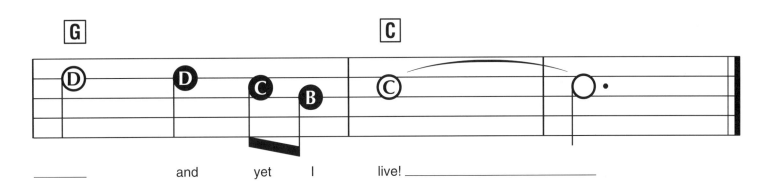

_____   and   yet   I   live! _____

Can't Live a Day

Registration 3
Rhythm: Pop Ballad

Words and Music by Ty Lacy,
Connie Harrington and Joe Beck

I could live life a - lone _____ and
I could trav - el the world, _____ see

nev - er fill the long - ings of my heart, the
all the won - ders beau - ti - ful and new. They'd

heal - ing warmth of some - one's ___ arms. And I could
on - ly make me think of _____ You. And I could

live with - out dreams _____ and nev - er know the
have all life of - fered, rich - es that were

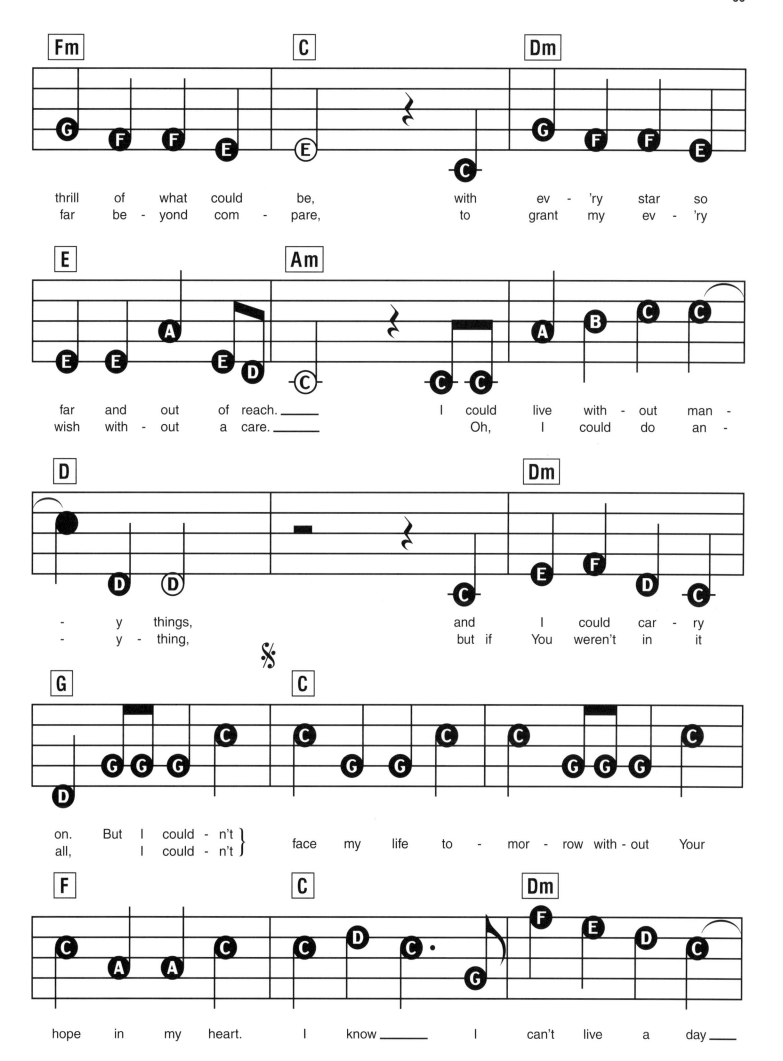

34

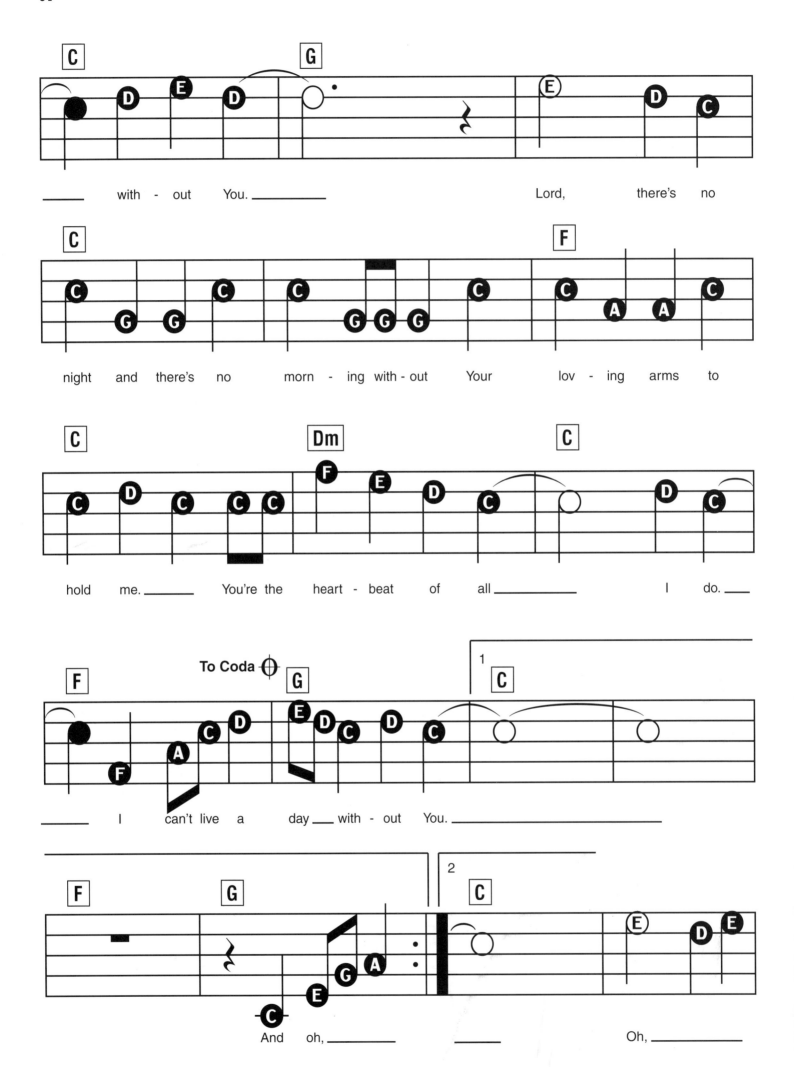

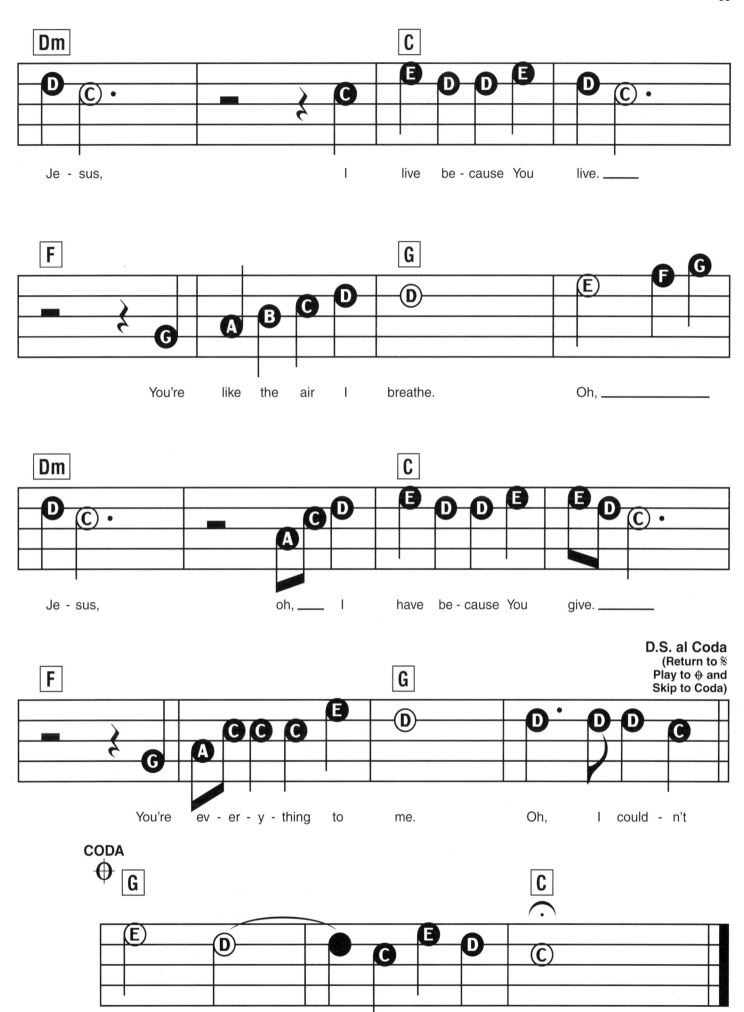

Je - sus,   I   live be - cause You   live. _____

You're   like the   air   I   breathe.   Oh, _____

Je - sus,   oh, ___ I   have be - cause You   give. _____

D.S. al Coda
(Return to 𝄋
Play to ⊕ and
Skip to Coda)

You're ev - er - y - thing to   me.   Oh,   I   could - n't

CODA

day _____ with - out You. _____

El Shaddai

Registration 6
Rhythm: Moderate Ballad

Words and Music by Michael Card
and John Thompson

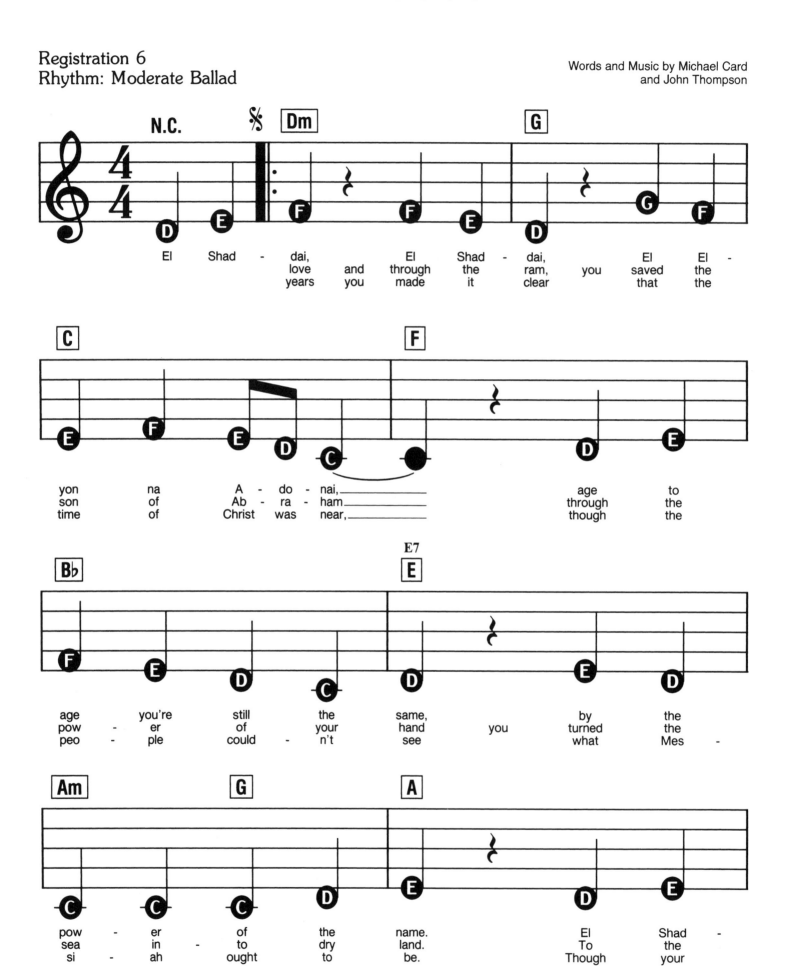

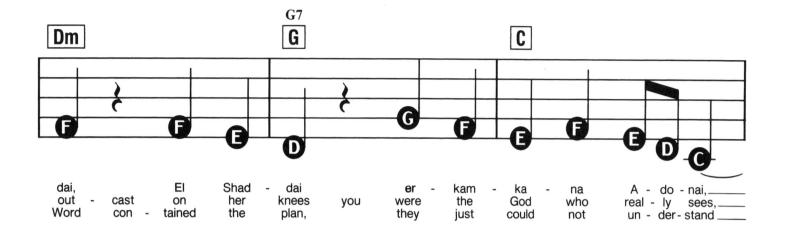

dai, El Shad - dai
out - cast on her knees you
Word con - tained the plan,

er kam - ka - na A - do - nai,_____
were they the just God could who not really sees,_____
un - der- stand_____

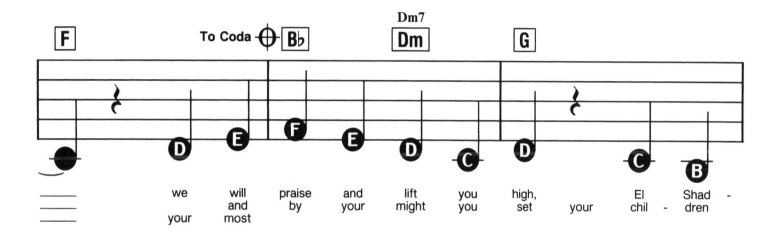

_____ we will praise and lift you high, El Shad -
_____ your and most by your might you set your chil - dren

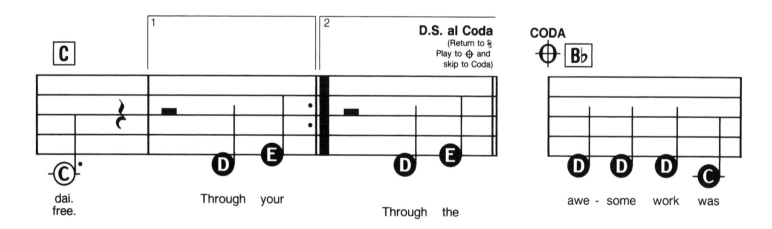

dai.
free.

Through your

Through the

awe - some work was

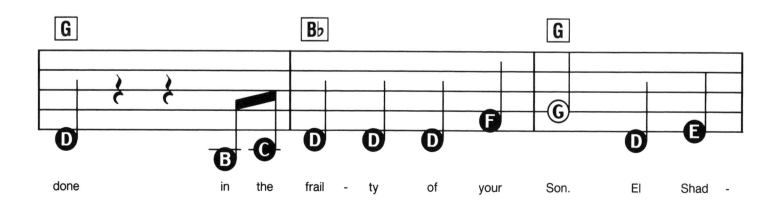

done in the frail - ty of your Son. El Shad -

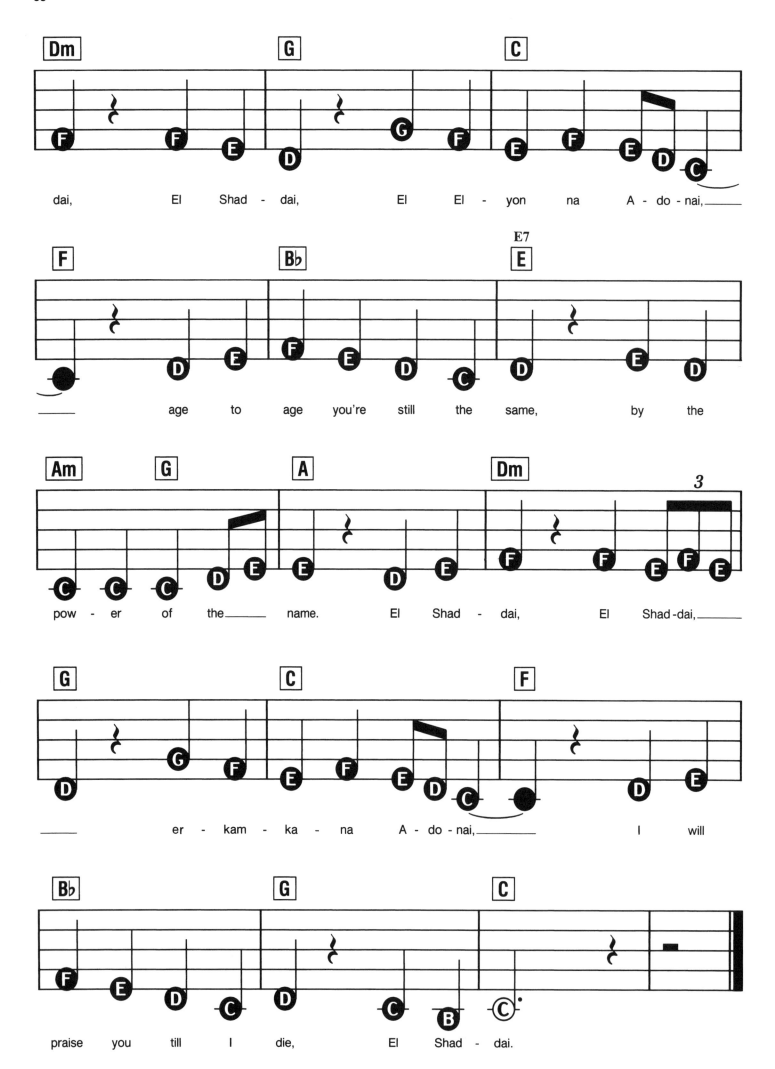

Faithful Friend

Registration 1
Rhythm: Ballad

Words and Music by Twila Paris
and Steven Curtis Chapman

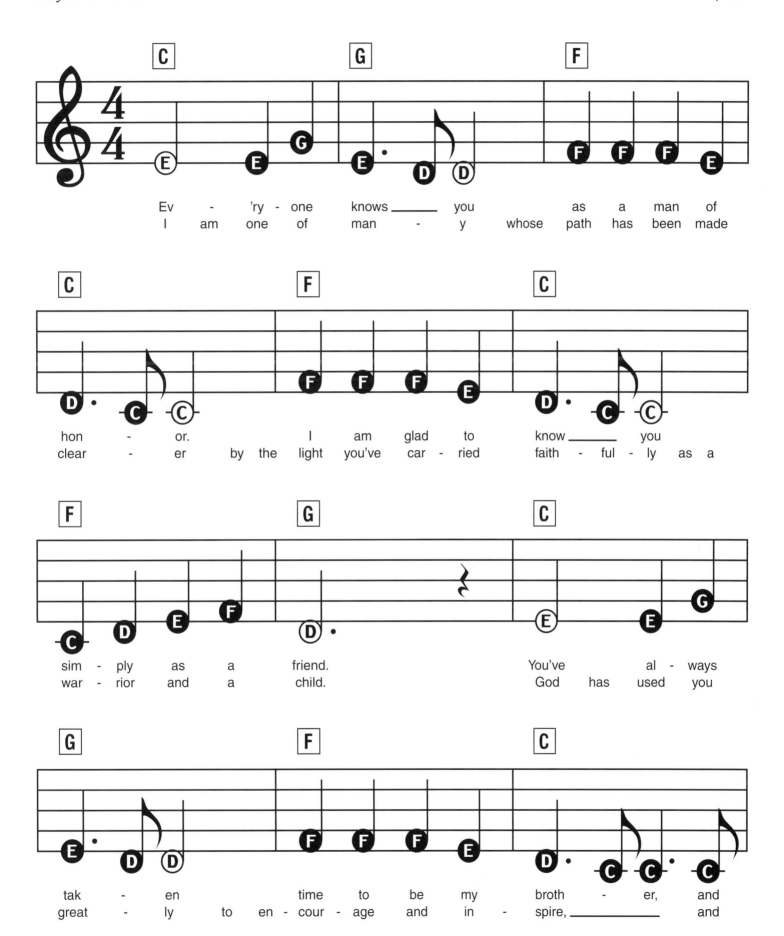

40

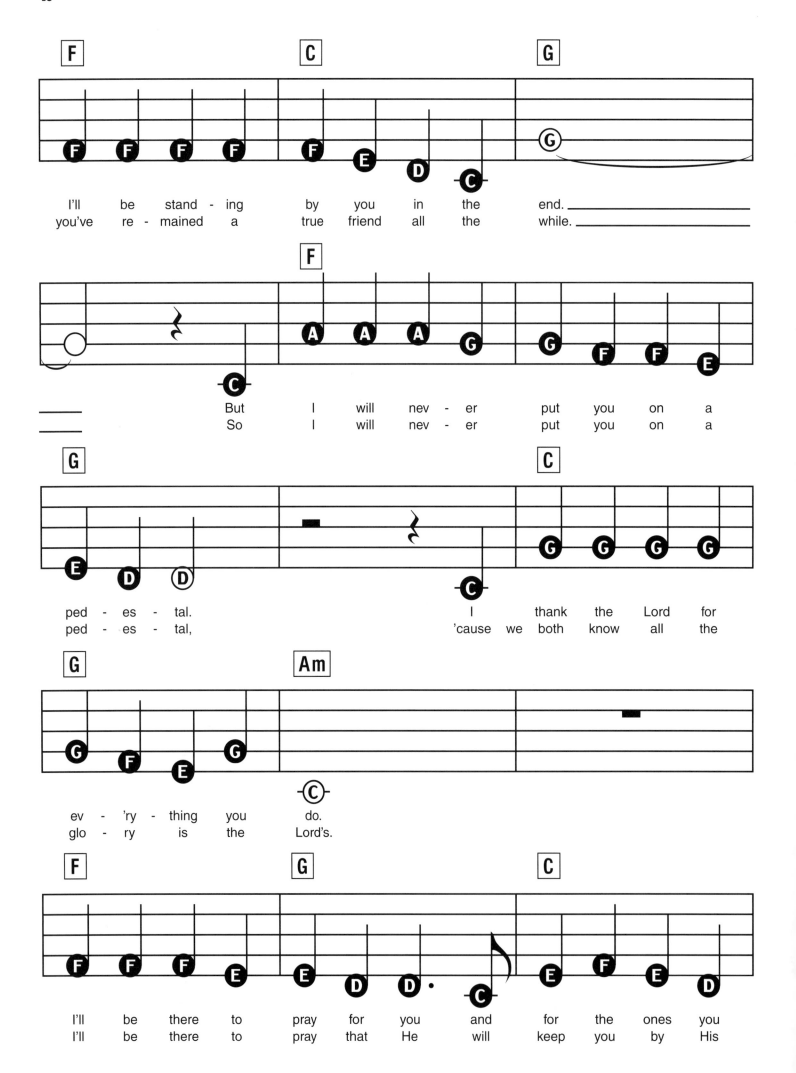

41

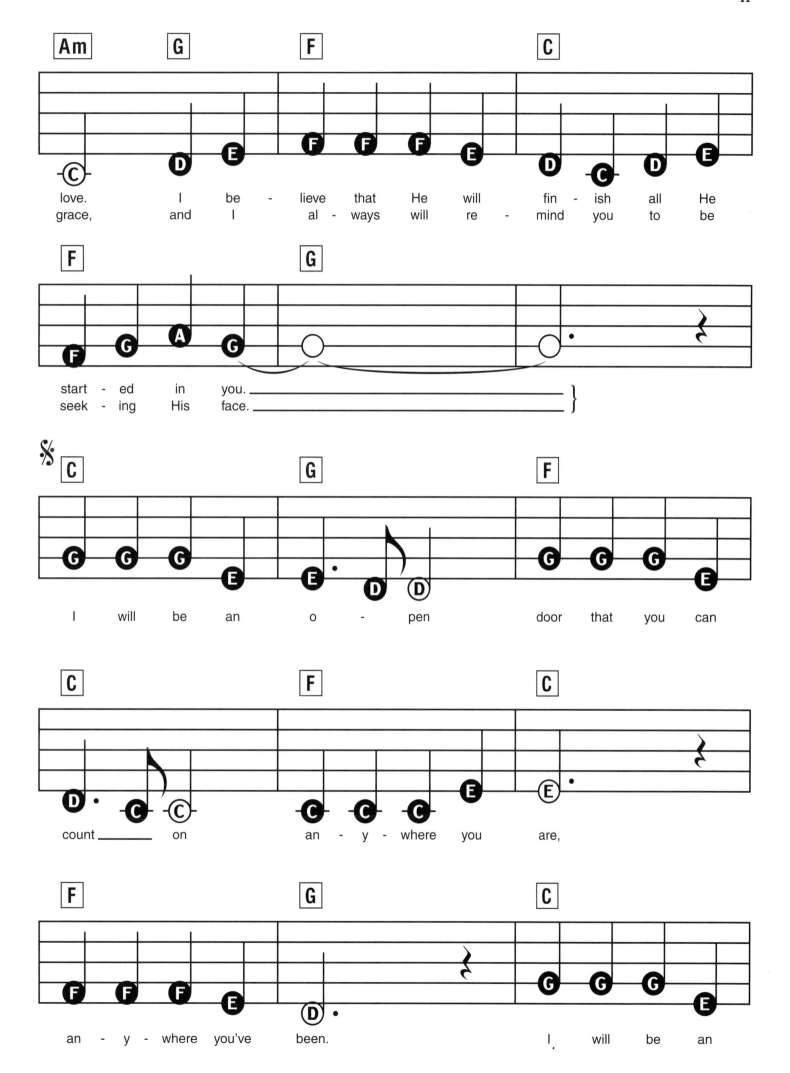

42

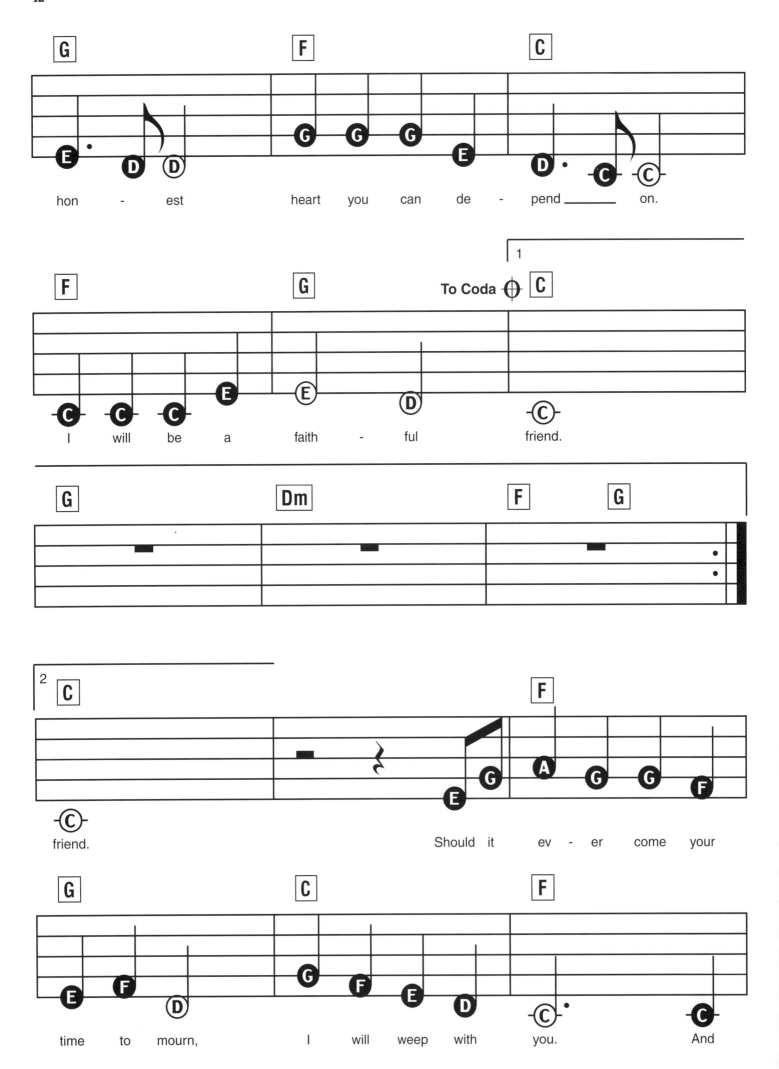

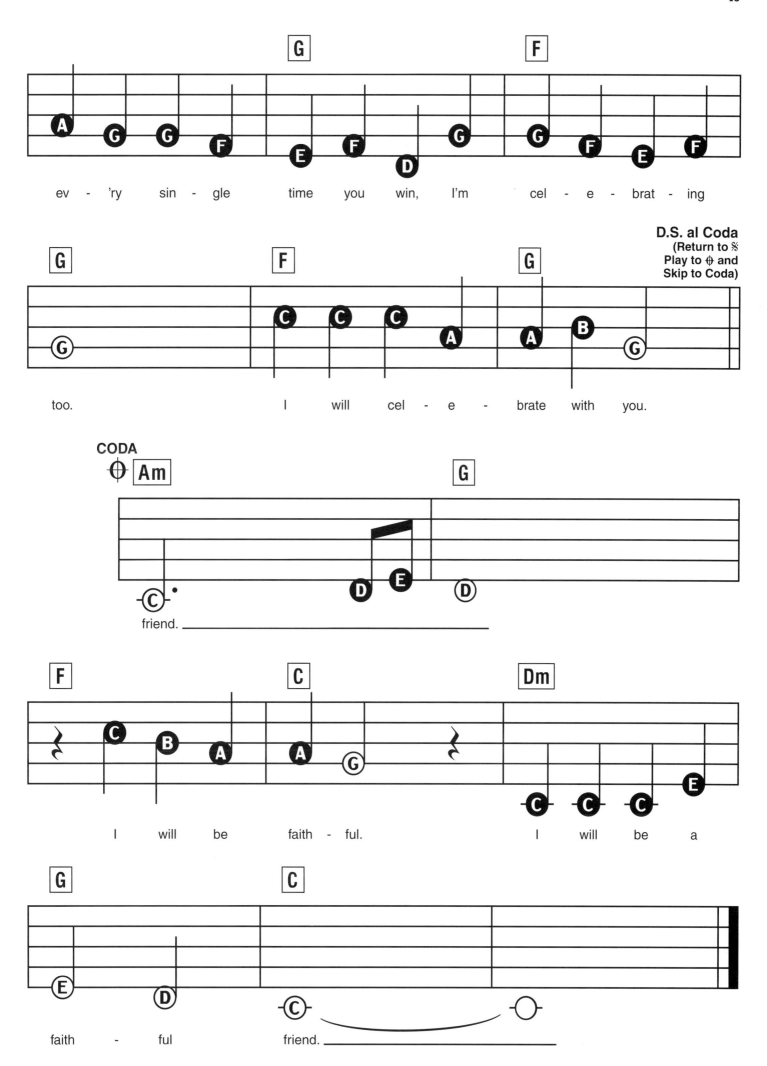

Father's Eyes

Registration 3
Rhythm: Ballad or Fox Trot

Words and Music by
Gary Chapman

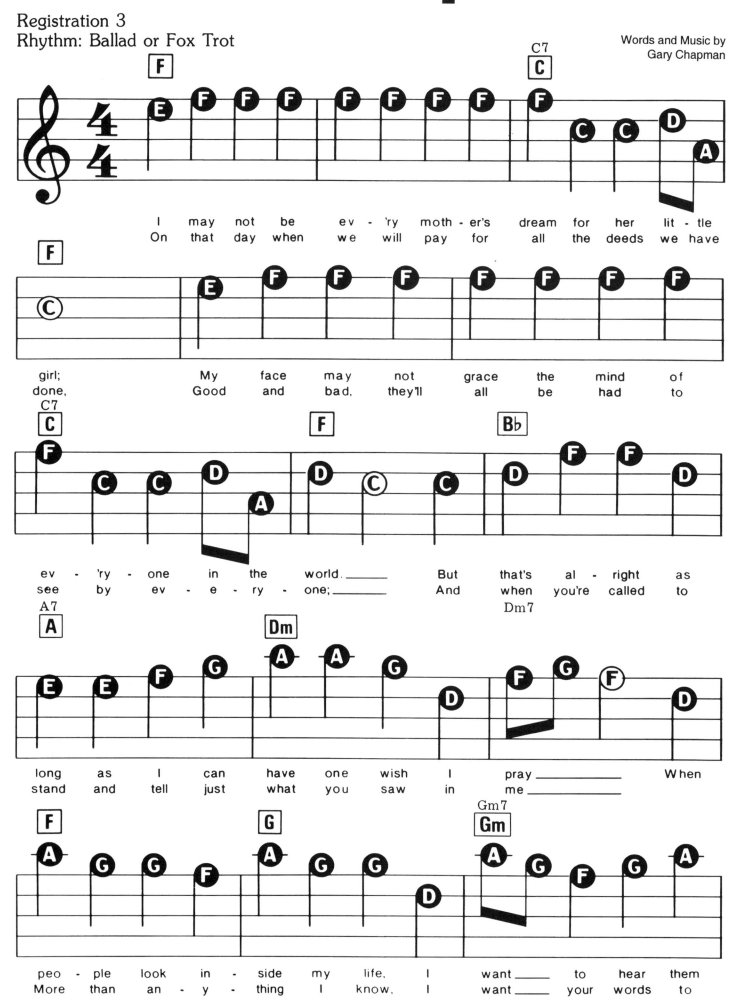

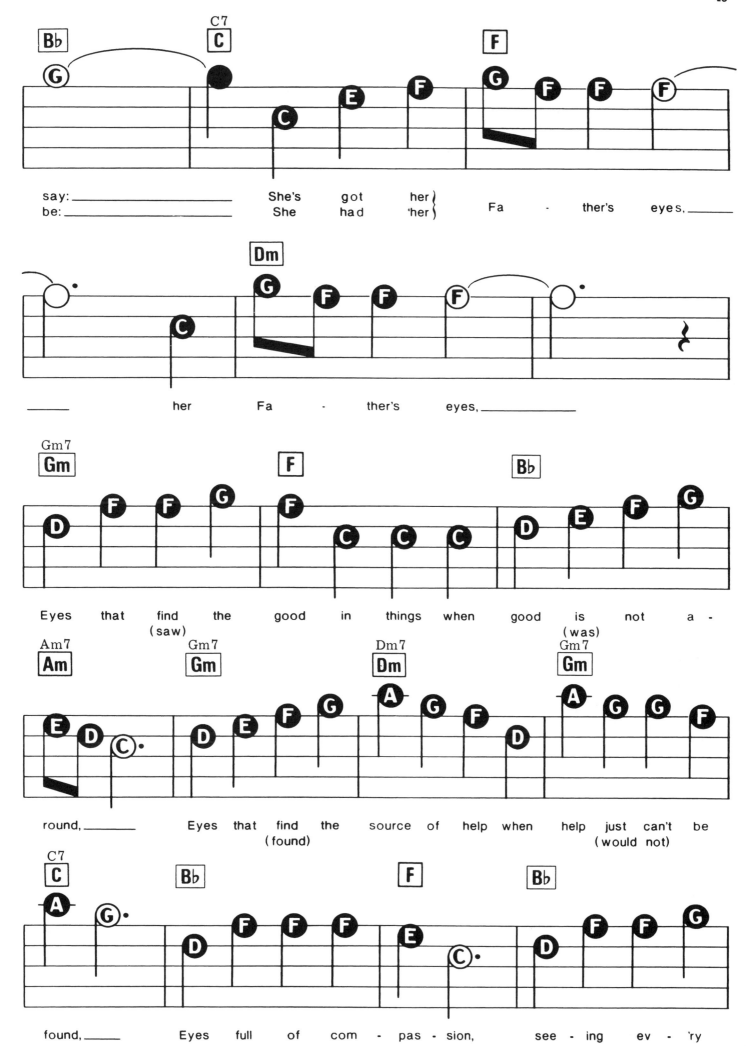

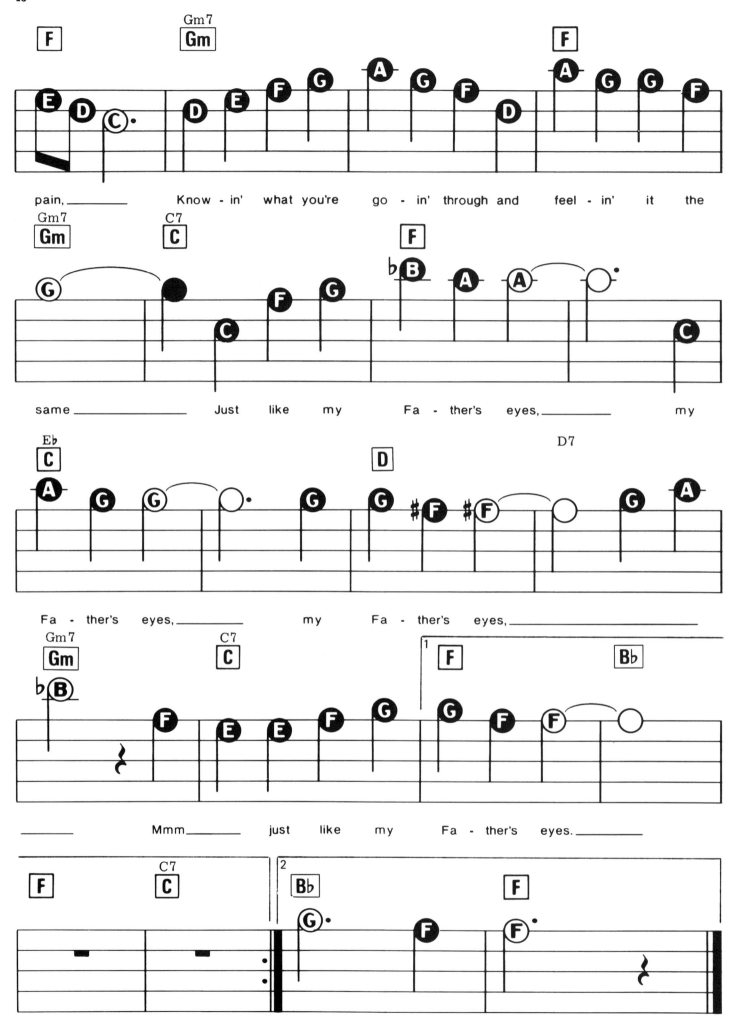

Fool for You

Registration 8
Rhythm: Pop

Words and Music by
Nichole Nordeman

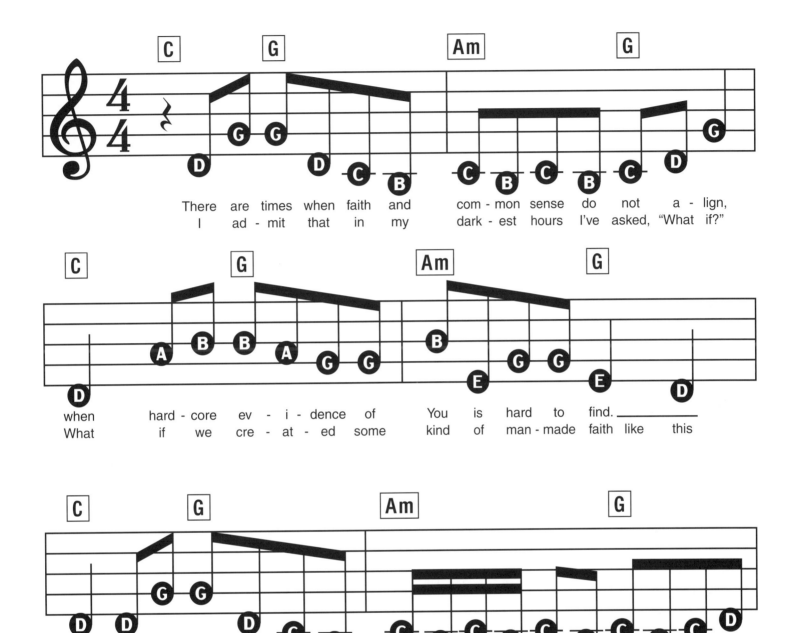

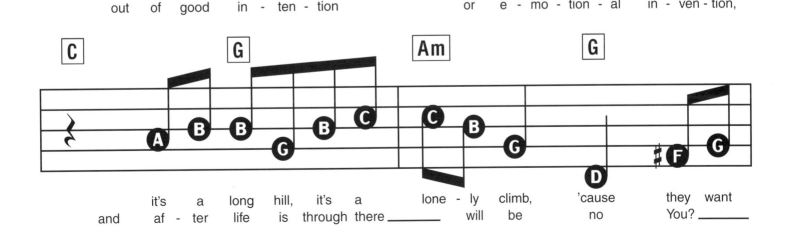

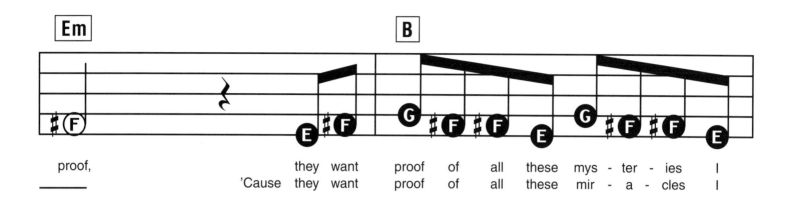

proof,   they   want   proof   of   all   these   mys - ter - ies   I

———   'Cause   they   want   proof   of   all   these   mir - a - cles   I

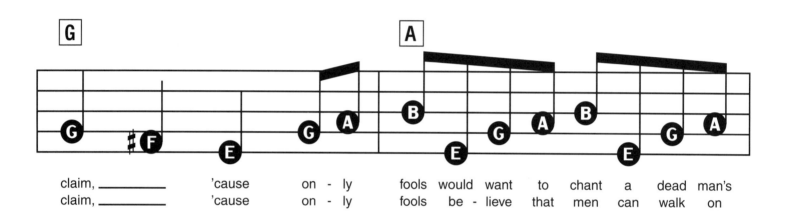

claim, ———   'cause   on - ly   fools   would   want   to   chant   a   dead   man's

claim, ———   'cause   on - ly   fools   be - lieve   that   men   can   walk   on

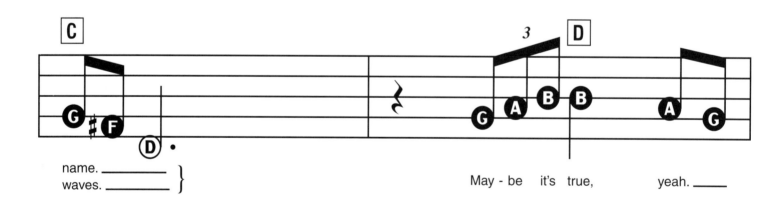

name. ———

waves. ———

May - be   it's   true,   yeah. ———

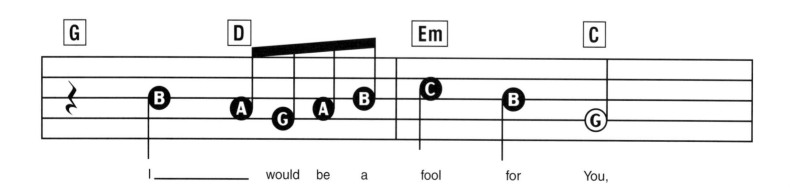

I ———   would   be   a   fool   for   You,

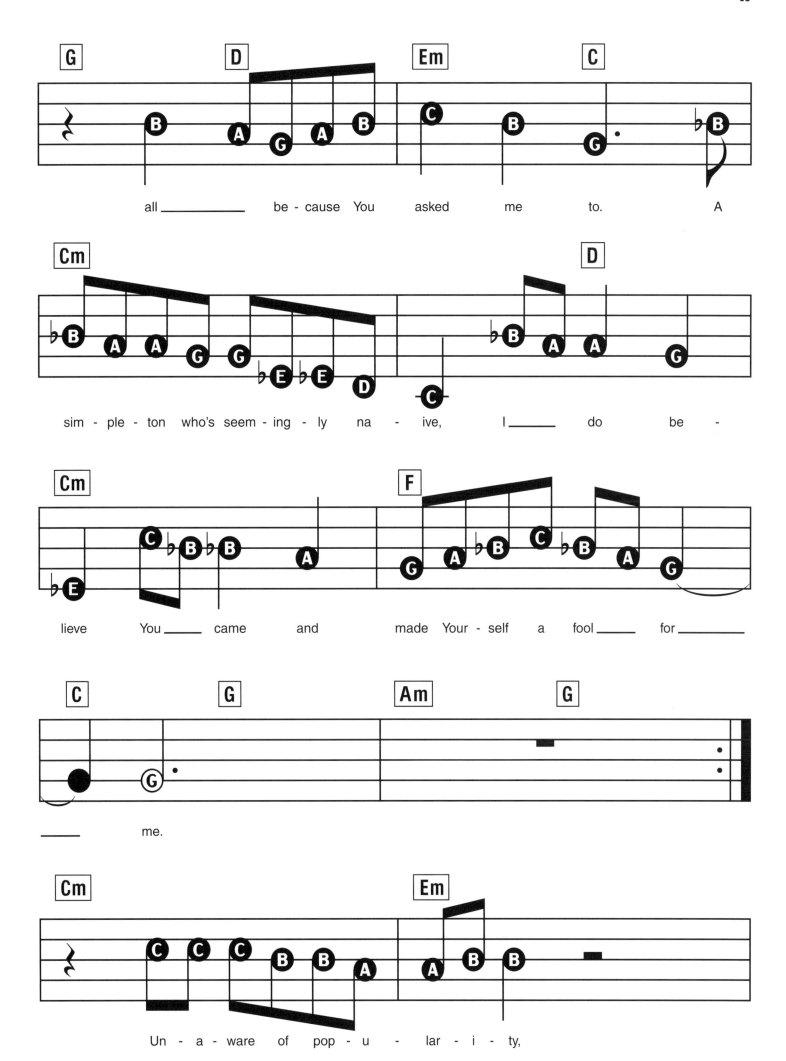

50

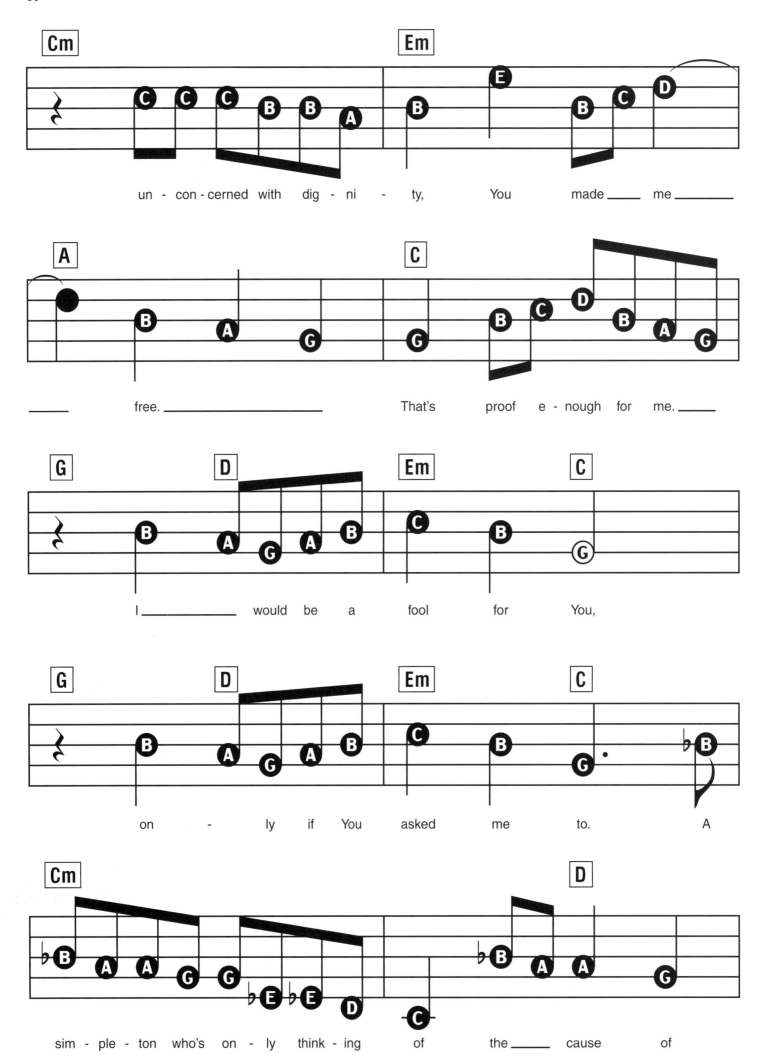

51

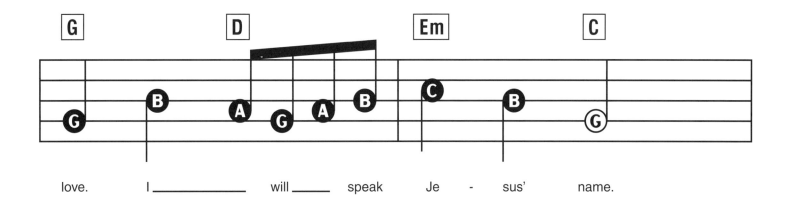

love. I _____ will _____ speak Je - sus' name.

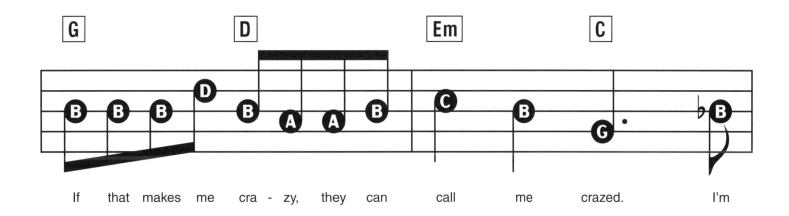

If that makes me cra - zy, they can call me crazed. I'm

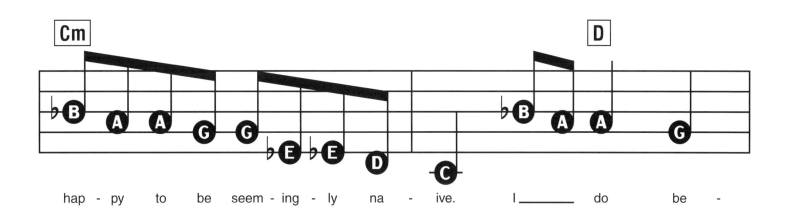

hap - py to be seem - ing - ly na - ive. I _____ do be -

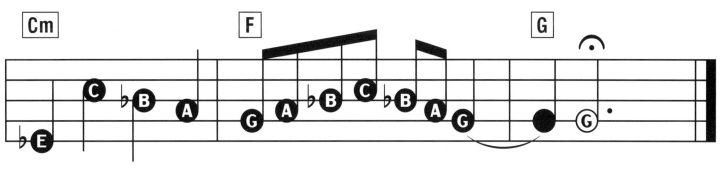

lieve You came and made your - self a fool __ for _____ me.

Find Us Faithful

Registration 3
Rhythm: 8 Beat or Ballad

Words and Music by
Jon Mohr

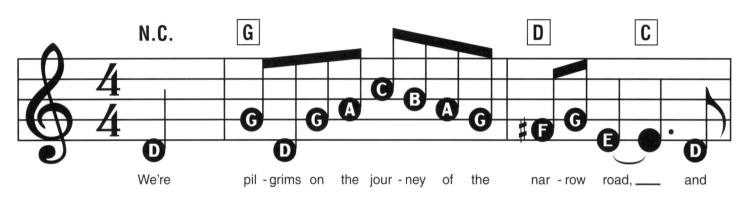

We're pil-grims on the jour-ney of the nar-row road, ___ and

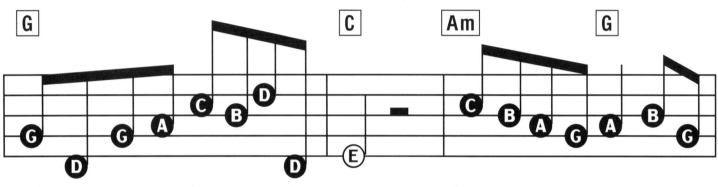

those who've gone be-fore us line the way. Cheer-ing on the faith-ful, en-

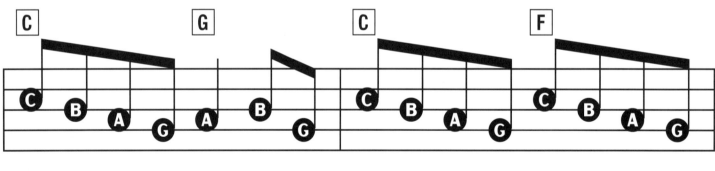

cour-ag-ing the wea-ry, their lives a stir-ring tes-ta-ment to

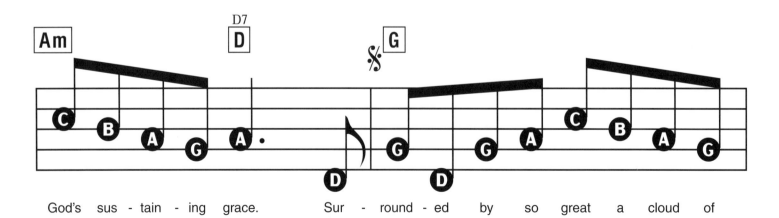

God's sus-tain-ing grace. Sur-round-ed by so great a cloud of

53

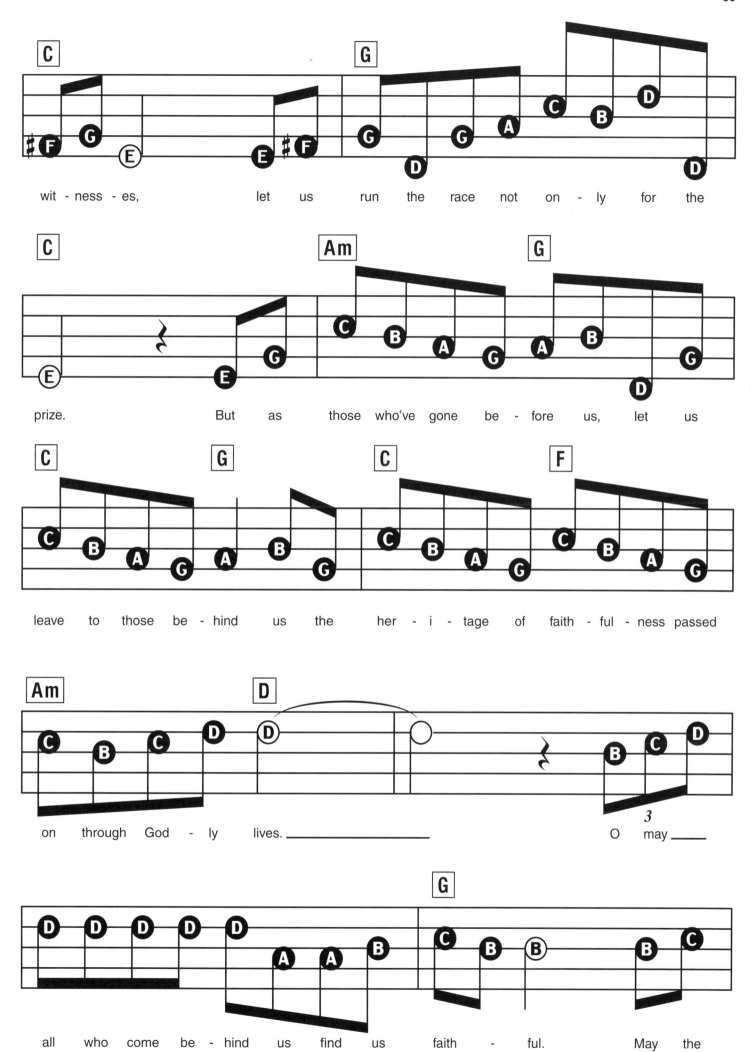

54

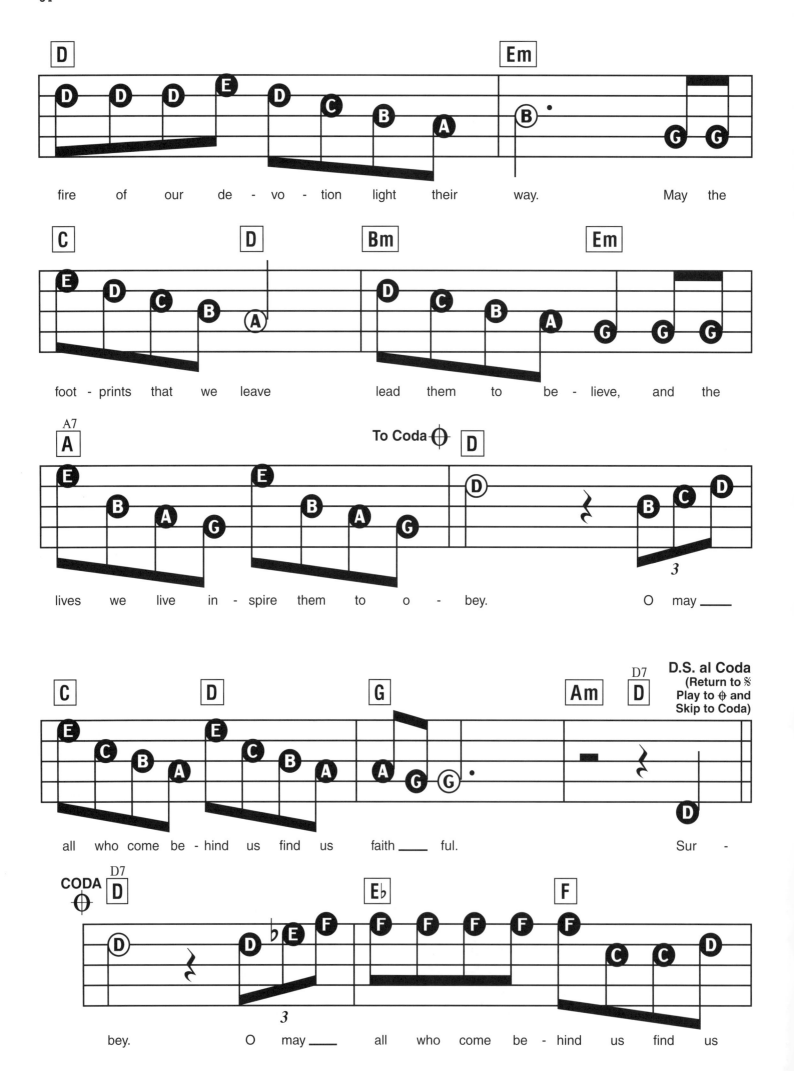

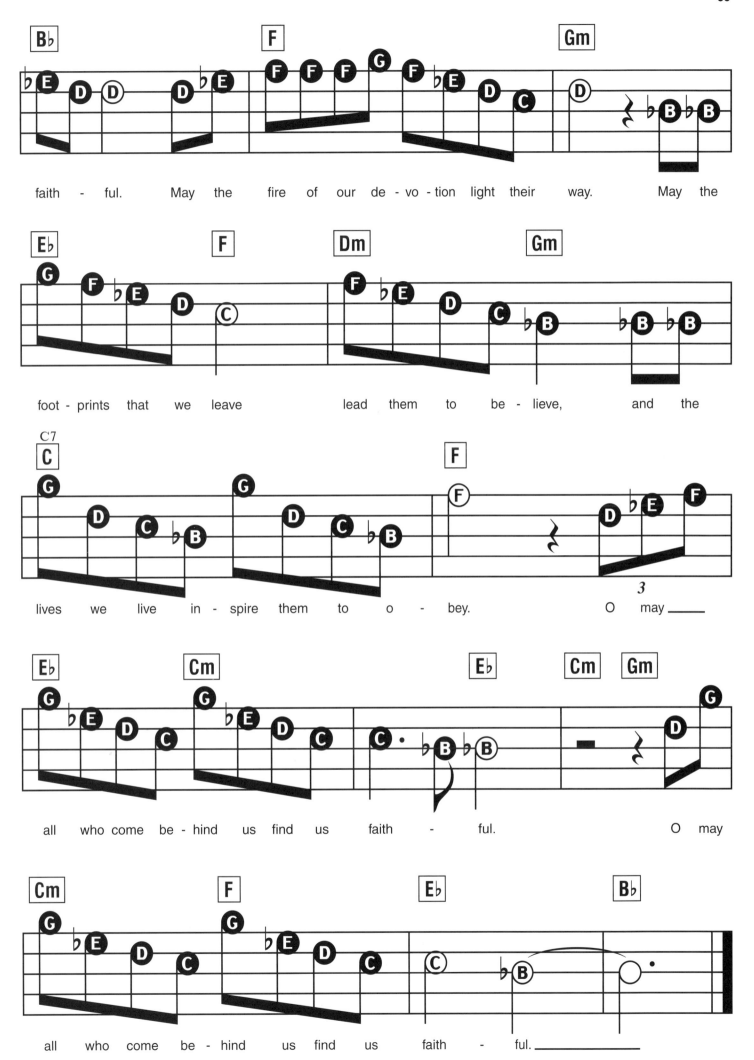

Friends

Registration 4
Rhythm: Rock

Words and Music by Michael W. Smith
and Deborah D. Smith

57

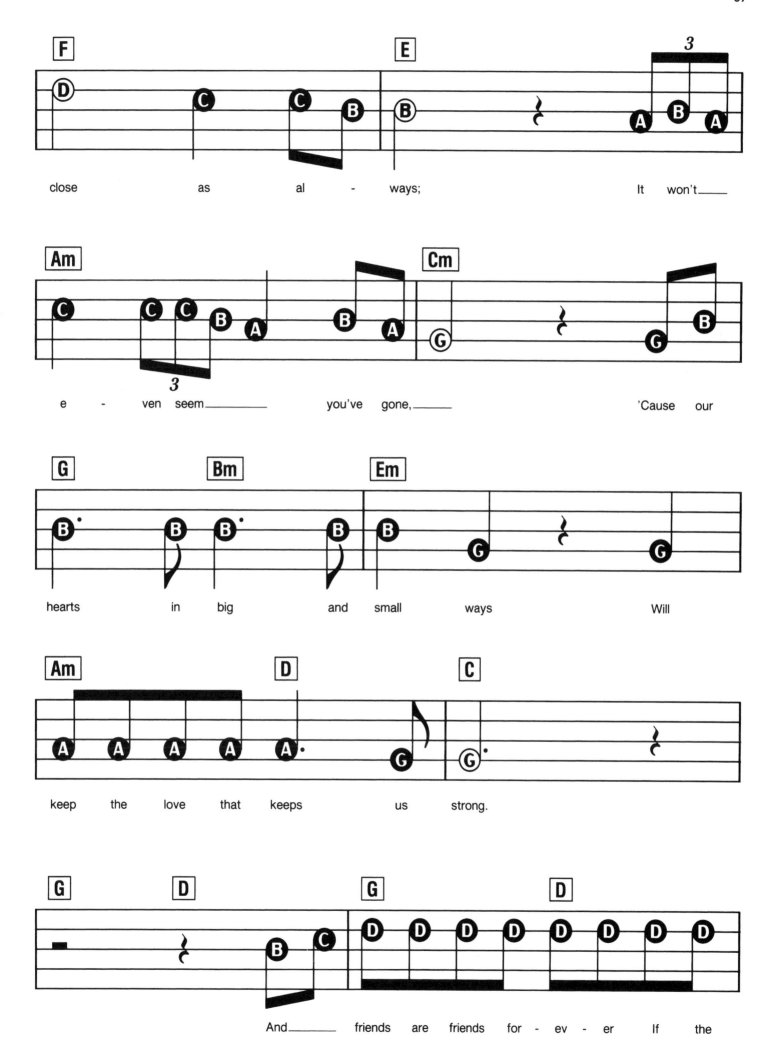

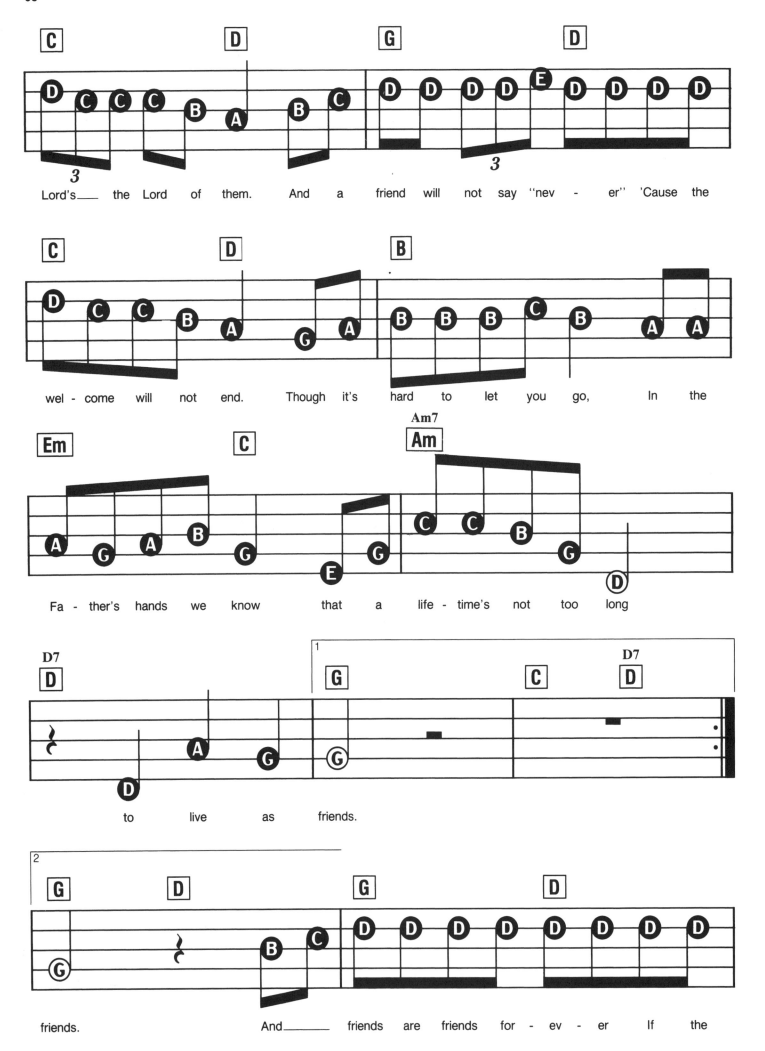

Go Light Your World

Registration 3
Rhythm: Ballad

Words and Music by
Chris Rice

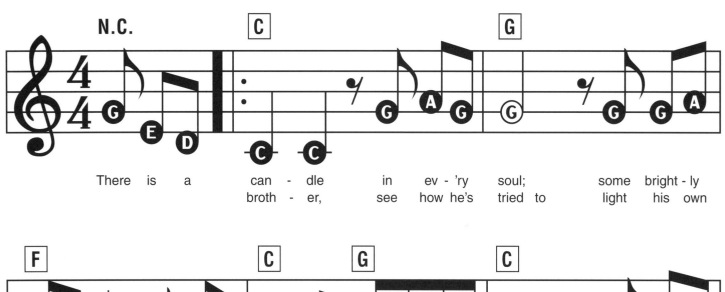

There is a can - dle in ev - 'ry soul; some bright - ly
broth - er, see how he's tried to light his own

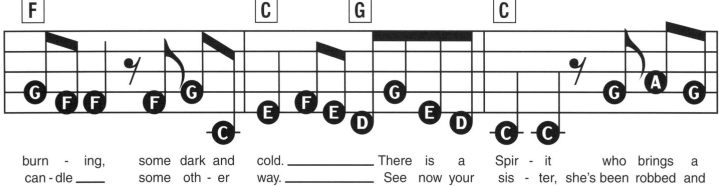

burn - ing, some dark and cold. _____ There is a Spir - it who brings a
can - dle ___ some oth - er way. _____ See now your sis - ter, she's been robbed and

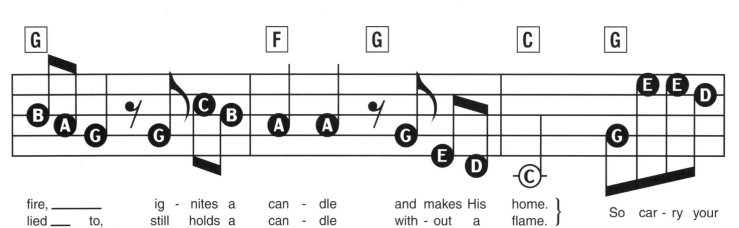

fire, _____ ig - nites a can - dle and makes His home. }
lied ___ to, still holds a can - dle with - out a flame. }

So car - ry your

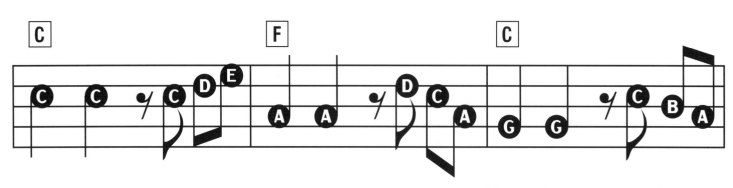

can - dle, run to the dark - ness, seek out the { hope - less, con - fused and
                                                 { lone - ly, the tired and

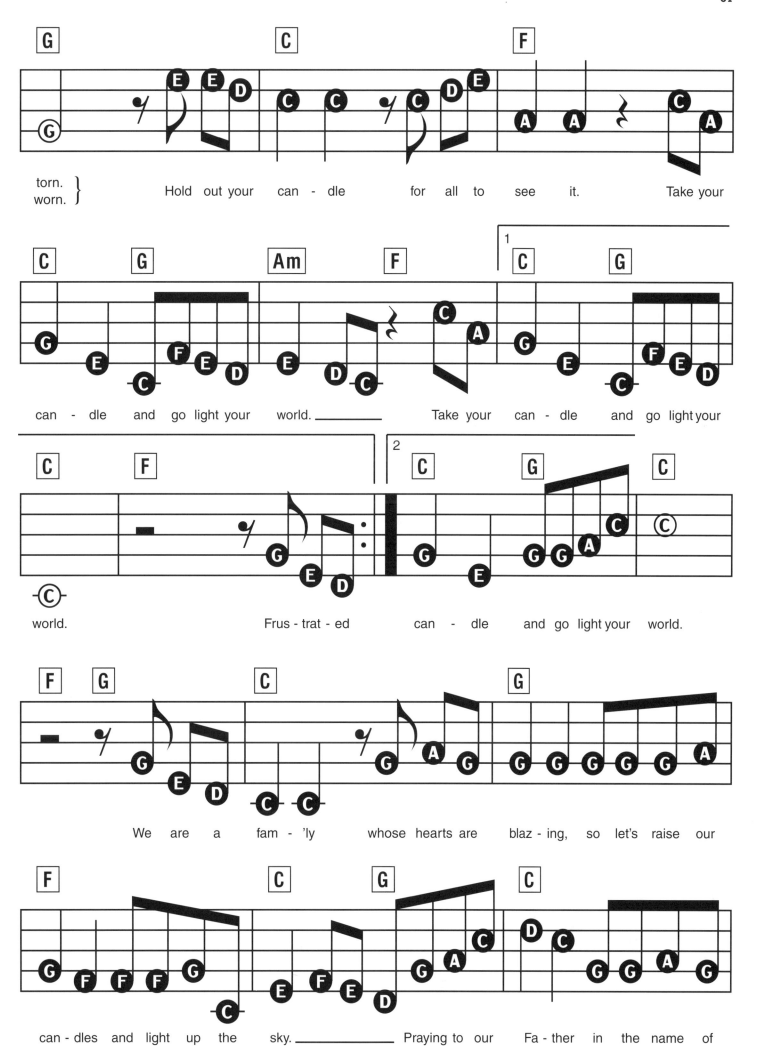

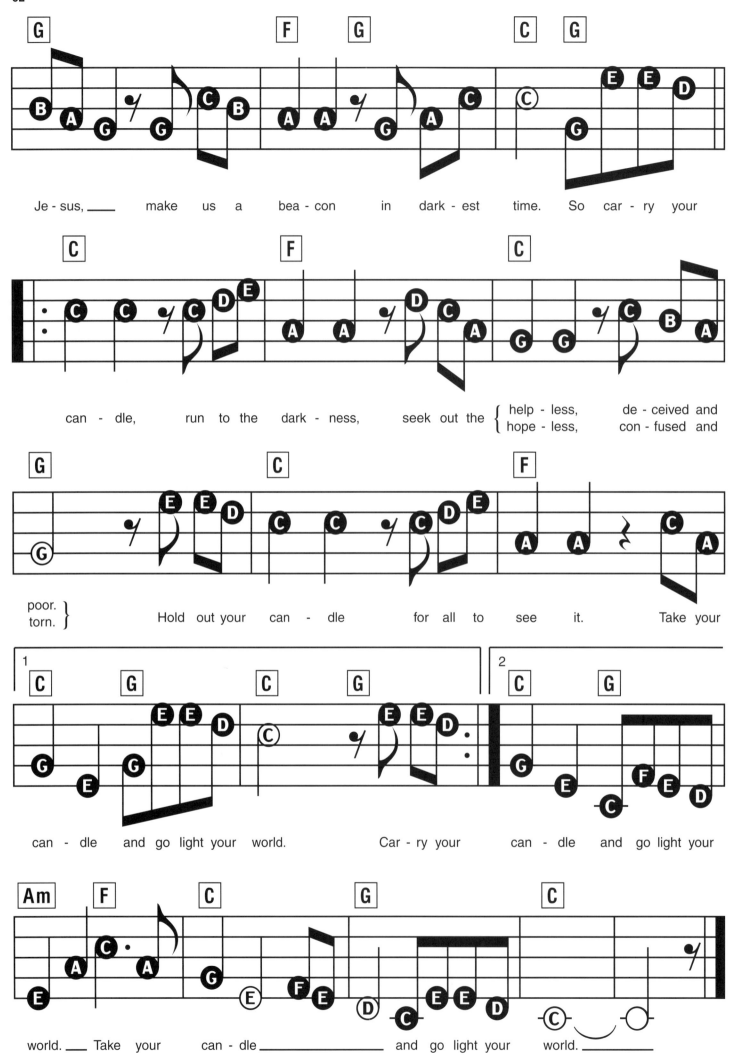

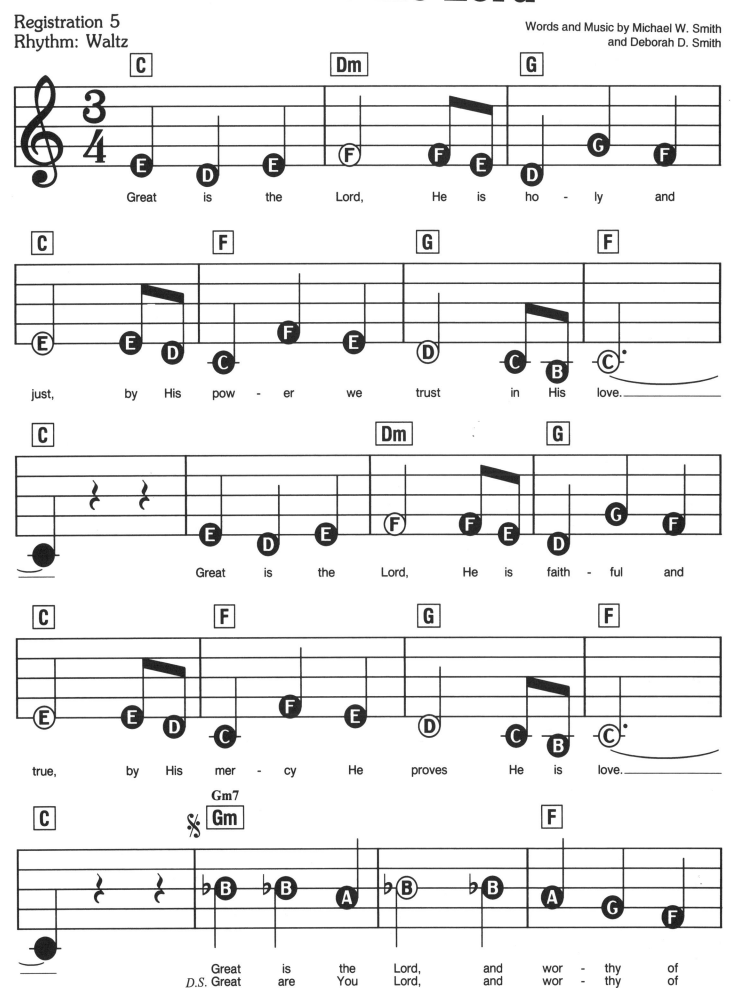

64

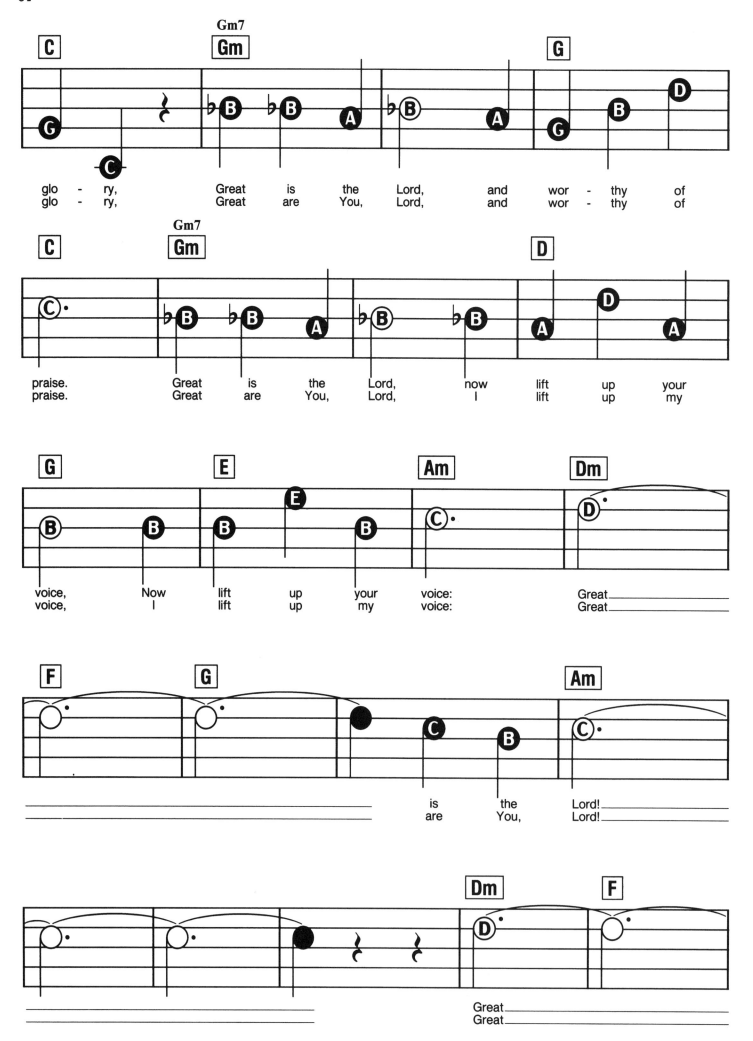

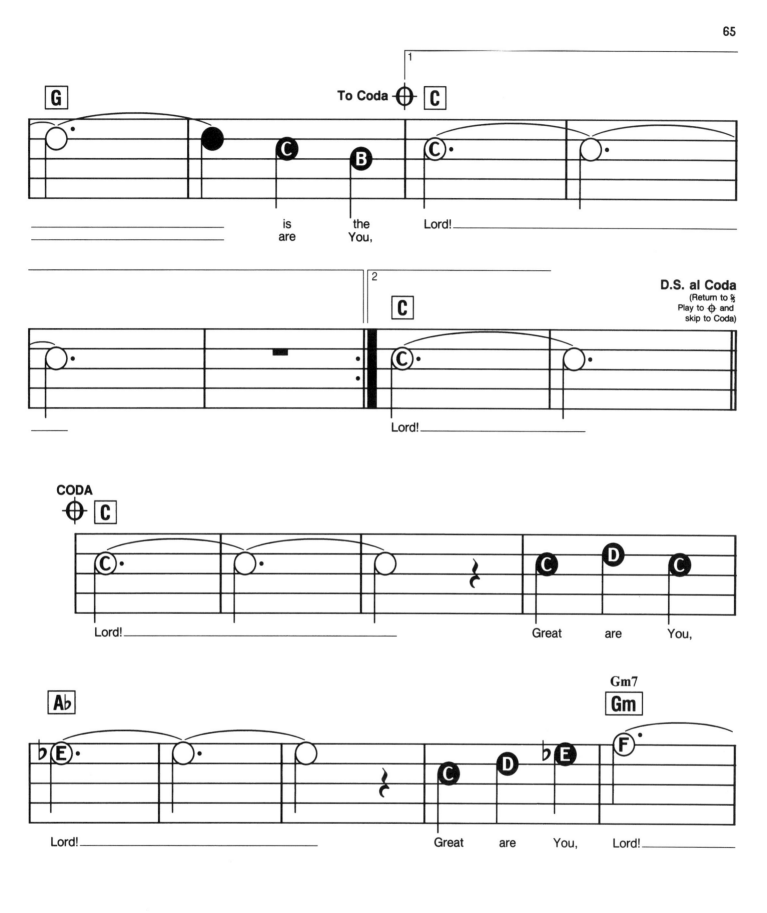

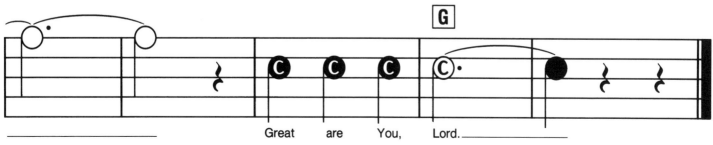

God Is in Control

Registration 7
Rhythm: Pop or 16 Beat

Words and Music by
Twila Paris

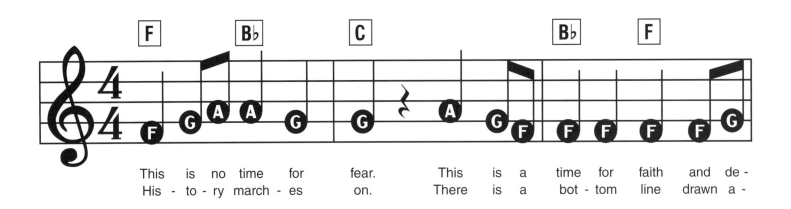

This is no time for fear. This is a time for faith and de-
His- to- ry march- es on. There is a bot- tom line drawn a-

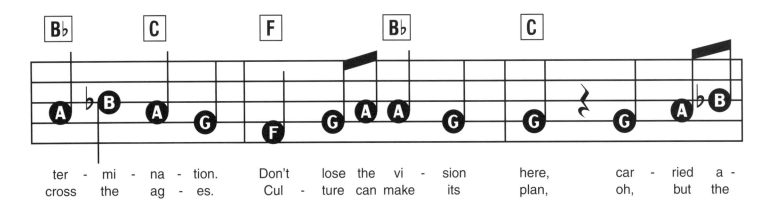

ter- mi- na- tion. Don't lose the vi- sion here, car- ried a-
cross the ag- es. Cul- ture can make its plan, oh, but the

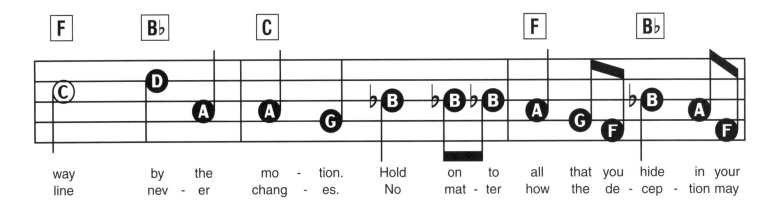

way by the mo- tion. Hold on to all that you hide in your
line nev- er chang- es. No mat- ter how the de- cep- tion may

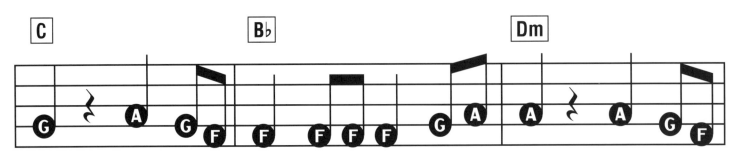

heart. There is one thing that has al- ways been true. It holds the
fly, there is one thing that has al- ways been true. It will be

67

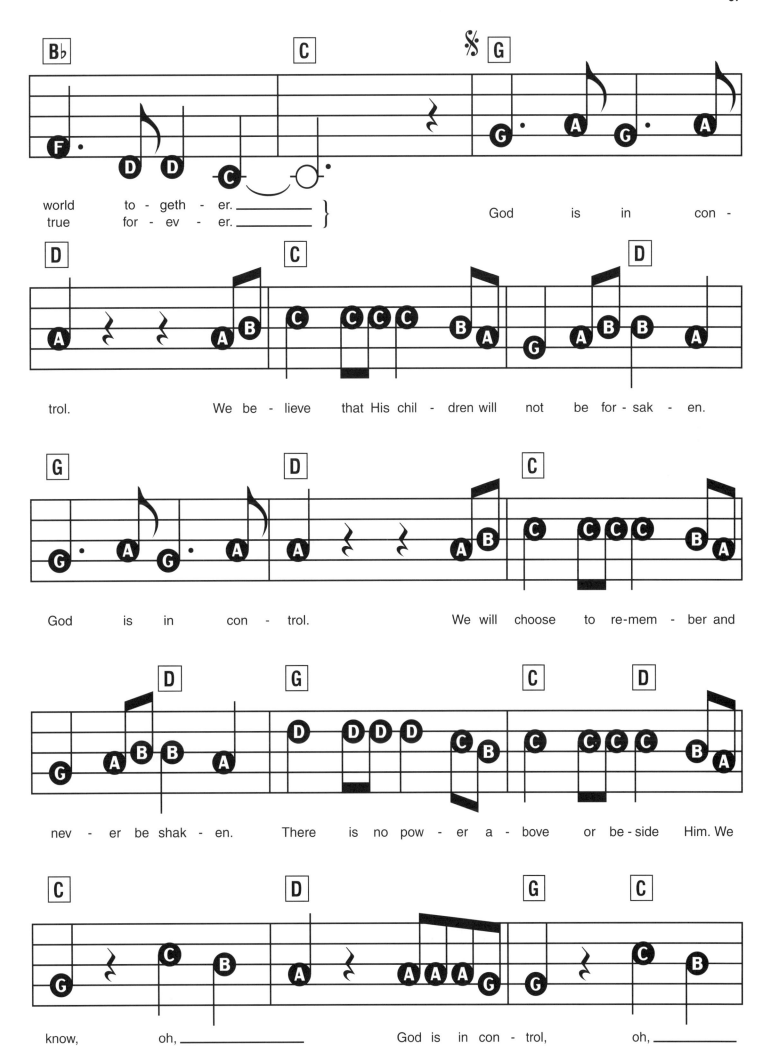

68

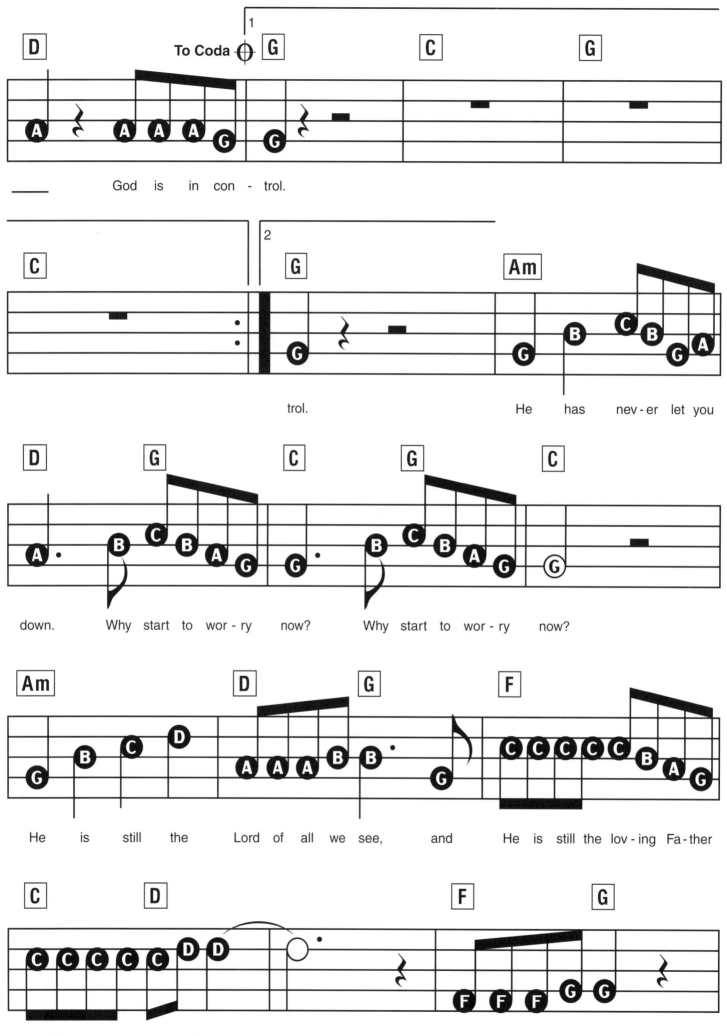

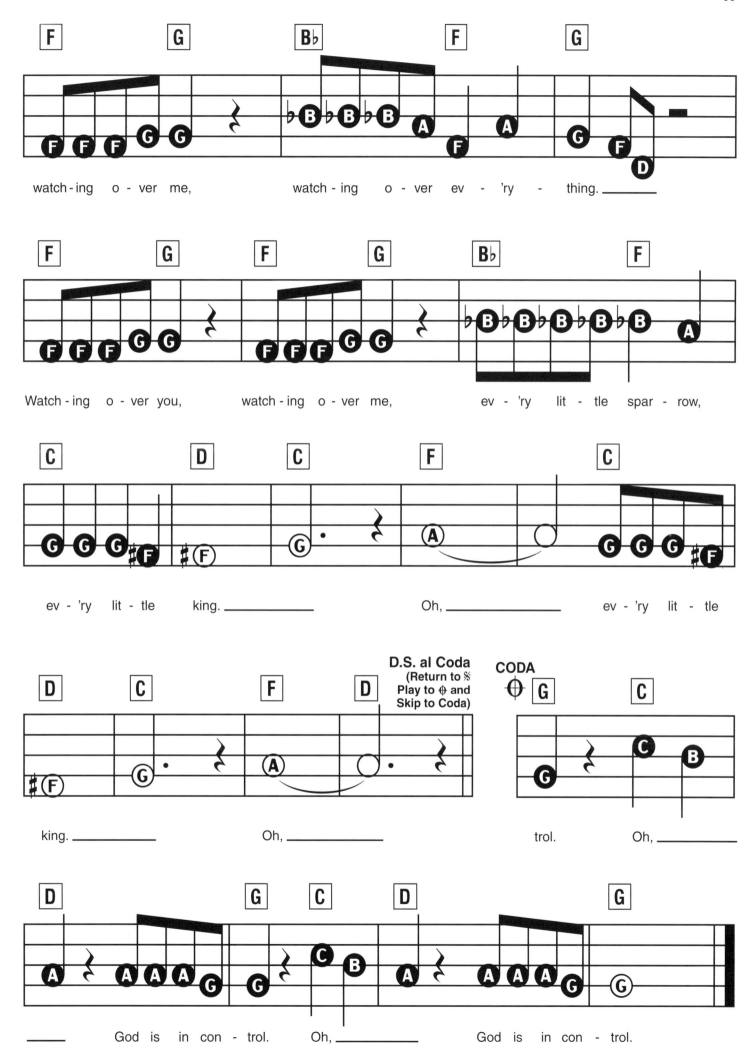

The Great Adventure

Registration 5
Rhythm: Rock or Pops

Words and Music by Steven Curtis Chapman
and Geoff Moore

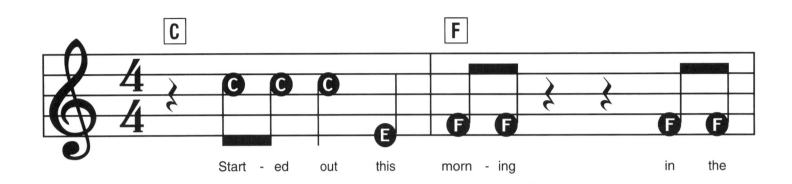

Start - ed out this morn - ing in the

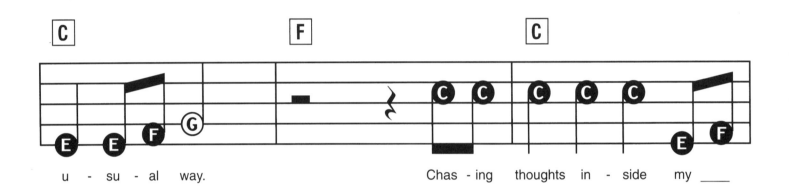

u - su - al way. Chas - ing thoughts in - side my ___

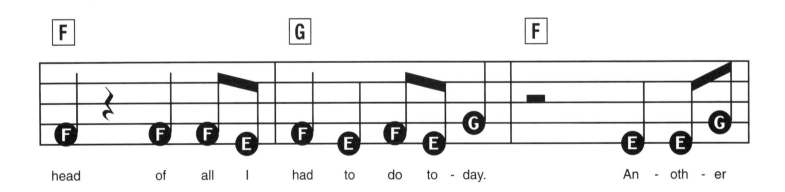

head of all I had to do to - day. An - oth - er

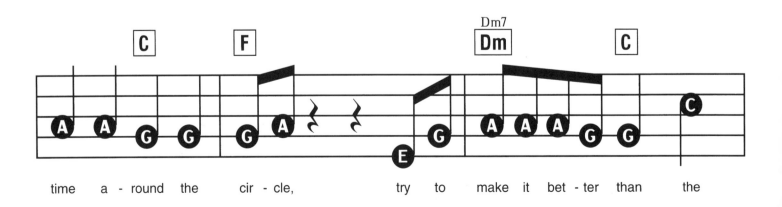

time a - round the cir - cle, try to make it bet - ter than the

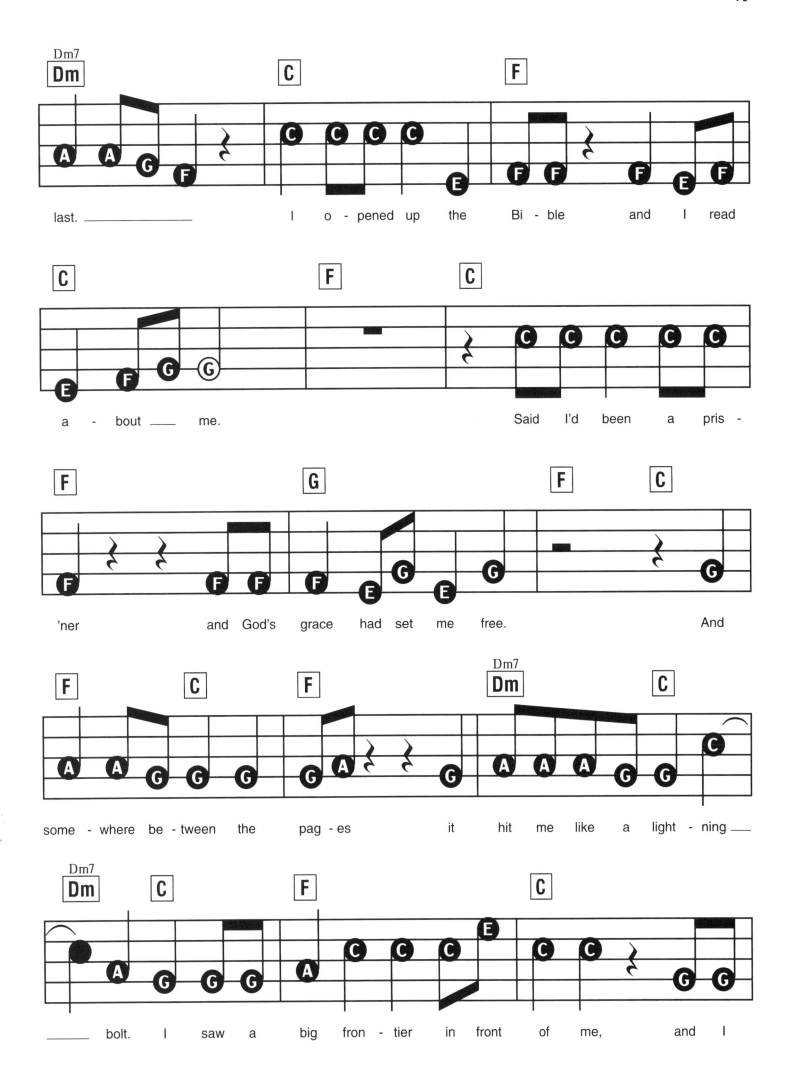

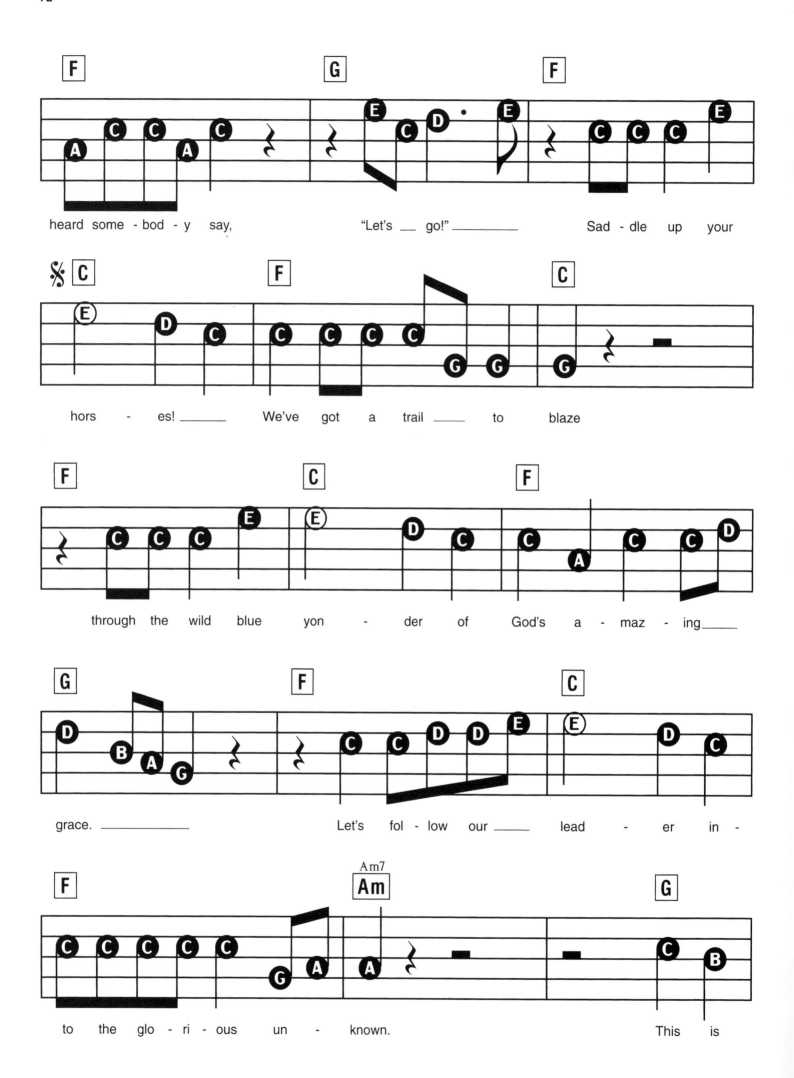

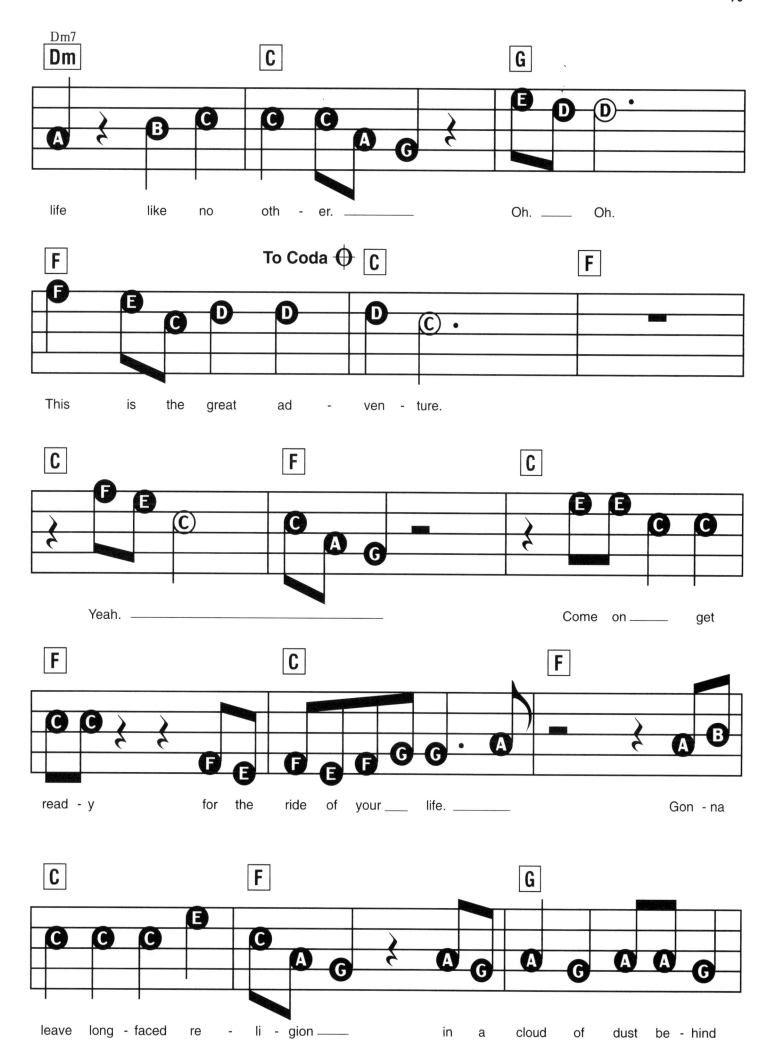

74

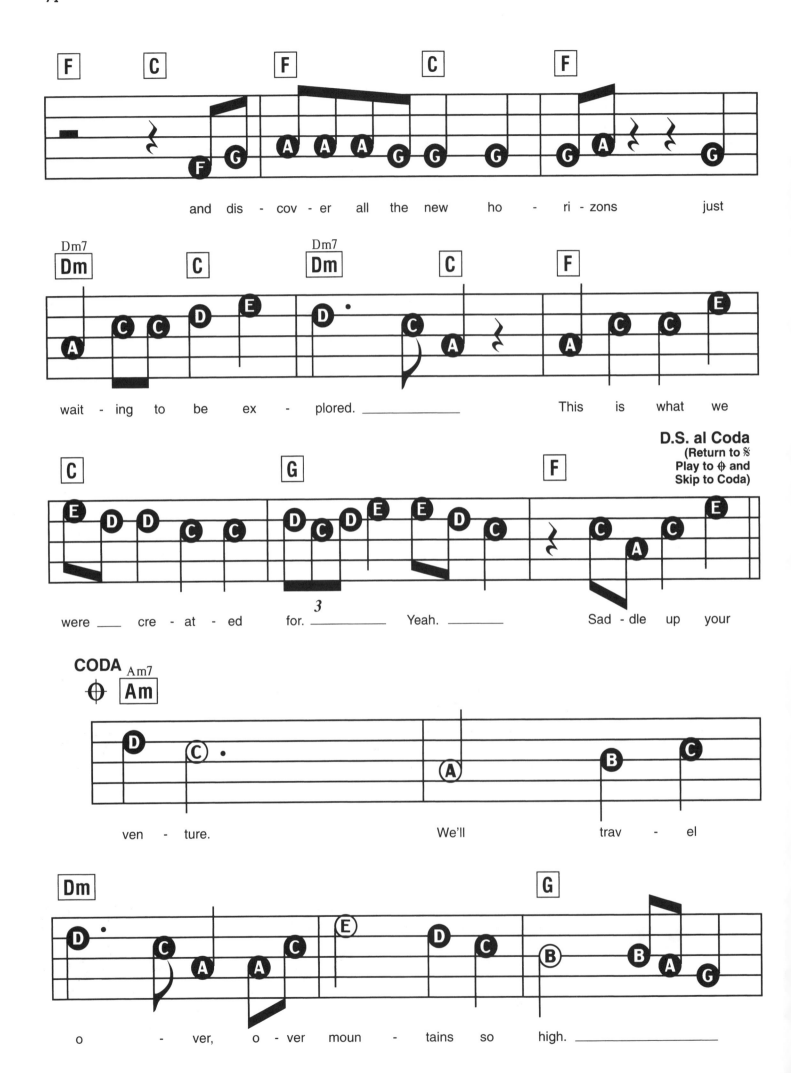

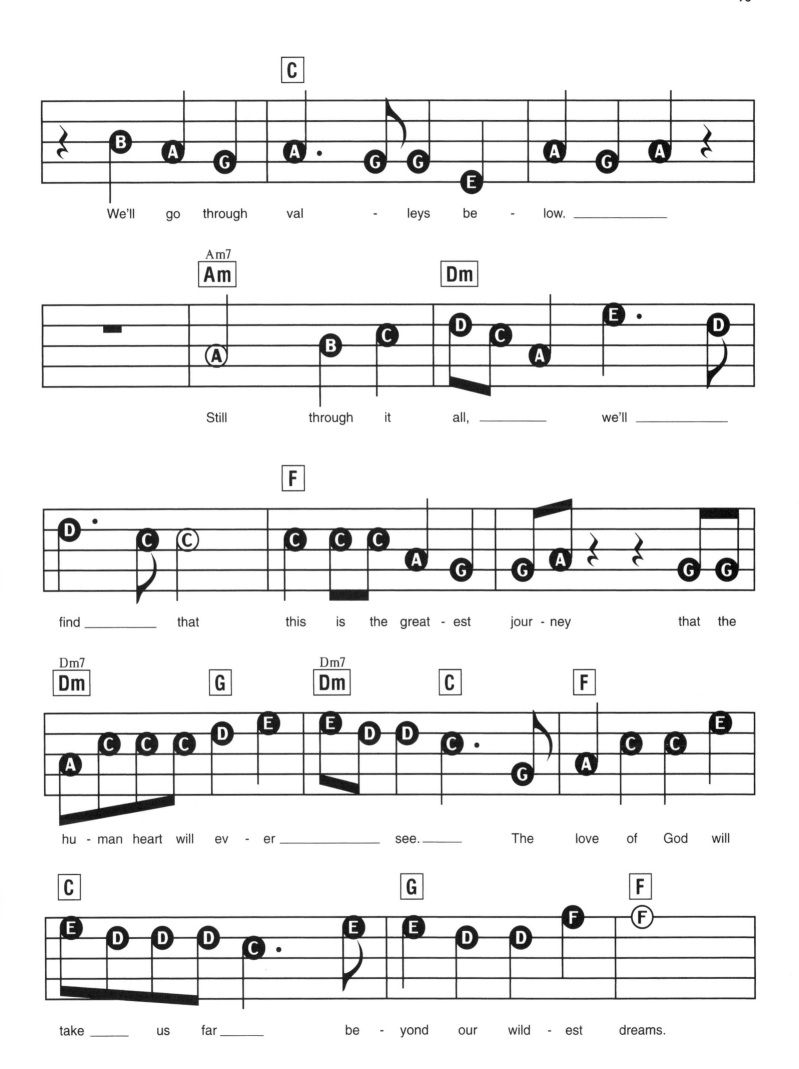

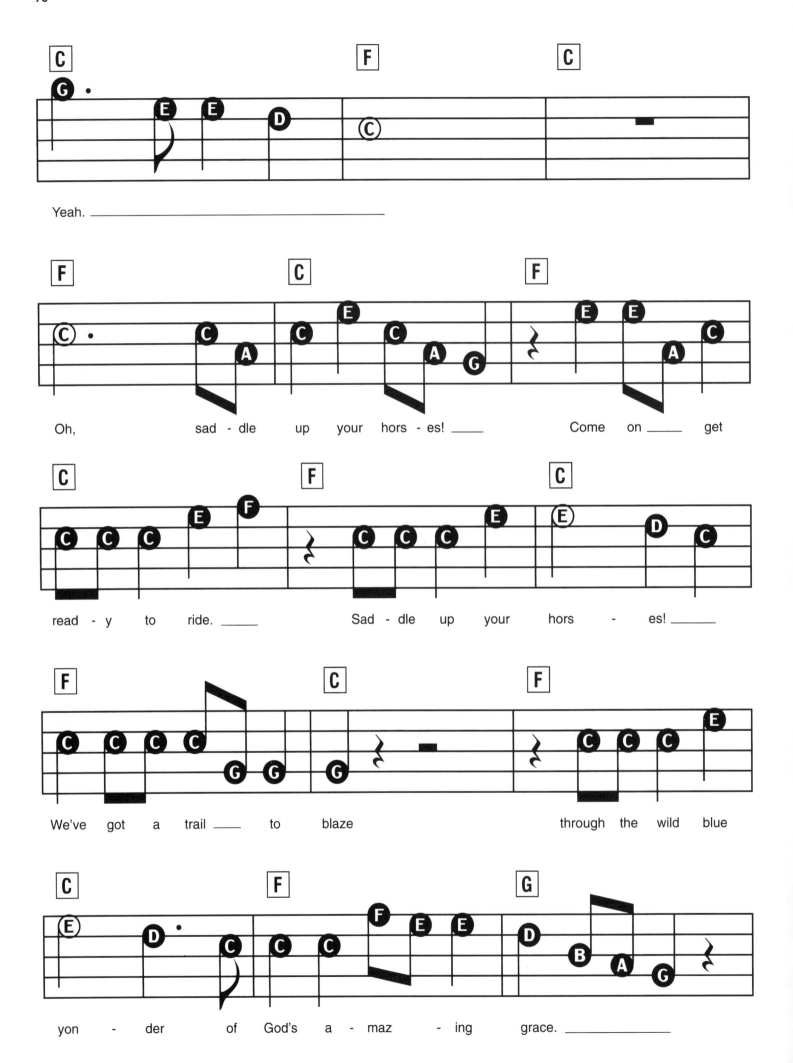

77

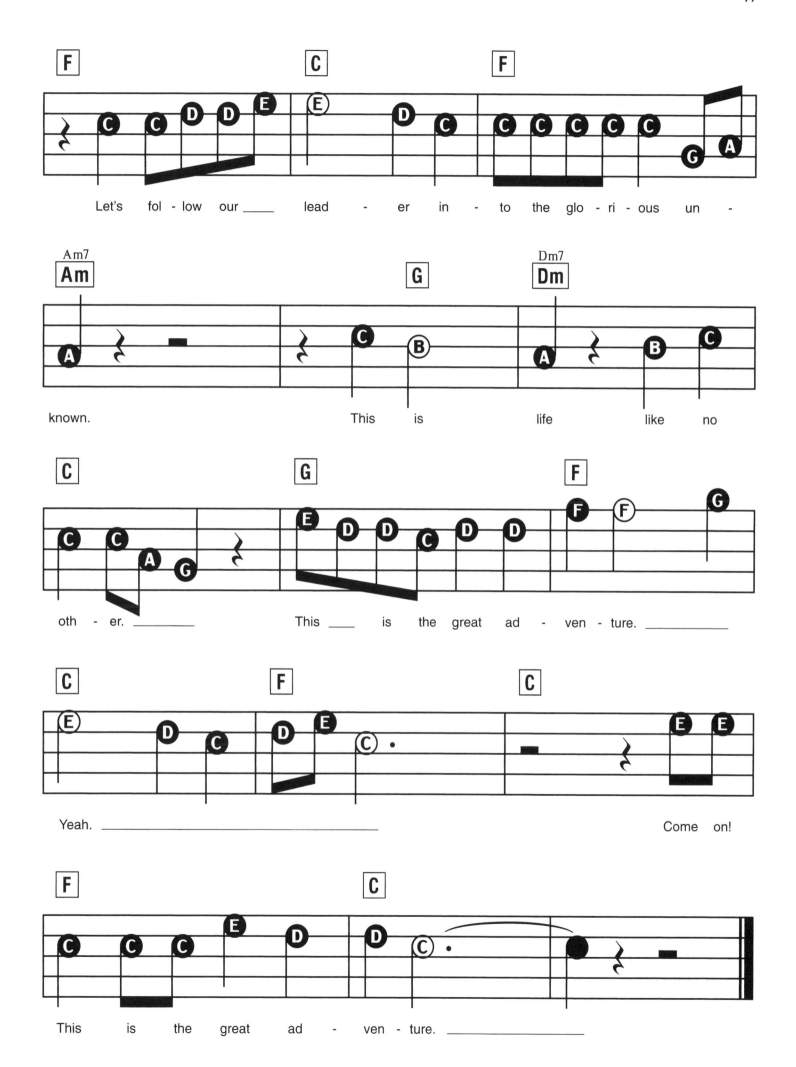

The Great Divide

Registration 1
Rhythm: Ballad

Words and Music by Matt Huesmann
and Grant Cunningham

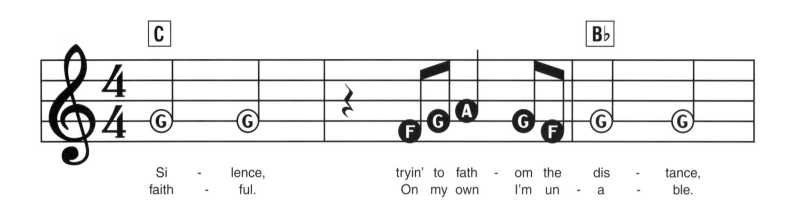

Si - lence, tryin' to fath - om the dis - tance,
faith - ful. On my own I'm un - a - ble.

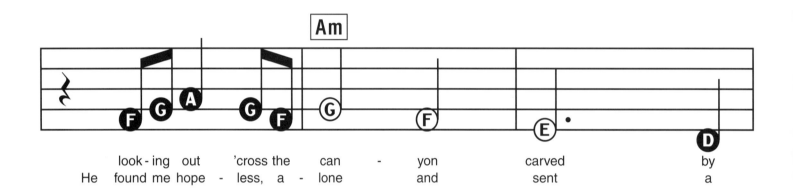

look - ing out 'cross the can - yon carved by
He found me hope - less, a - lone and sent a

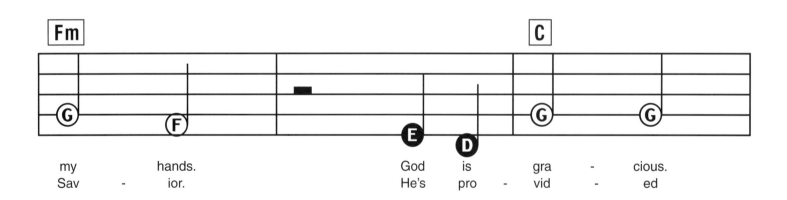

my hands. God is gra - cious.
Sav - ior. He's pro - vid - ed

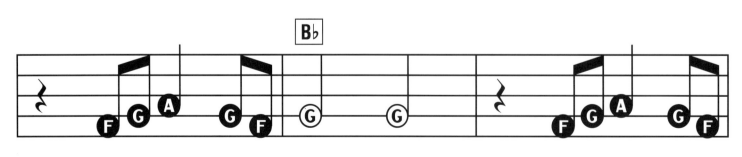

Sin would still sep - a - rate us were it not for the
a path and prom - ised to guide us safe - ly past all the

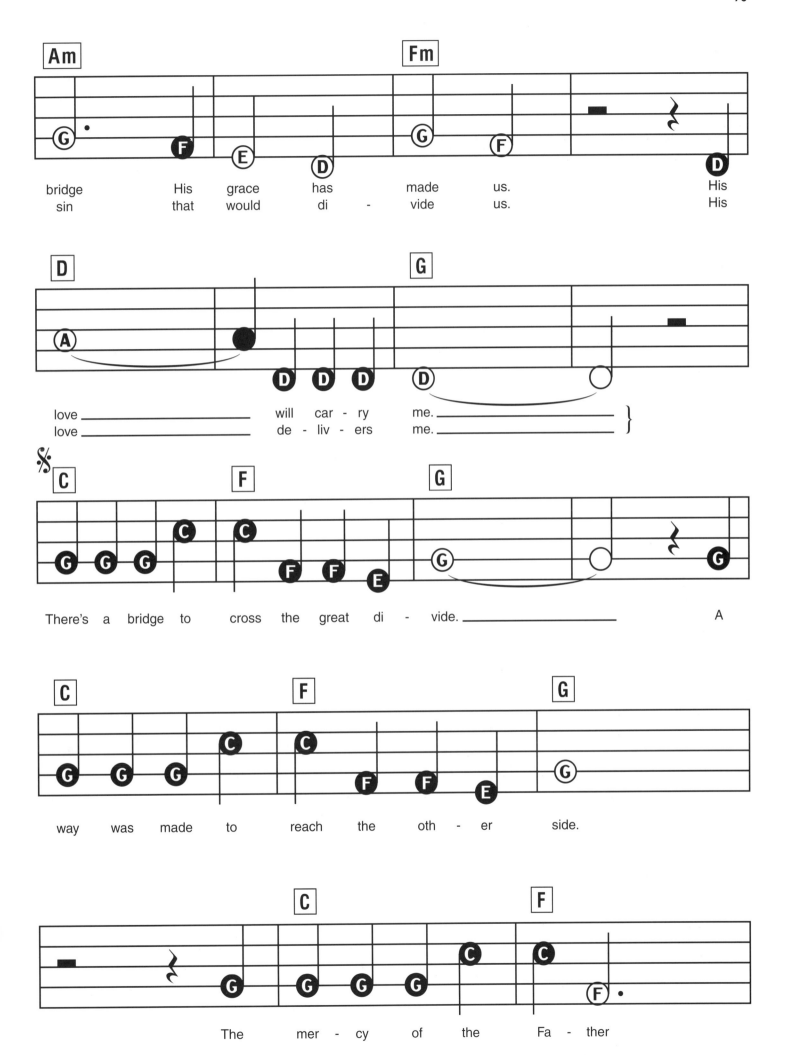

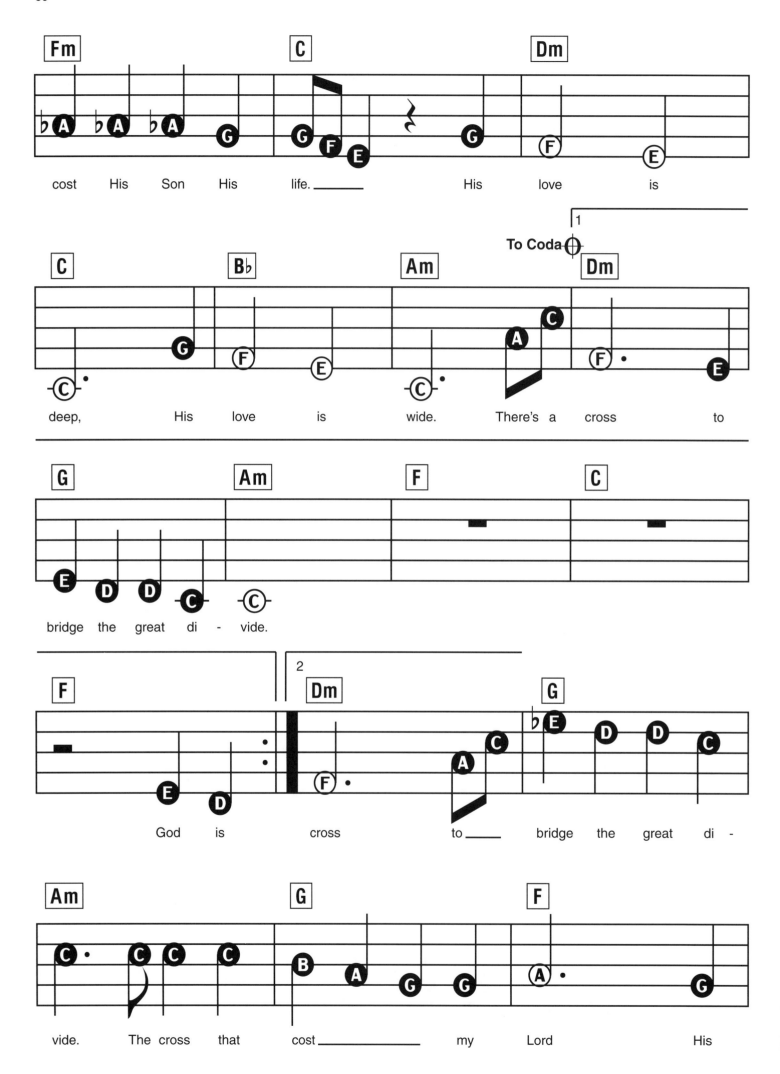

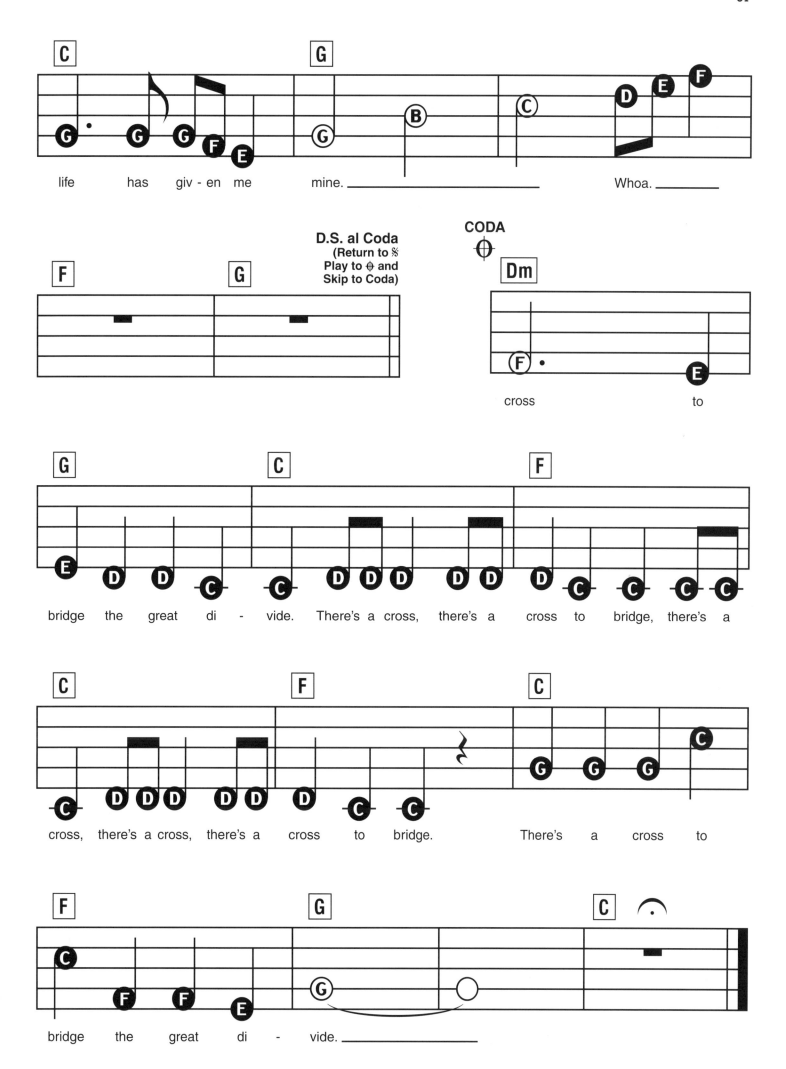

Heaven in the Real World

Registration 4
Rhythm: 8 Beat or Rock

Words and Music by
Steven Curtis Chapman

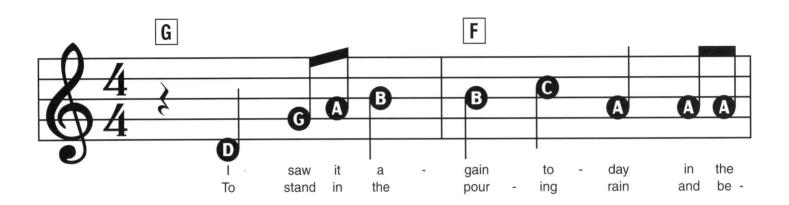

I saw it a - gain to - day in the
To stand in the pour - ing day rain and be -

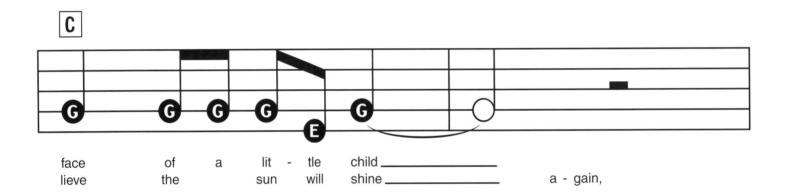

face of a lit - tle child _____
lieve of the sun will shine _____ a - gain,

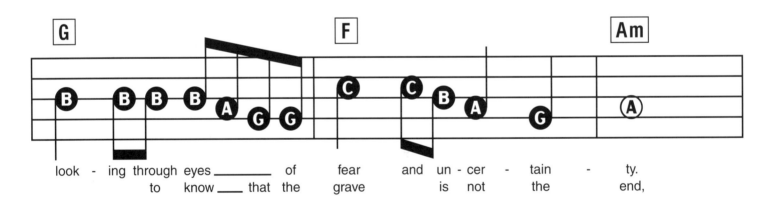

look - ing through eyes _____ of fear and un - cer - tain - ty.
to know ___ that the grave is not the end,

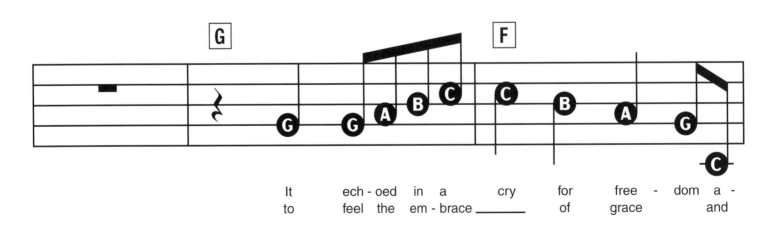

It ech - oed in a cry for free - dom a -
to feel the em - brace _____ of grace and

83

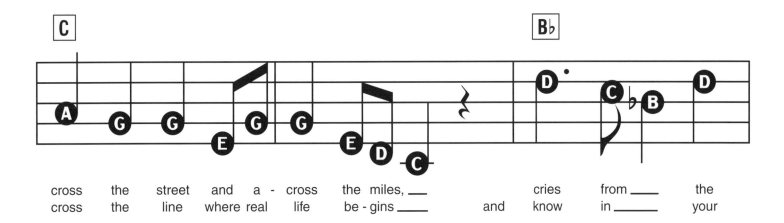

cross the street and a-cross the miles, ___ cries from ___ the
cross the line where real life be-gins ___ and know in ___ your

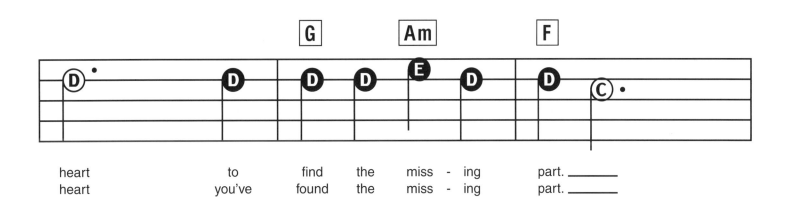

heart to find the miss-ing part. ___
heart you've found the miss-ing part. ___

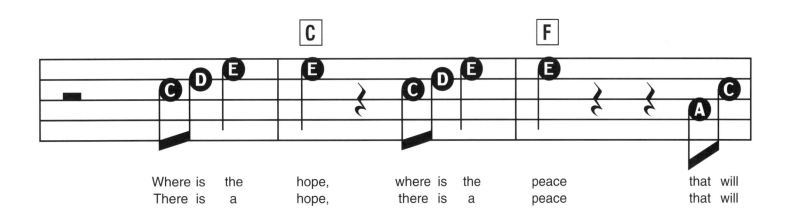

Where is the hope, where is the peace that will
There is a hope, where there is a peace that will

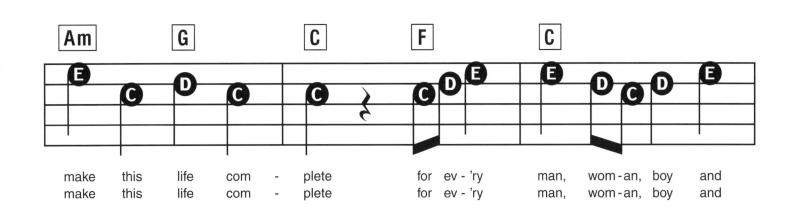

make this life com-plete for ev-'ry man, wom-an, boy and
make this life com-plete for ev-'ry man, wom-an, boy and

84

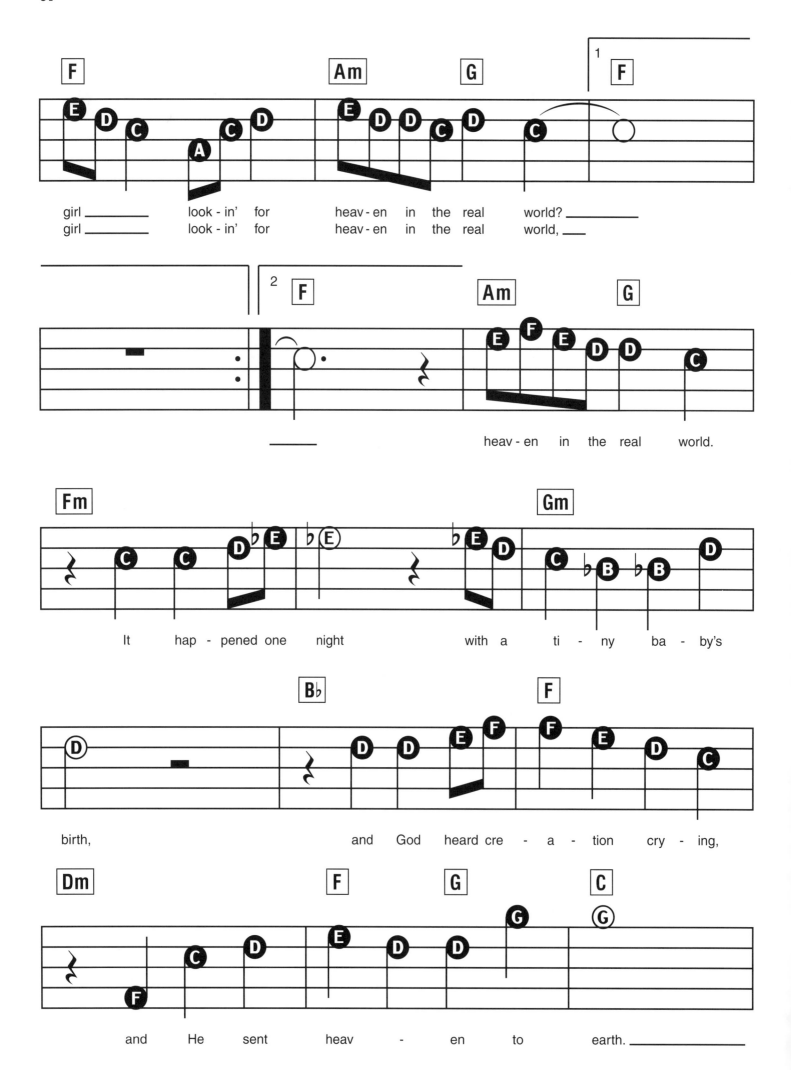

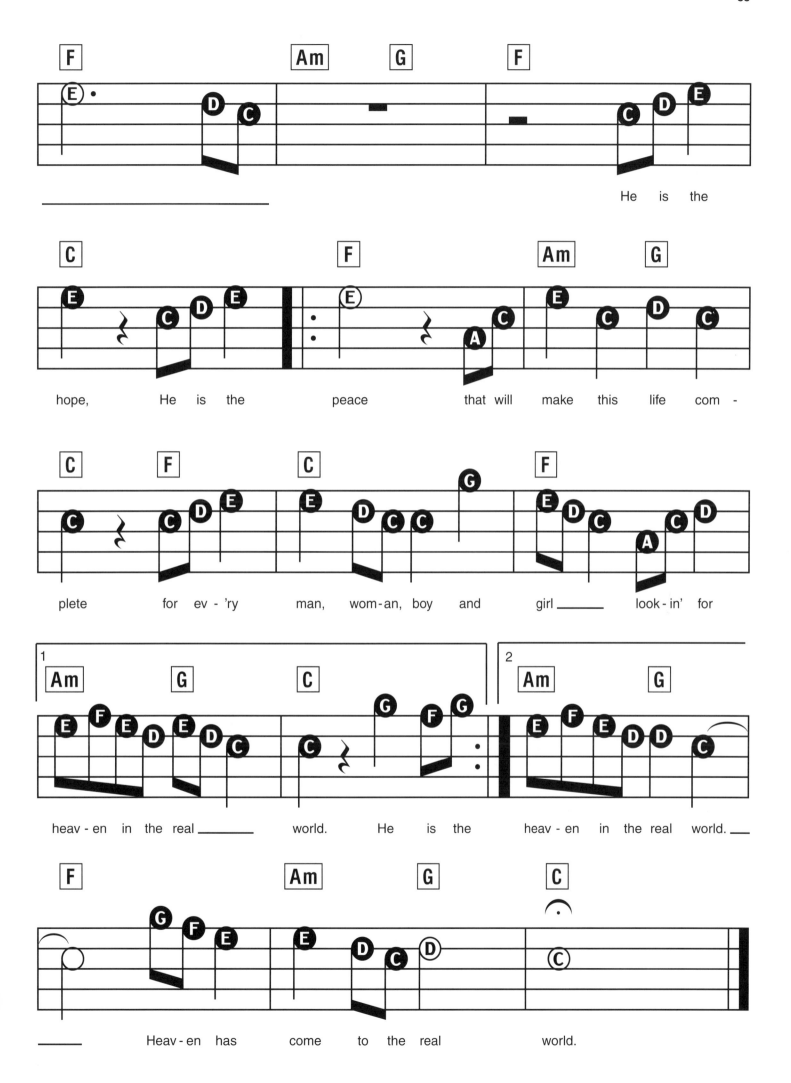

Here I Am

Registration 5
Rhythm: Rock or 8 Beat

Words and Music by Rebecca St. James,
Bill Deaton and Eric Champion

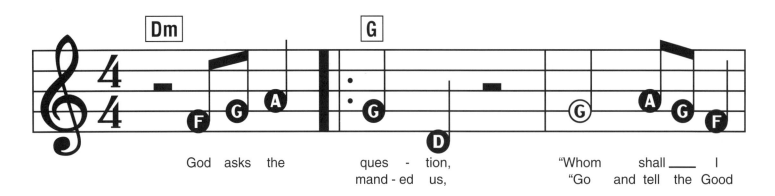

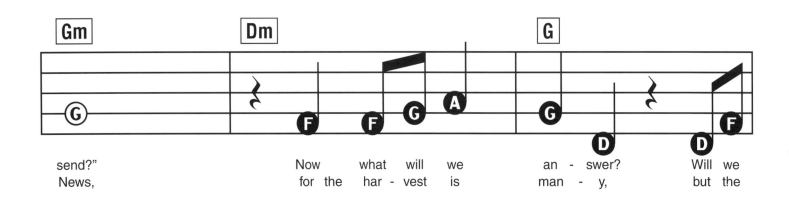

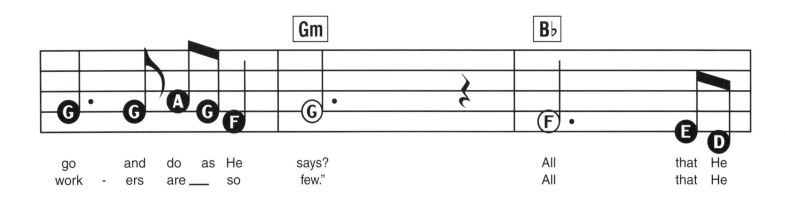

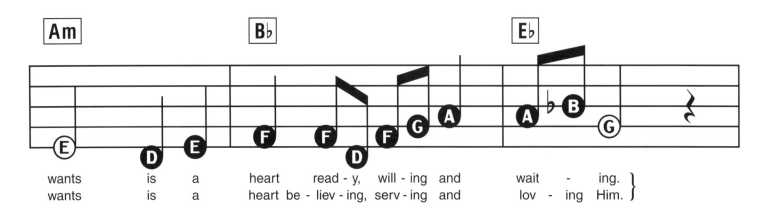

87

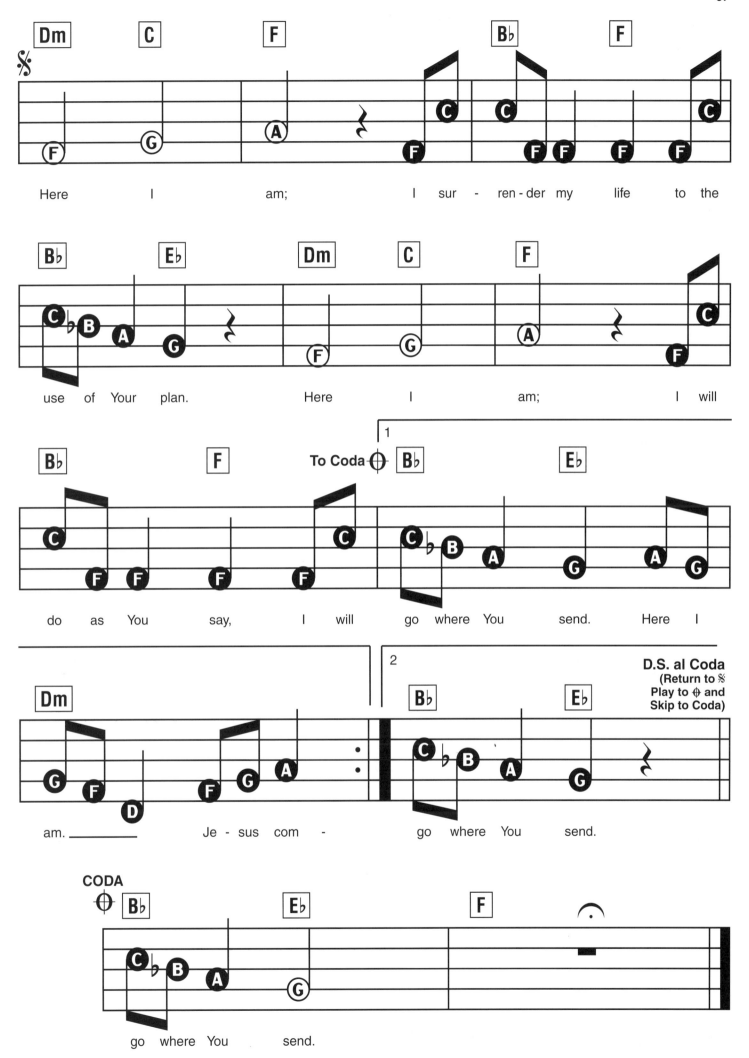

His Strength Is Perfect

Registration 1
Rhythm: Ballad

Words and Music by Steven Curtis Chapman
and Jerry Salley

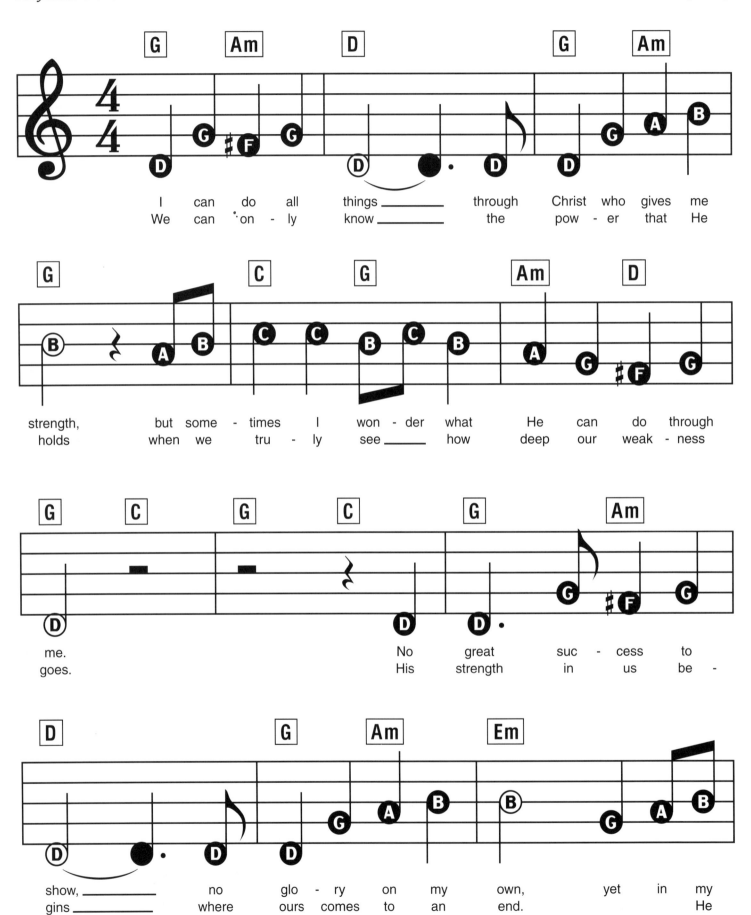

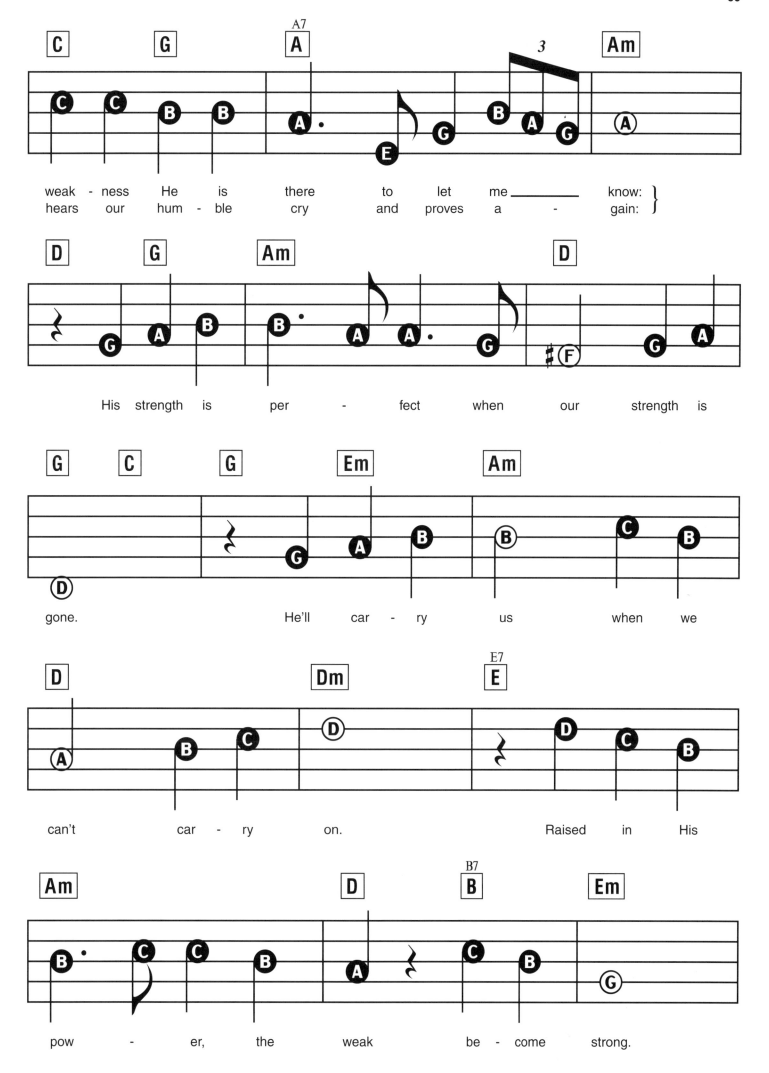

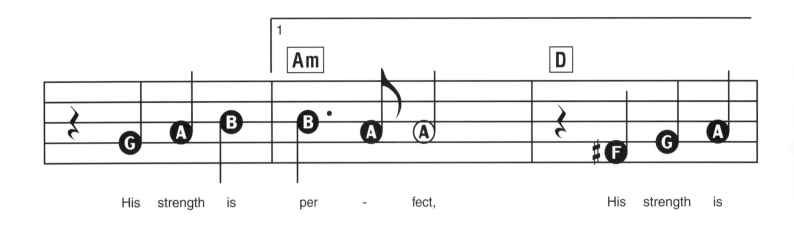

His strength is per - fect, His strength is

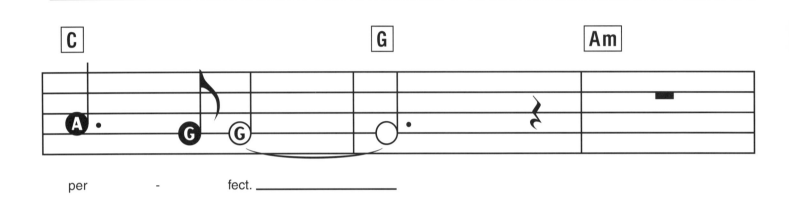

per - fect. _____

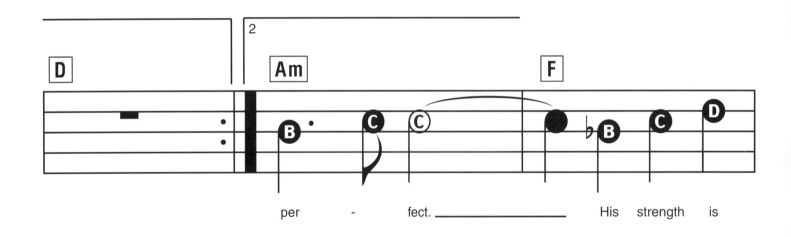

per - fect. _____ His strength is

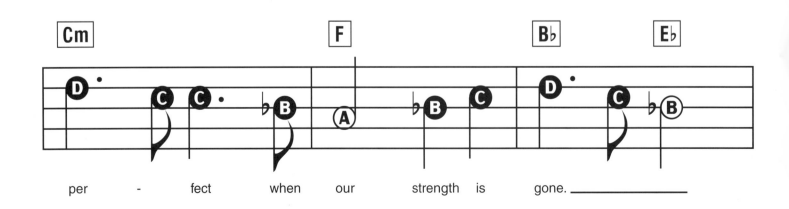

per - fect when our strength is gone. _____

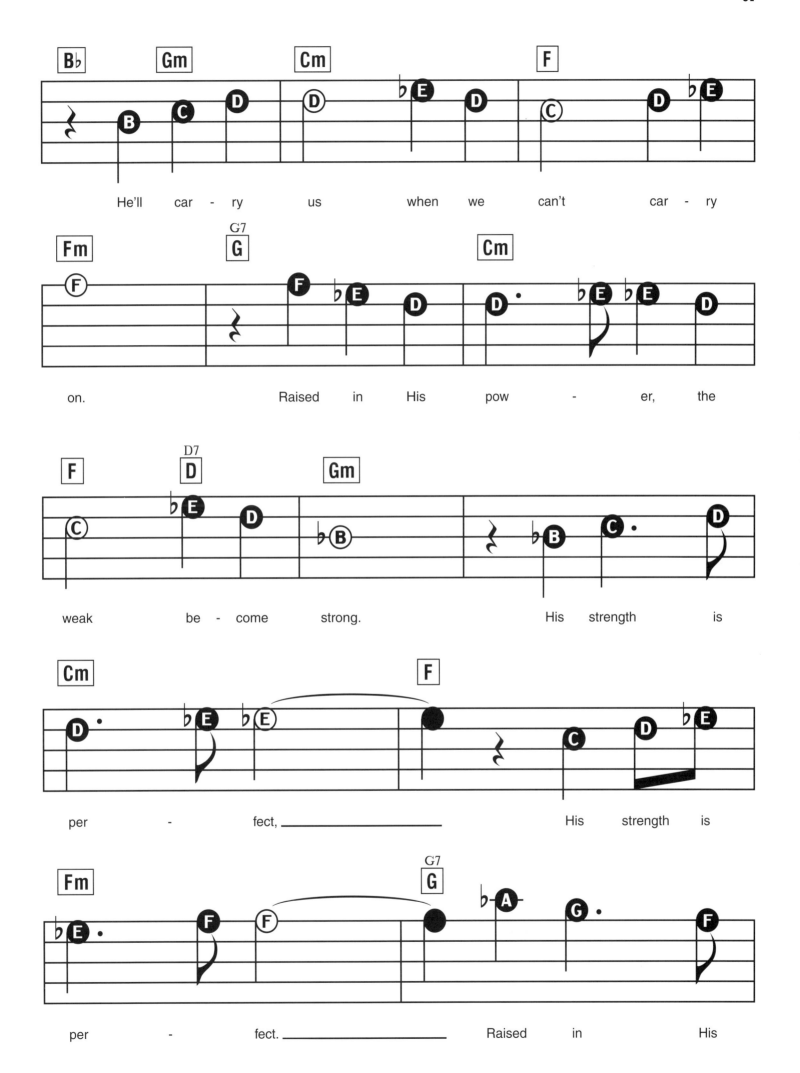

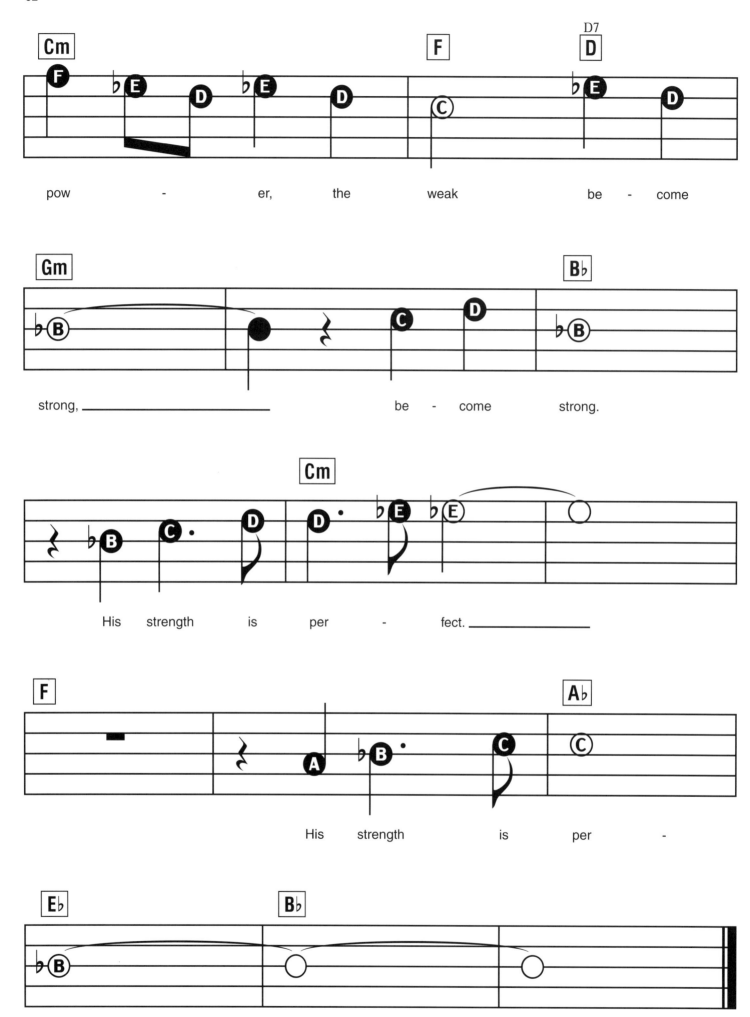

I Will Be Here

Registration 8
Rhythm: Ballad

Words and Music by
Steven Curtis Chapman

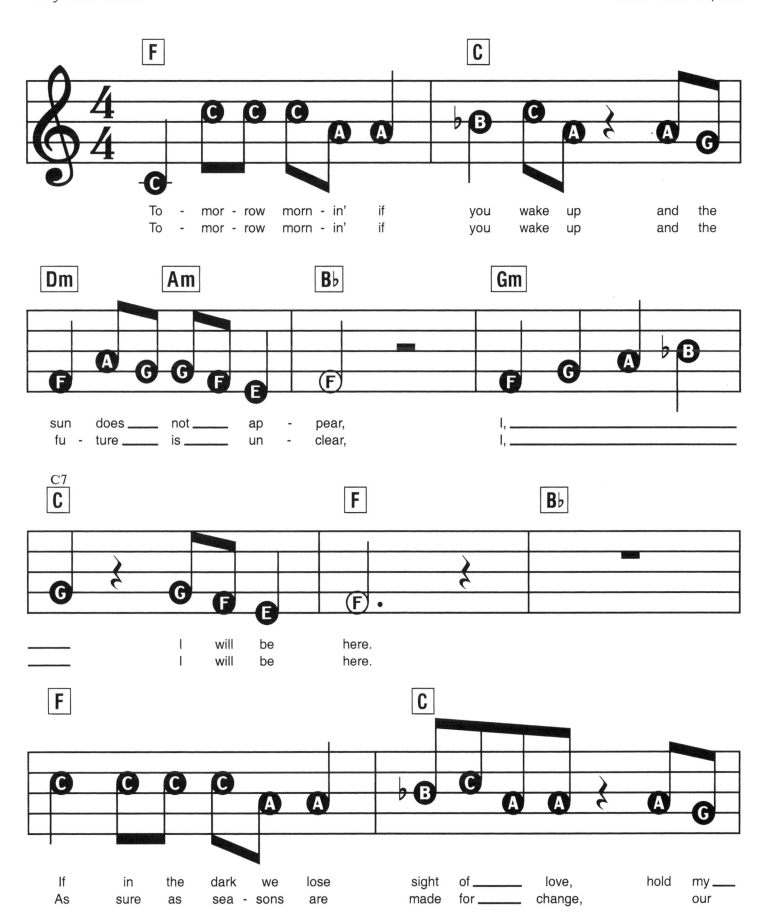

94

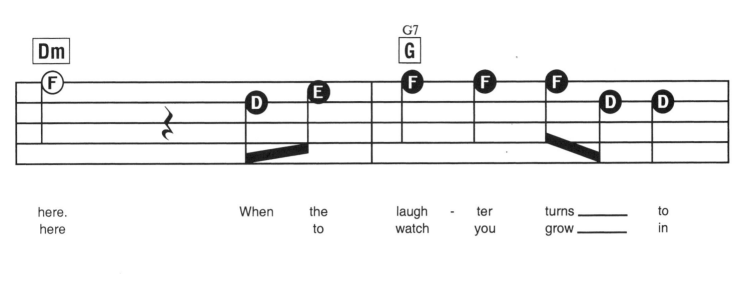

here.   When the laugh - ter turns _____ to
here   to watch you grow _____ in

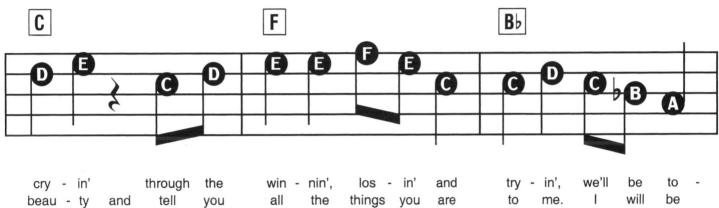

cry - in' through the win - nin', los - in' and try - in', we'll be to -
beau - ty and tell you all the things you are to me. I will be

To Coda

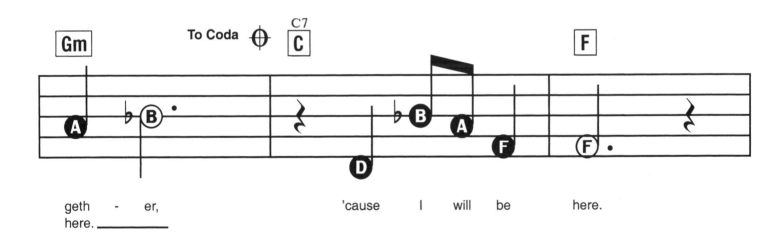

geth - er,   'cause I will be here.
here. _____

D.C. al Coda
(Return to beginning
Play to ⊕ and
Skip to Coda)

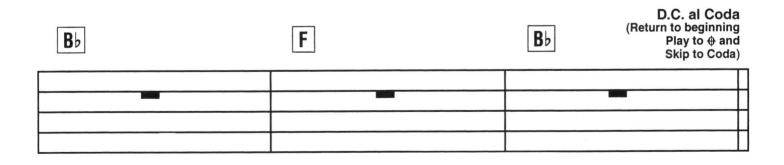

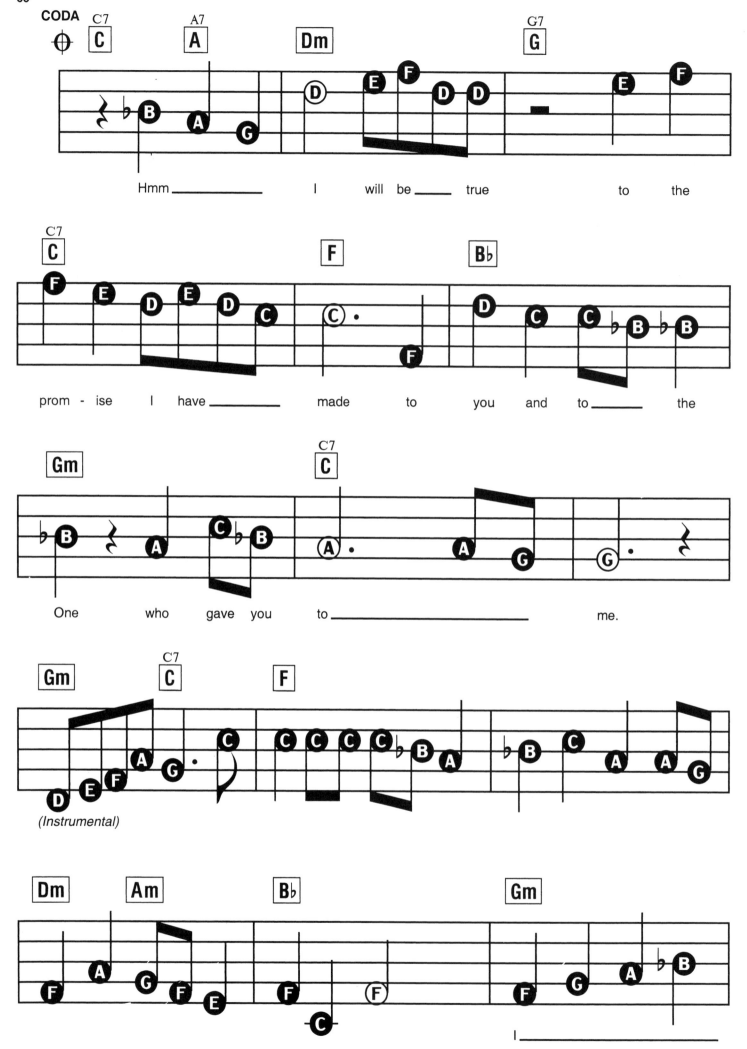

CODA

Hmm _____ I will be ___ true to the

prom - ise I have _____ made to you and to ___ the

One who gave you to _____ me.

(Instrumental)

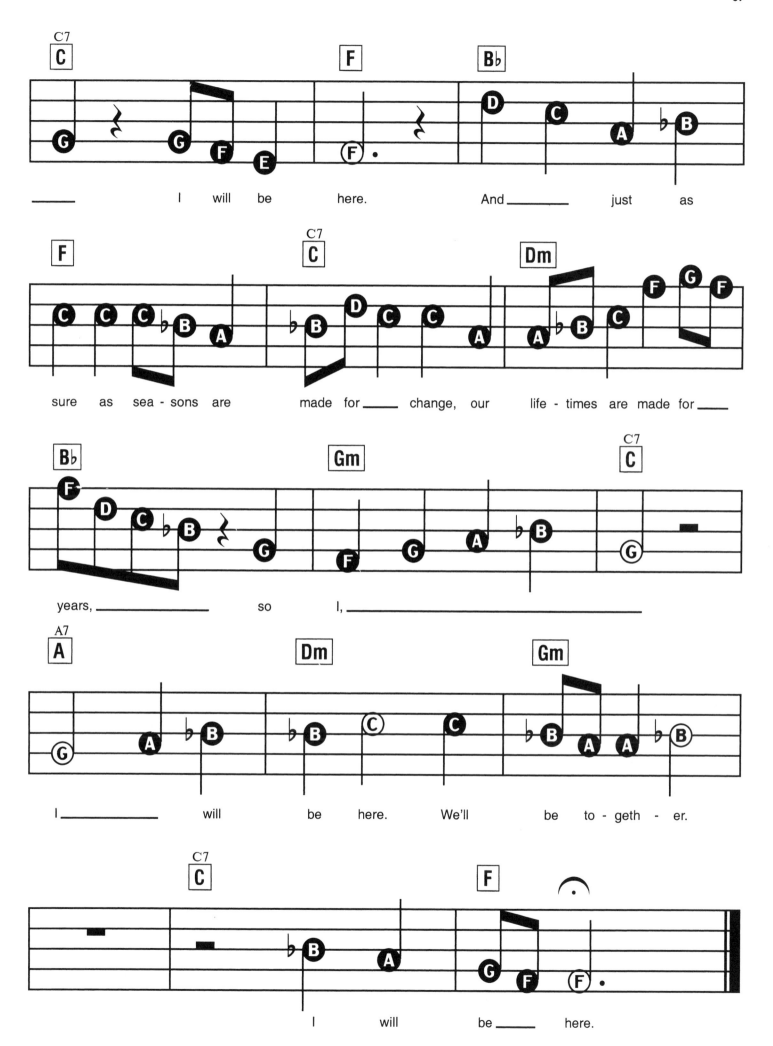

Holy

Registration 8
Rhythm: Pop or 8 Beat

Words and Music by Nichole Nordeman
and Mark Hammond

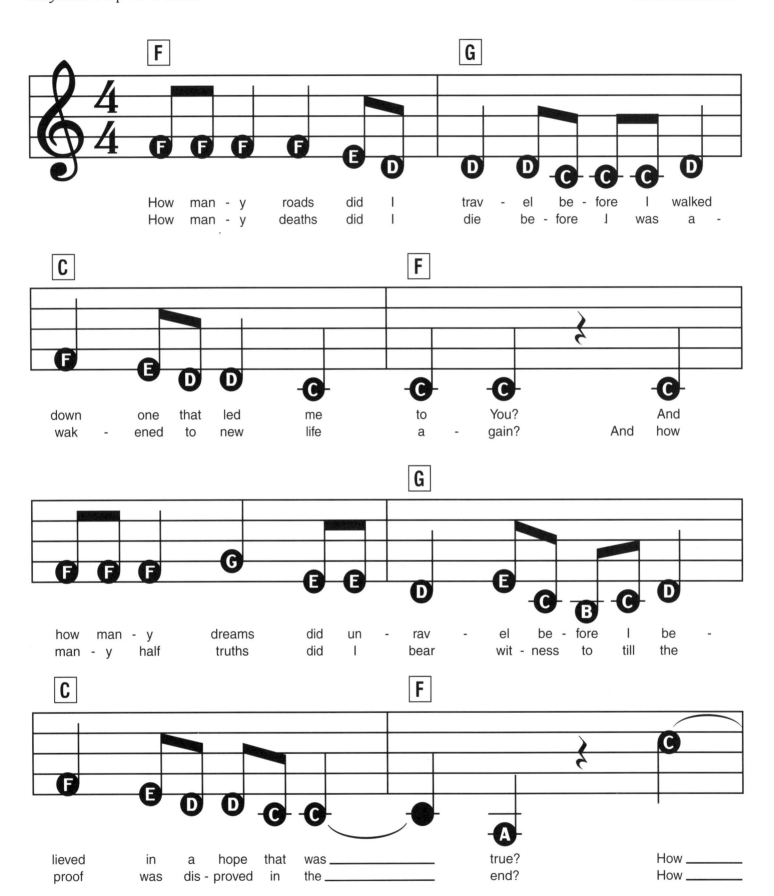

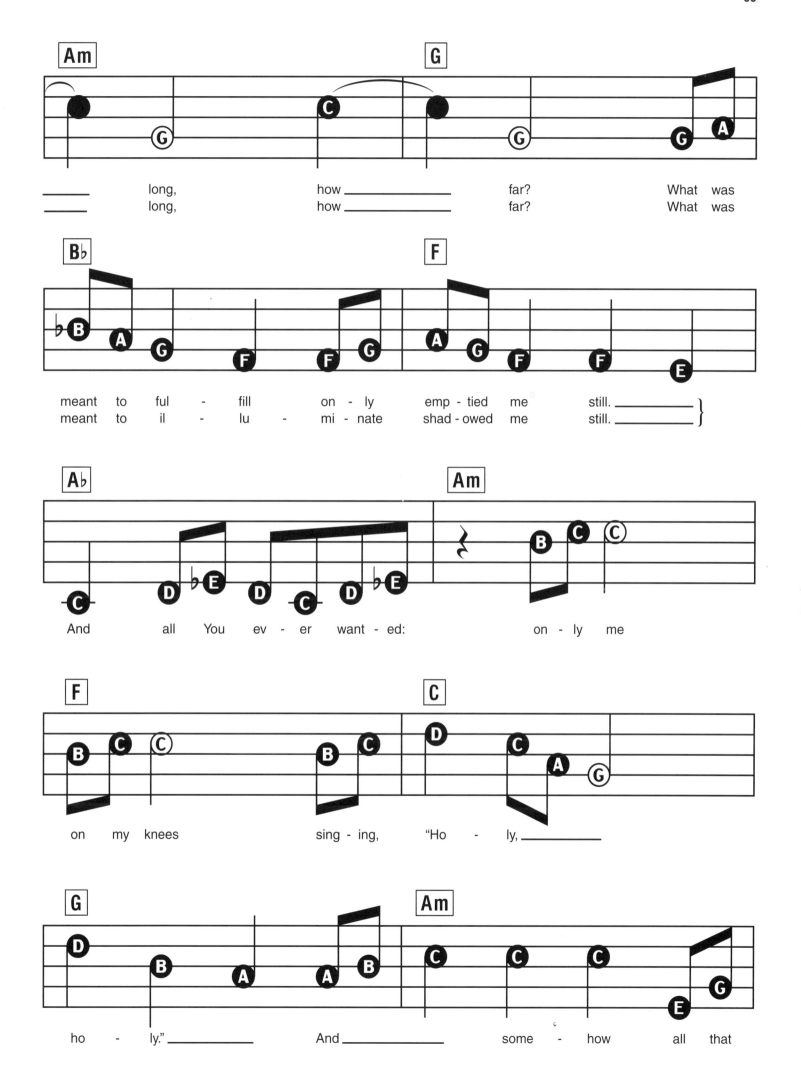

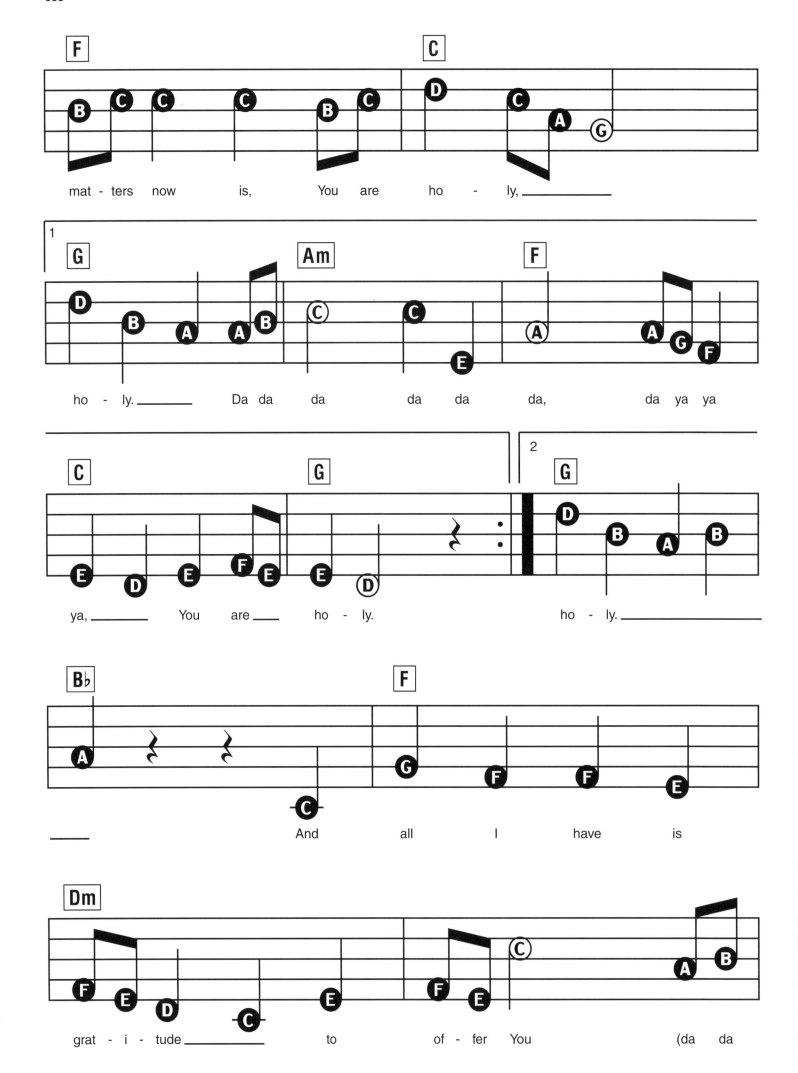

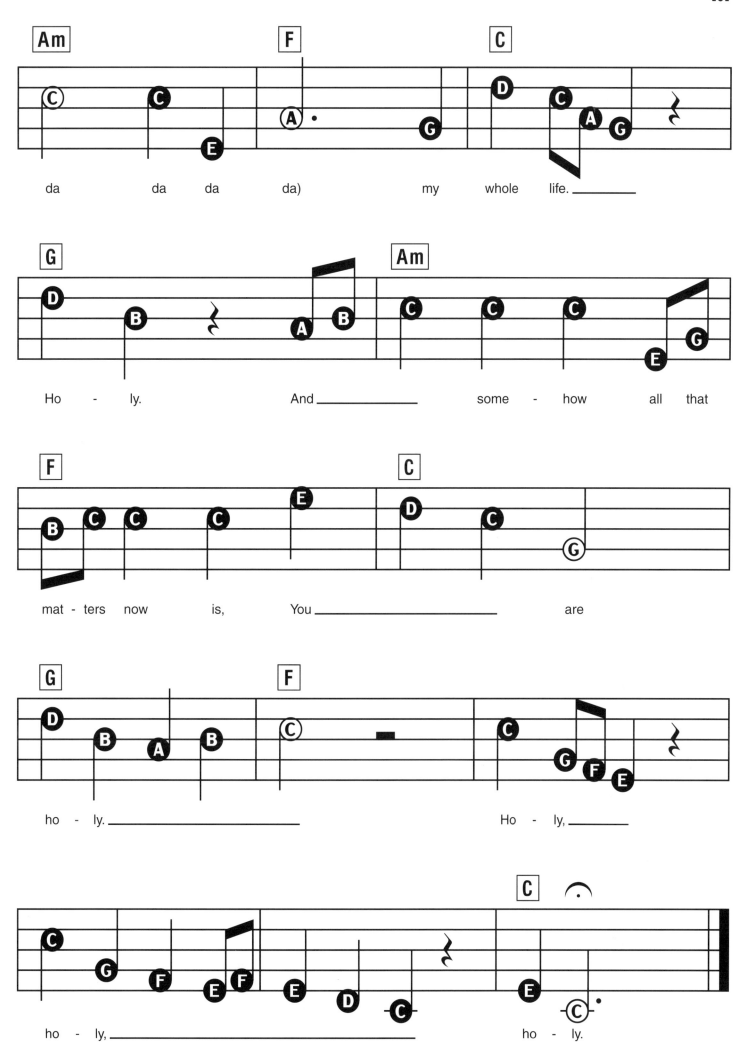

How Beautiful

Registration 3
Rhythm: Ballad or 8 Beat

Words and Music by
Twila Paris

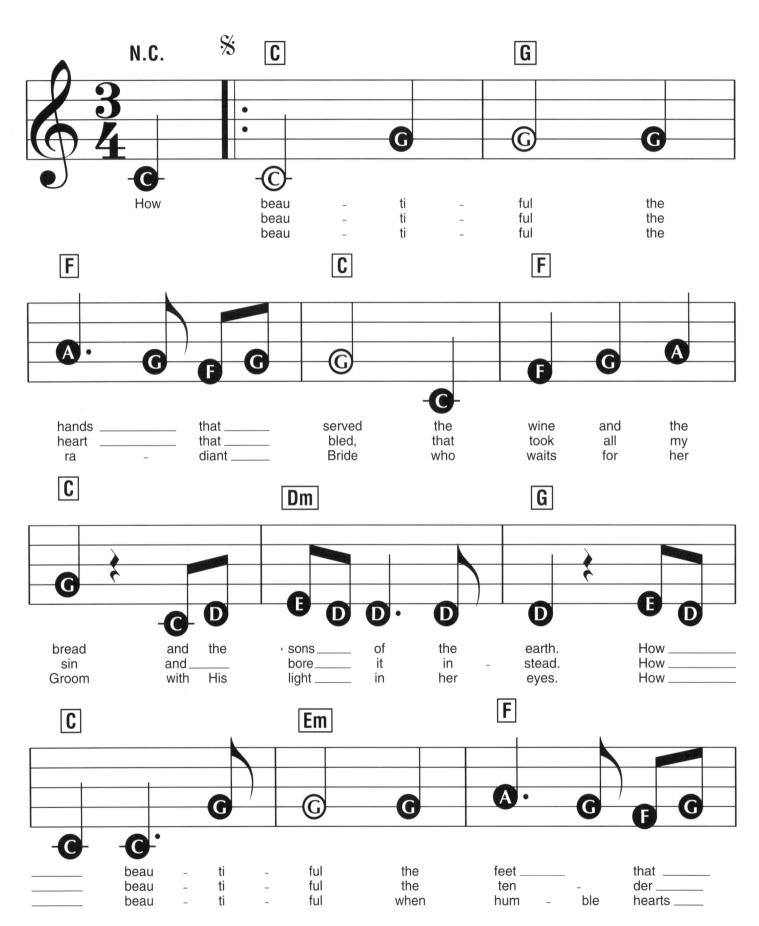

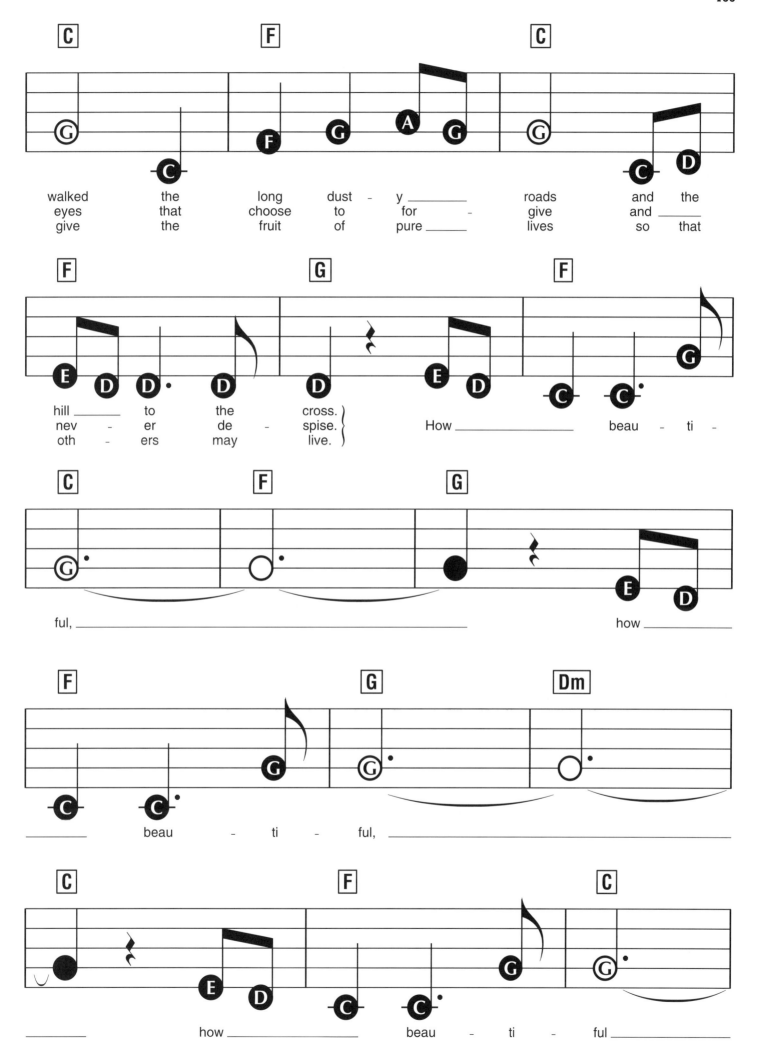

104

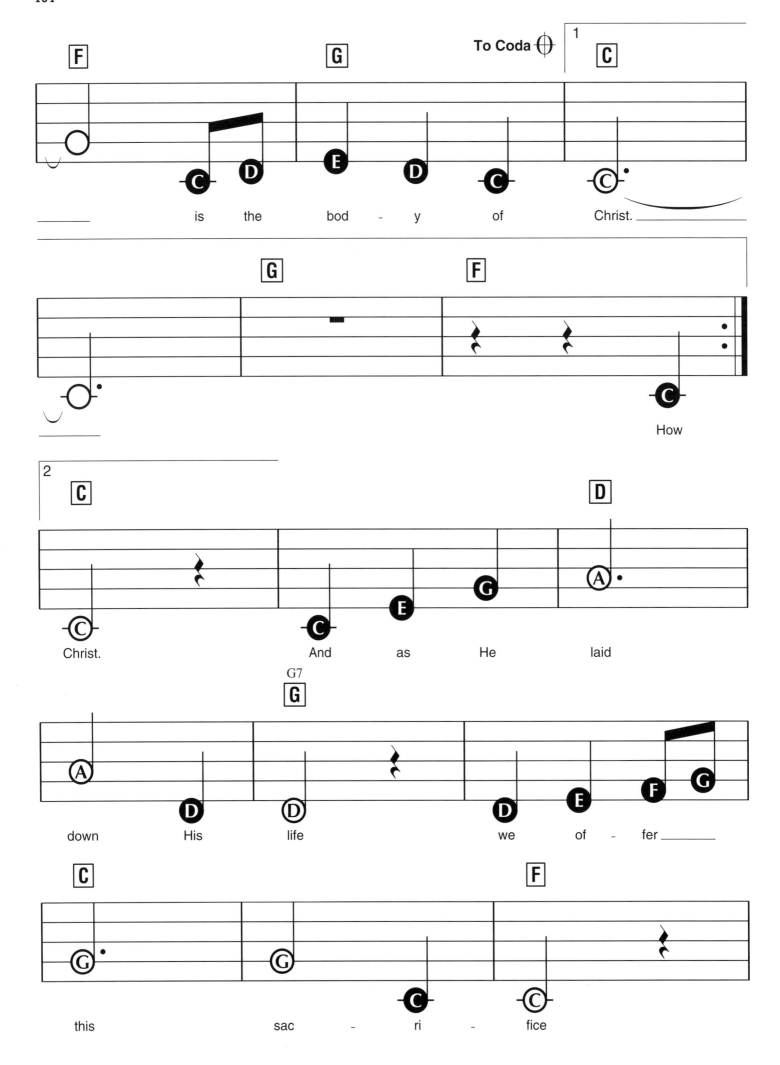

105

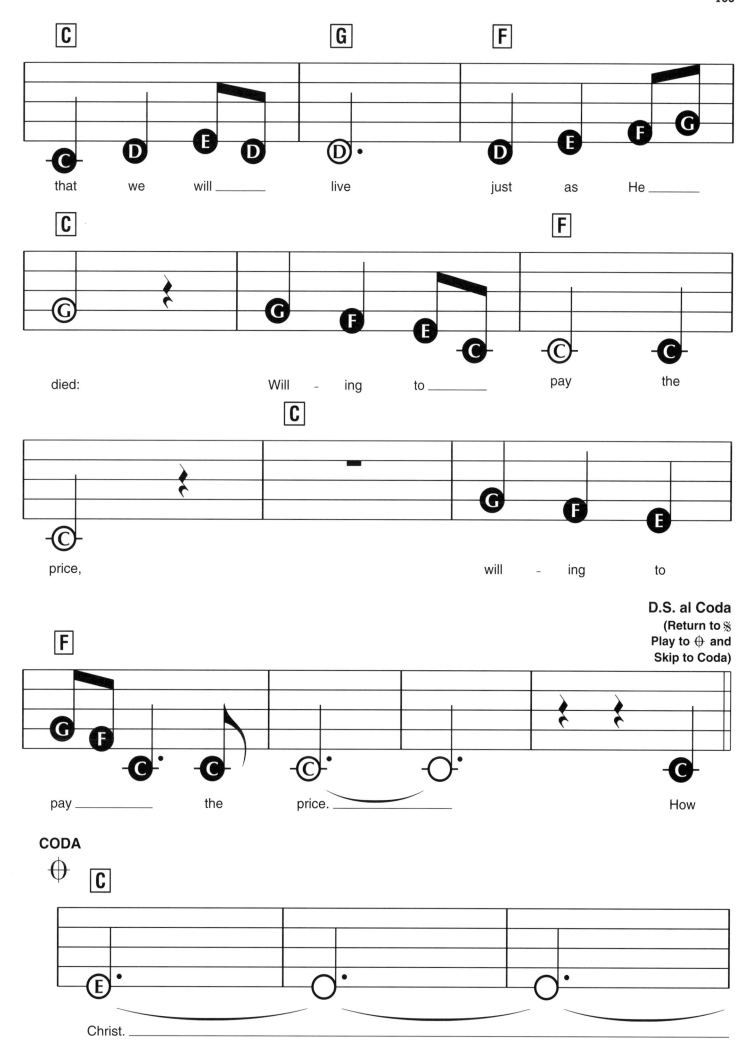

106

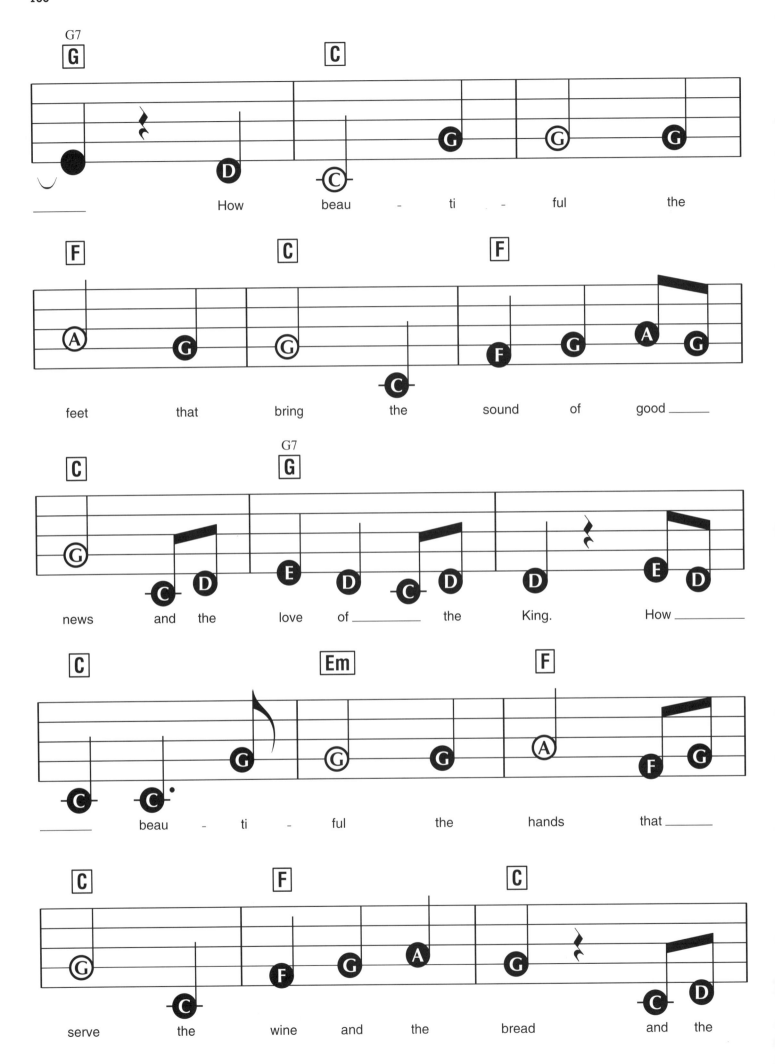

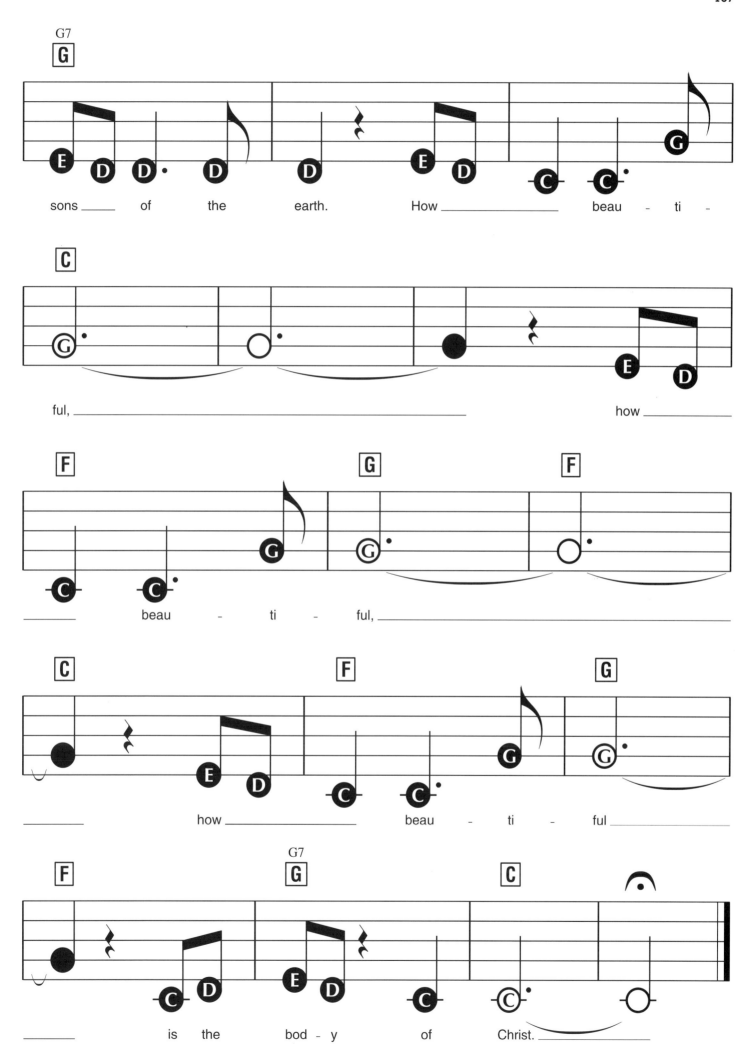

I Can Only Imagine

Registration 1
Rhythm: Ballad or 8 Beat

Words and Music by
Bart Millard

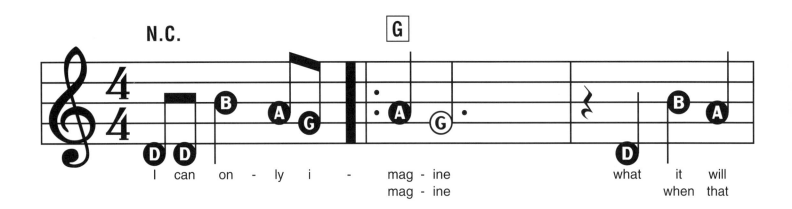

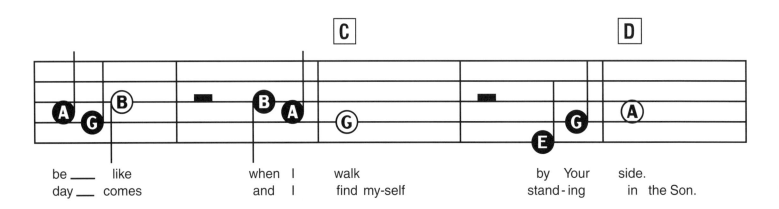

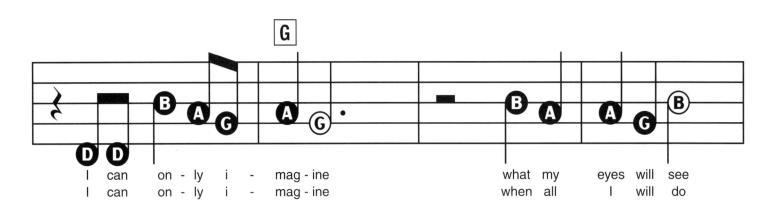

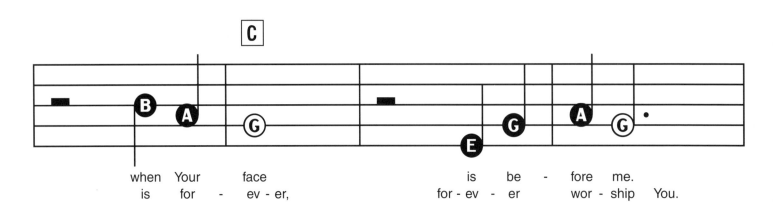

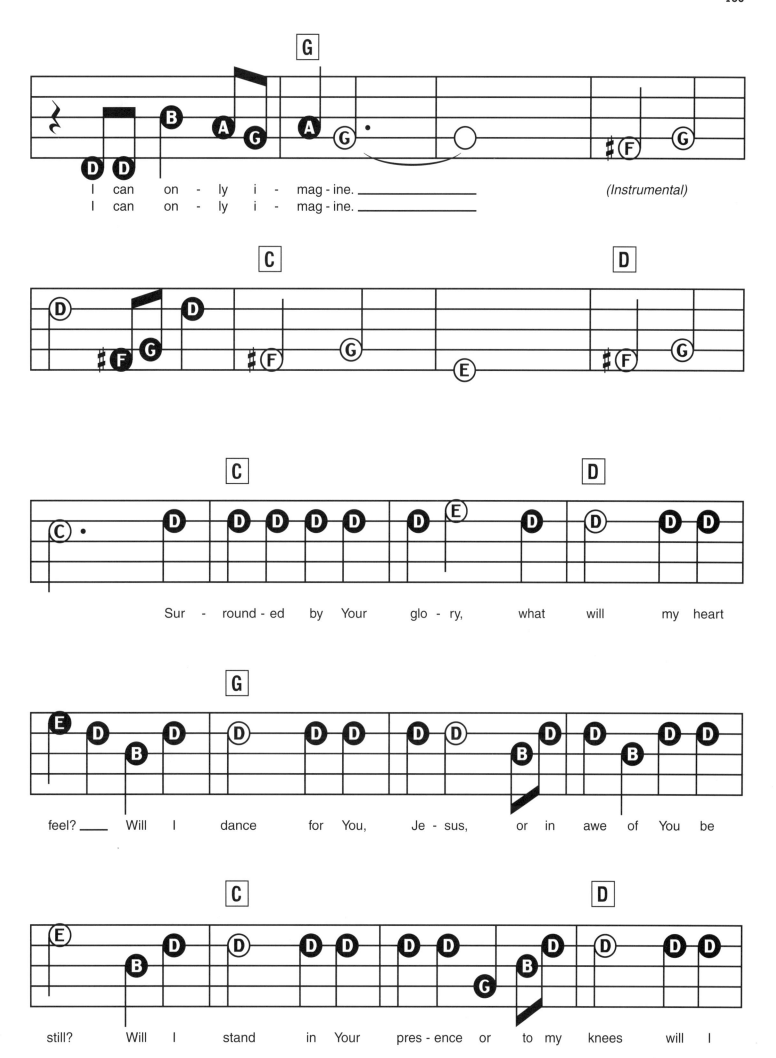

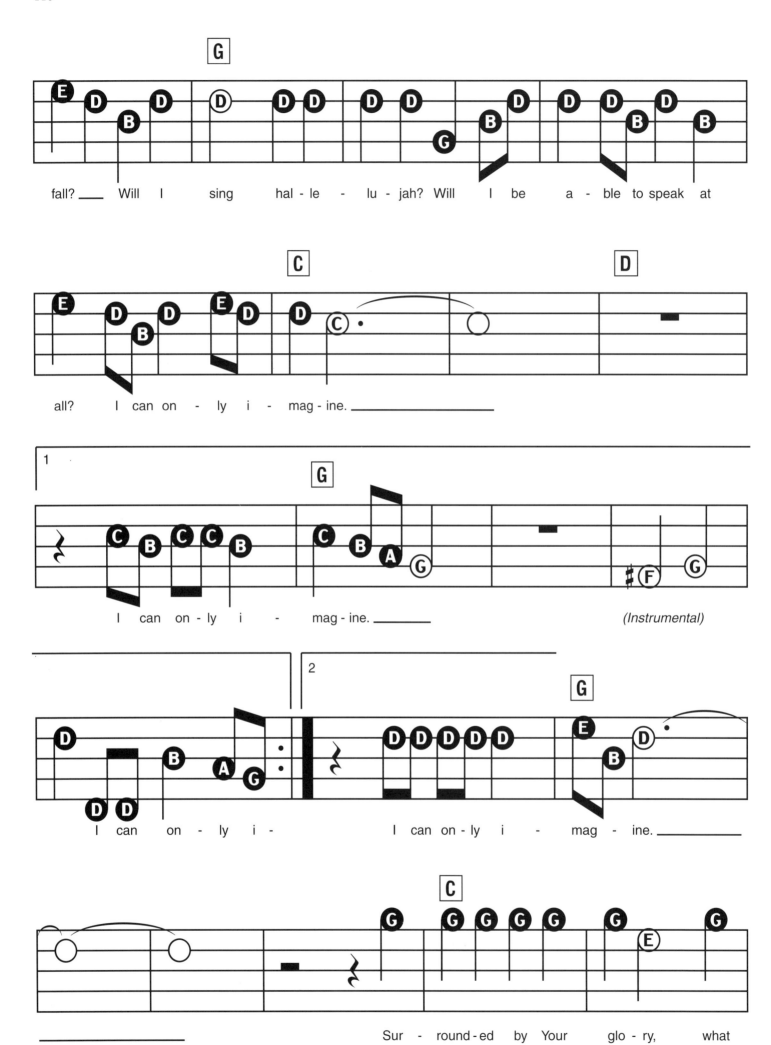

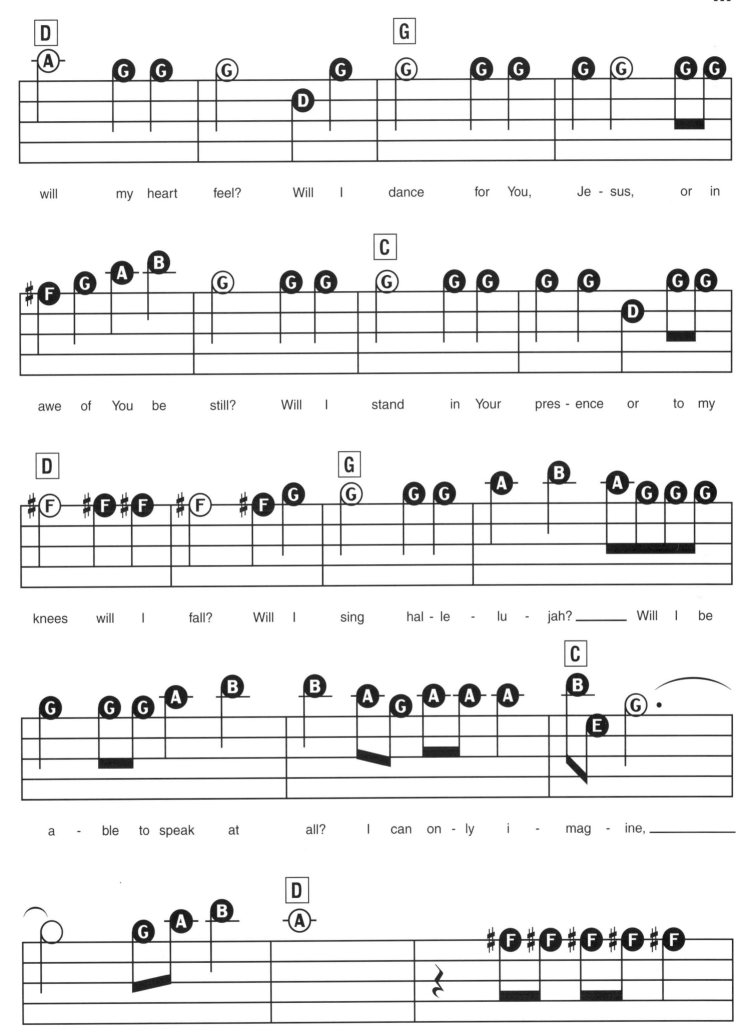

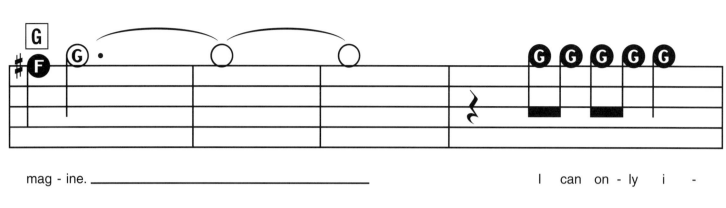

mag - ine. _____ I can on - ly i -

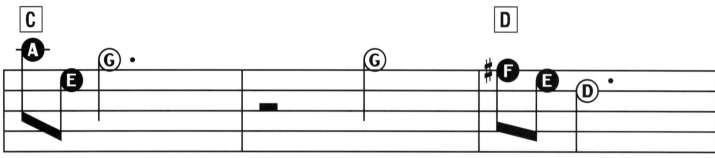

mag - ine, yeah, _____

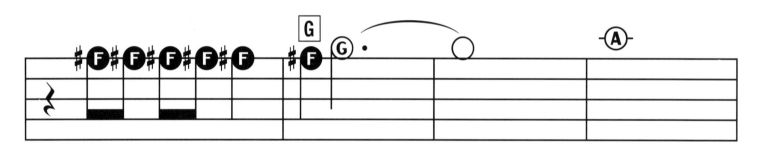

I can on - ly i - mag-ine. _____

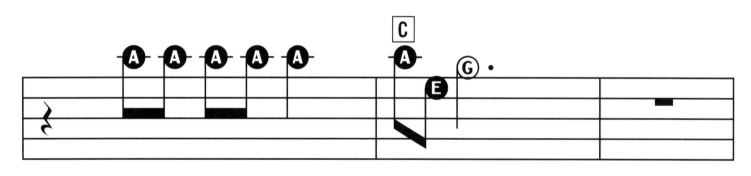

I can on - ly i - mag - ine,

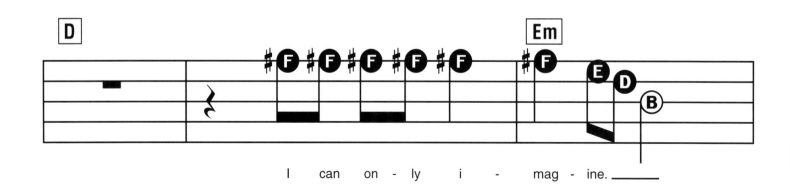

I can on - ly i - mag - ine. _____

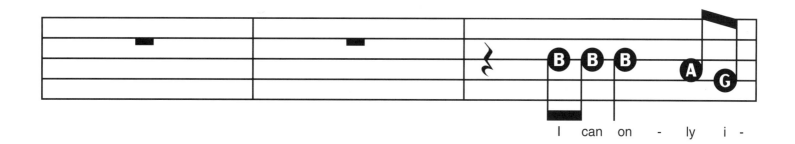

I can on - ly i -

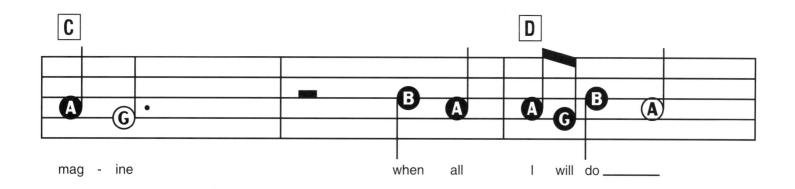

mag - ine   when all   I will do _____

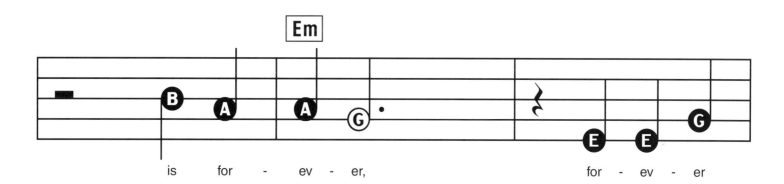

is for - ev - er,   for - ev - er

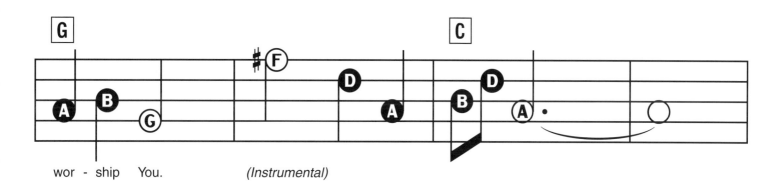

wor - ship You.   *(Instrumental)*

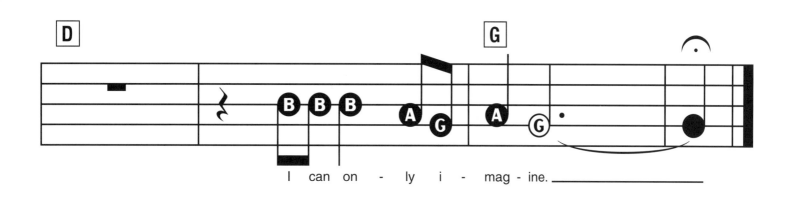

I can on - ly i - mag - ine. _____

If You Could See Me Now

Registration 3
Rhythm: Ballad

Words and Music by
Kim Noblitt

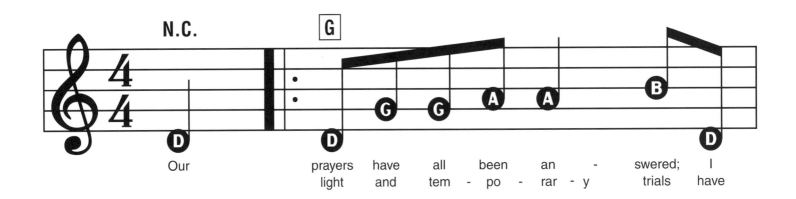

Our
prayers have all been an - swered; I
light and tem - po - rar - y trials have

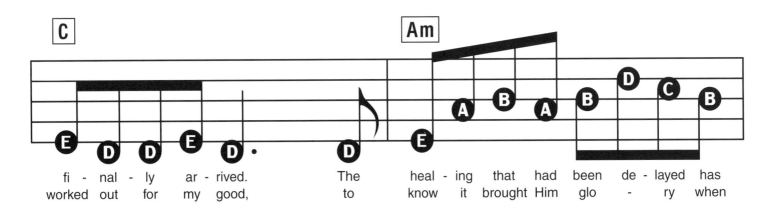

fi - nal - ly ar - rived. The
worked out for my good, to

heal - ing that had been de - layed has
know it brought Him glo - ry when

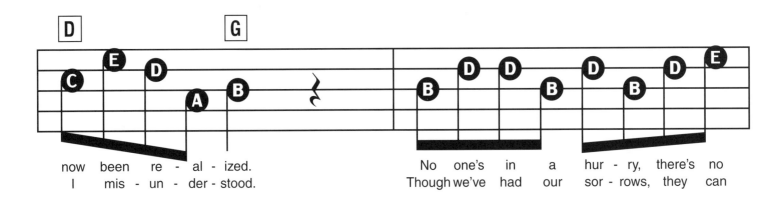

now been re - al - ized.
I mis - un - der - stood.

No one's in a hur - ry, there's no
Though we've had our sor - rows, they can

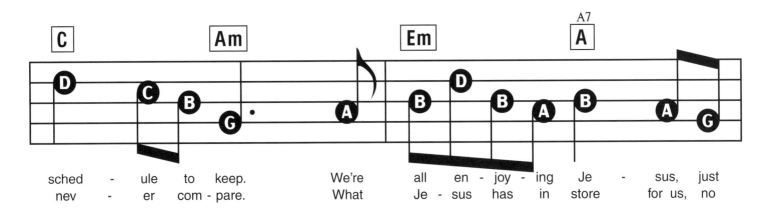

sched - ule to keep. We're
nev - er com - pare. What

all en - joy - ing Je - sus, just
Je - sus has in store for us, no

115

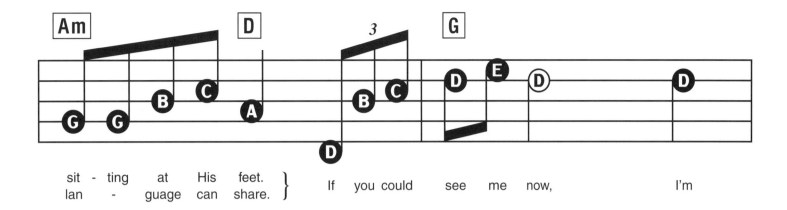

sit - ting   at   His   feet.   }   If   you   could   see   me   now,   I'm
lan - guage   can   share.

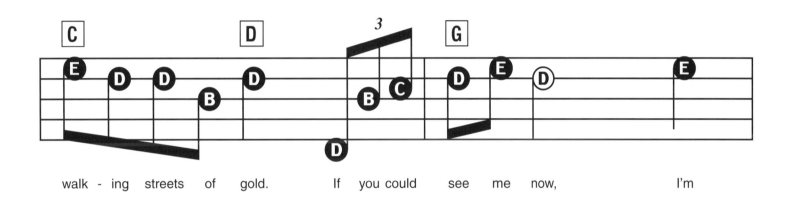

walk - ing   streets   of   gold.   If   you   could   see   me   now,   I'm

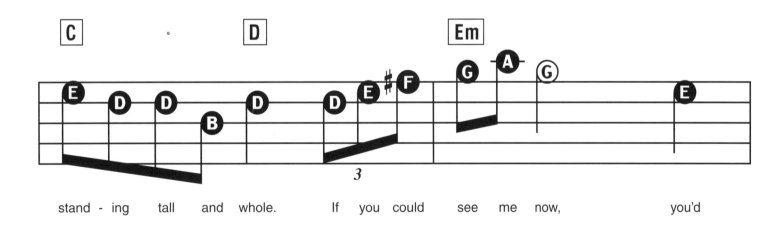

stand - ing   tall   and   whole.   If   you   could   see   me   now,   you'd

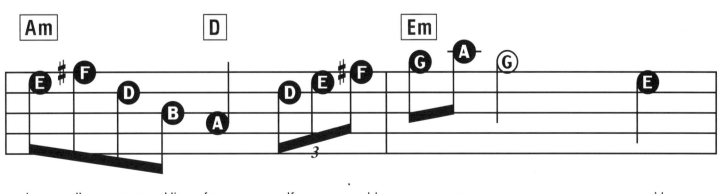

know   I've   seen   His   face.   If   you   could   see   me   now,   you'd

116

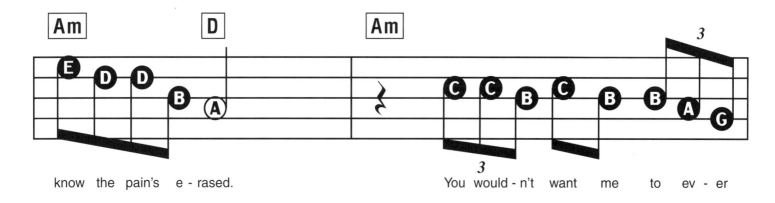

know the pain's e - rased.   You would - n't want me to ev - er

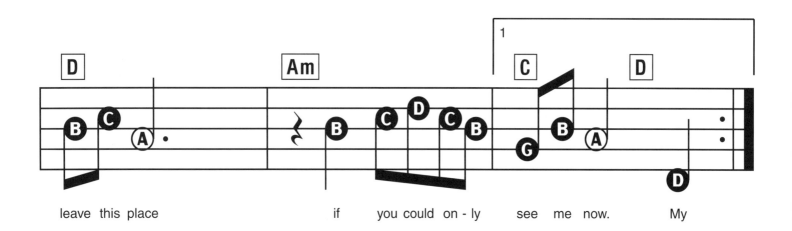

leave this place   if you could on - ly see me now. My

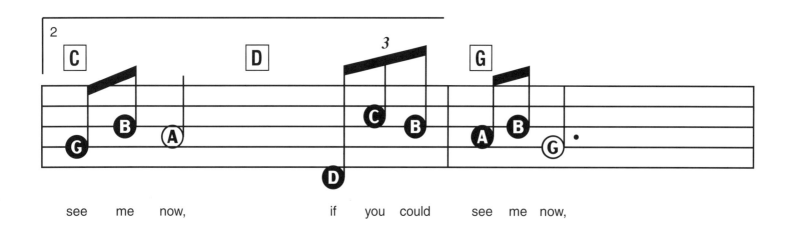

see me now,   if you could see me now,

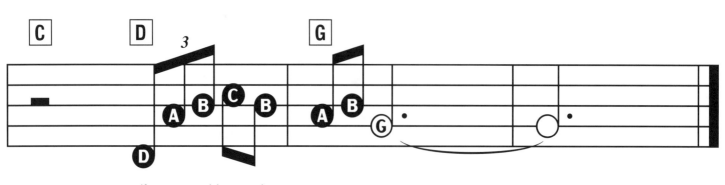

if you could on - ly see me now._____

Joy

Registration 4
Rhythm: Rock or 16 Beat

Words and Music by Peter Furler
and Steve Taylor

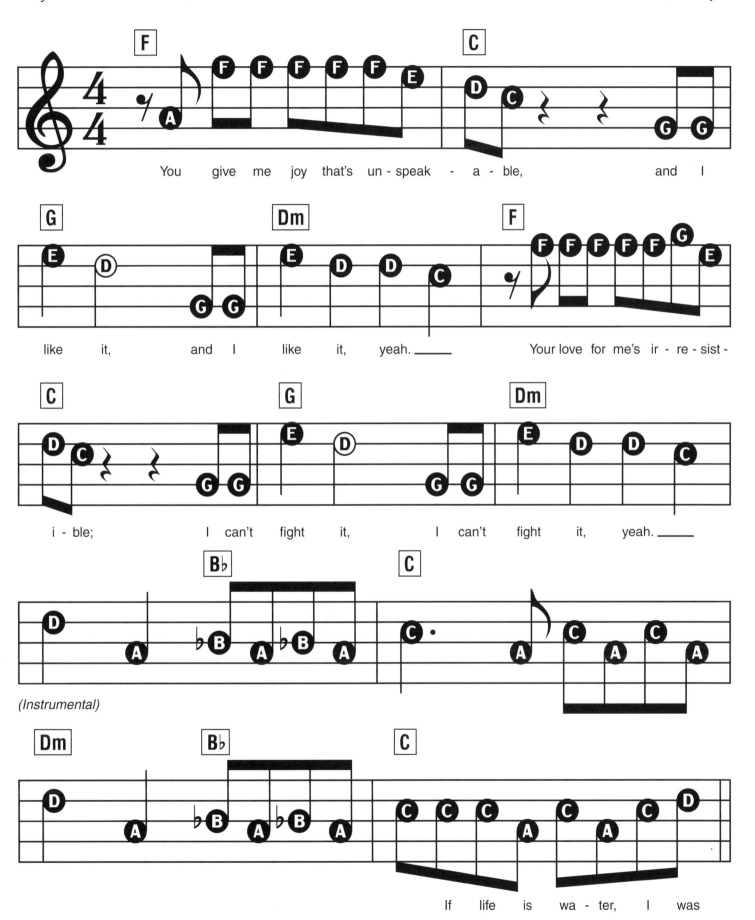

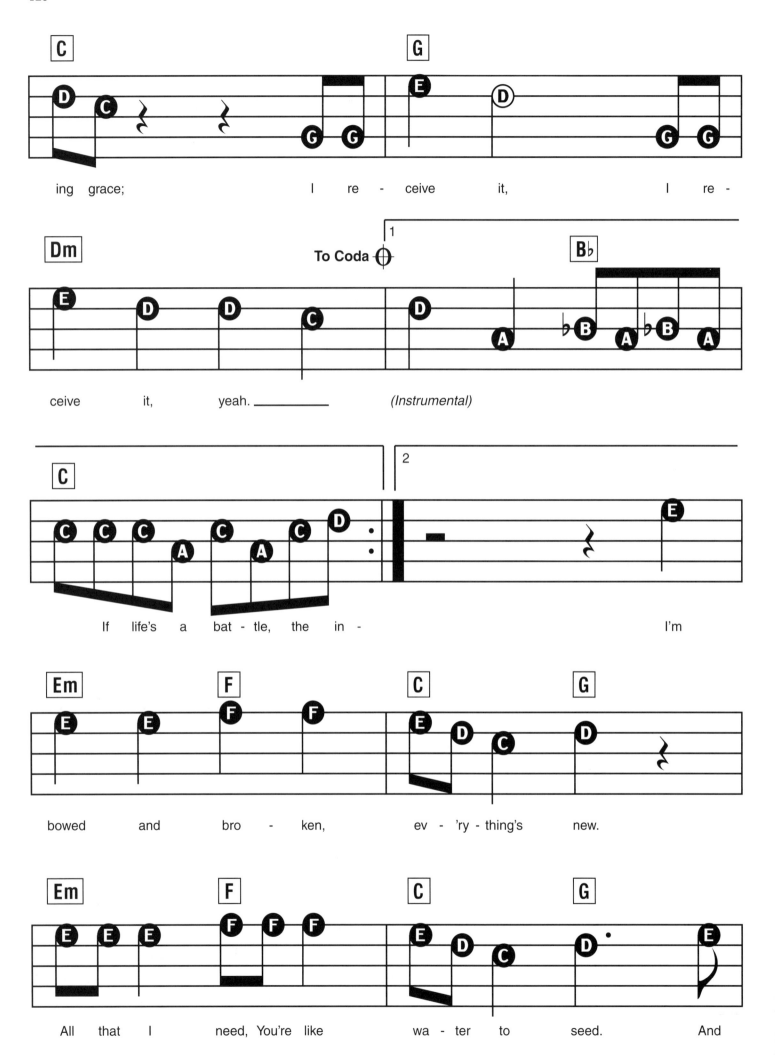

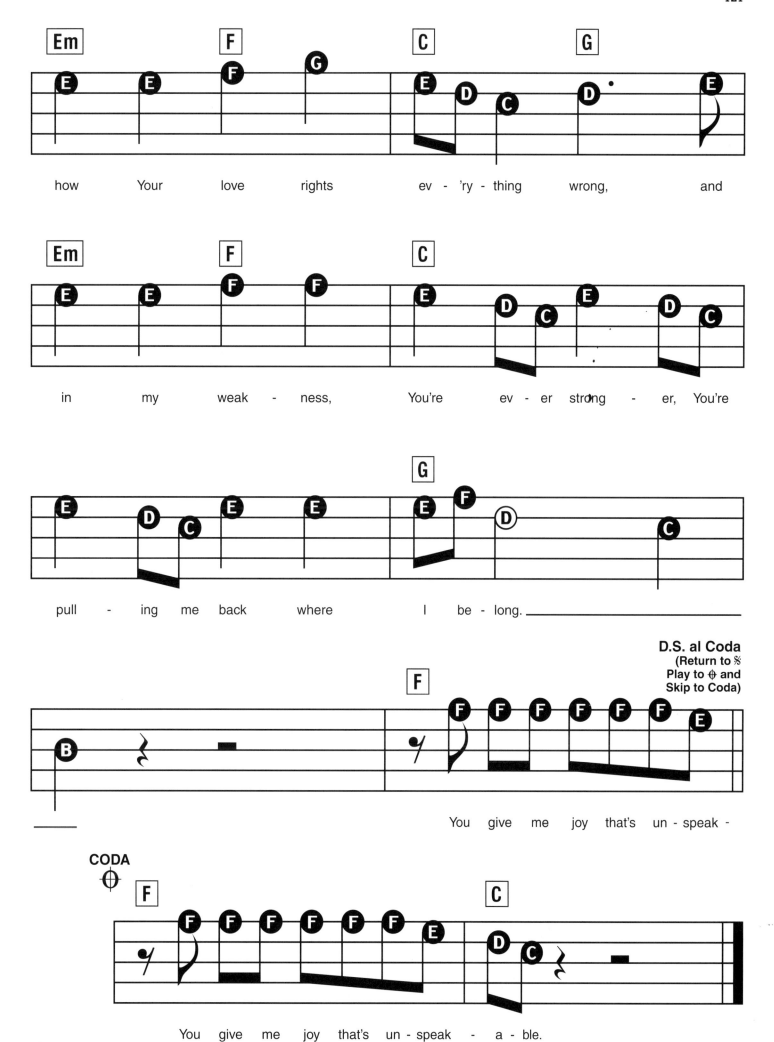

In the Name of the Lord

Registration 4
Rhythm: 8 Beat or Ballad

Words by Gloria Gaither, Phill McHugh and Sandi Patty
Music by Sandi Patty

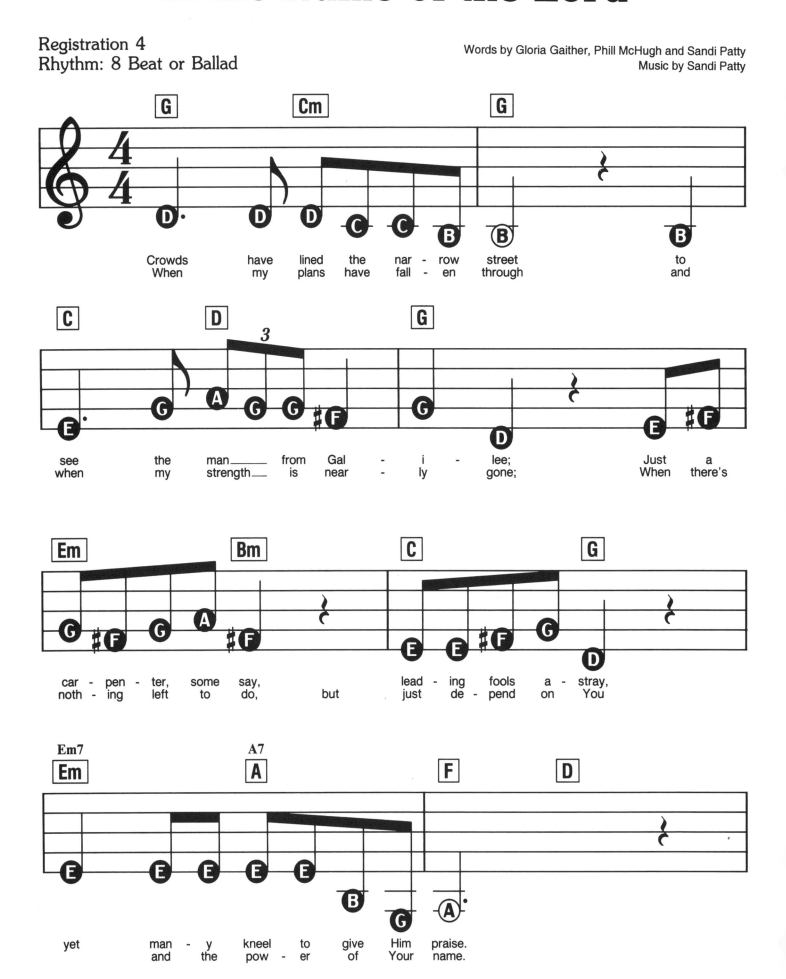

123

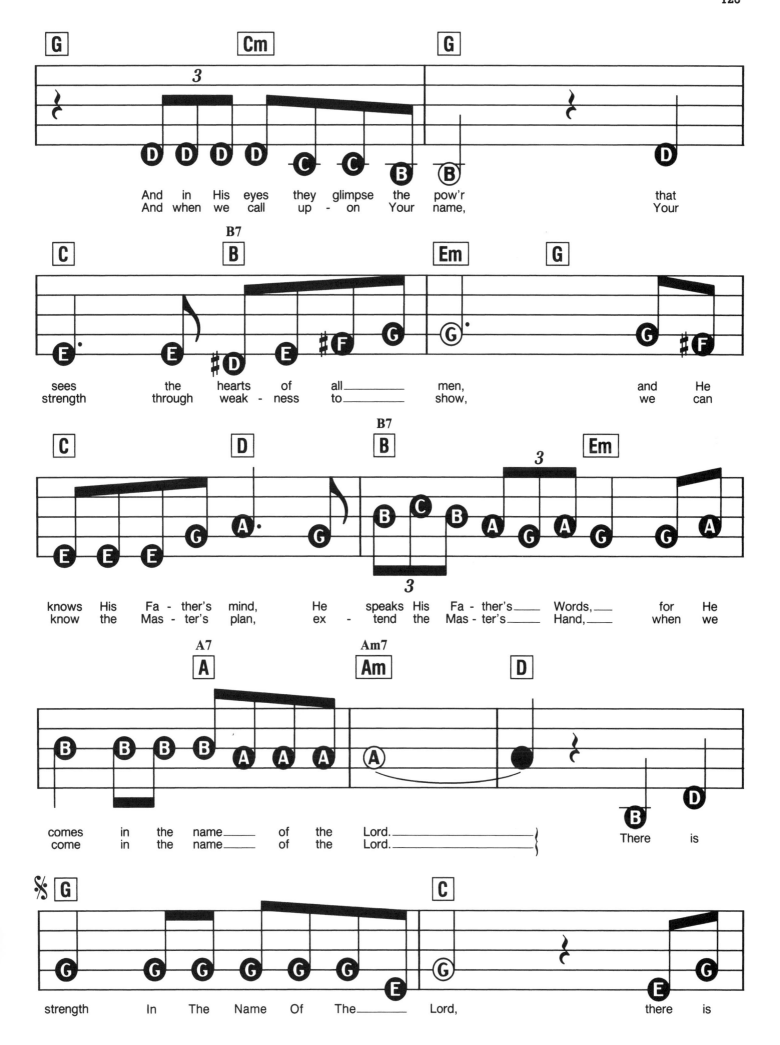

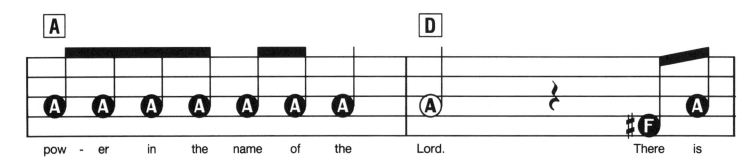

pow - er in the name of the Lord. There is

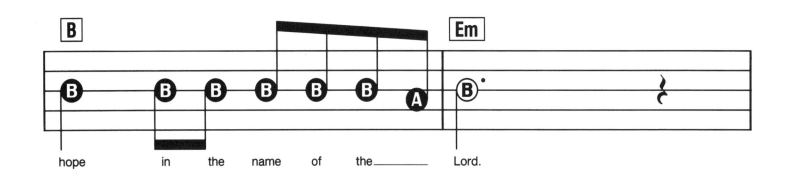

hope in the name of the_____ Lord.

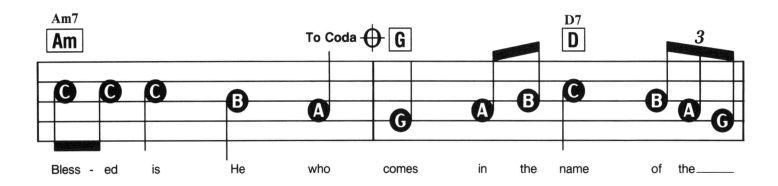

Bless - ed is He who comes in the name of the_____

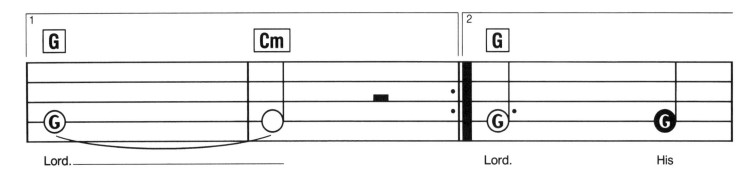

Lord._____ Lord. His

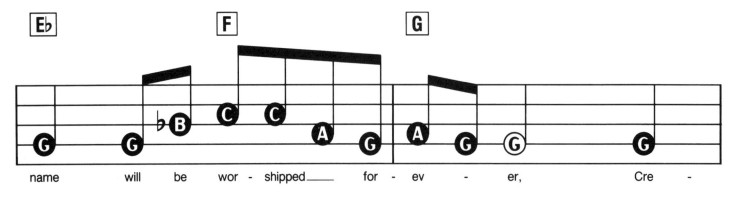

name will be wor - shipped_____ for - ev - er, Cre -

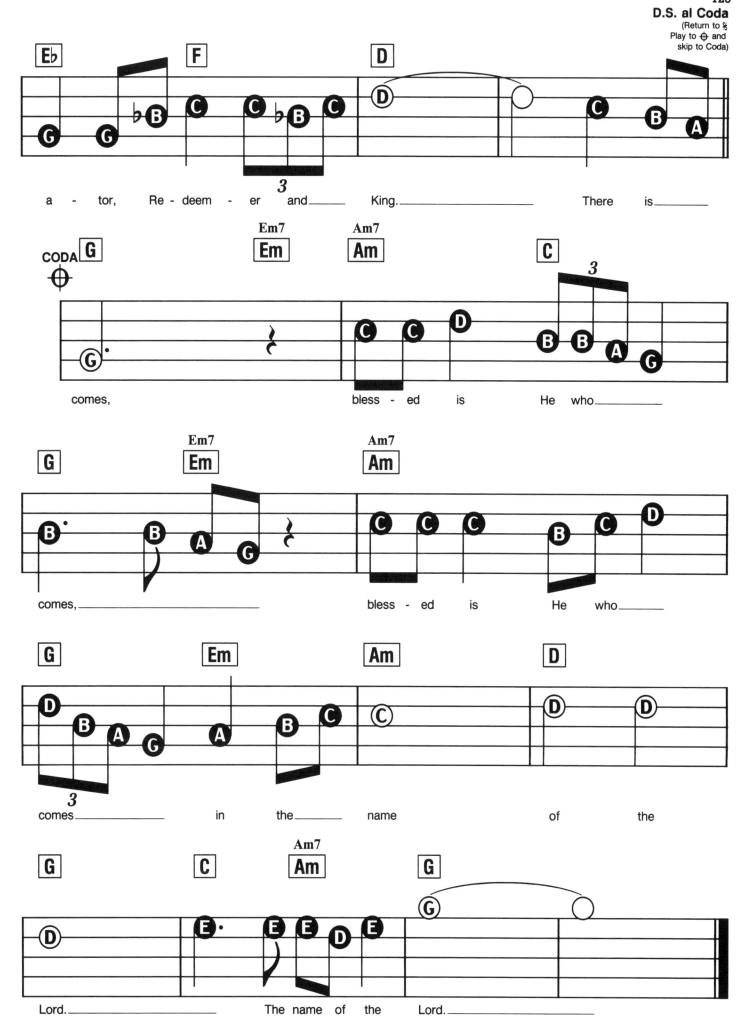

Jesus Will Still Be There

Registration 10
Rhythm: Ballad or 8 Beat

Words and Music by John Mandeville
and Robert Sterling

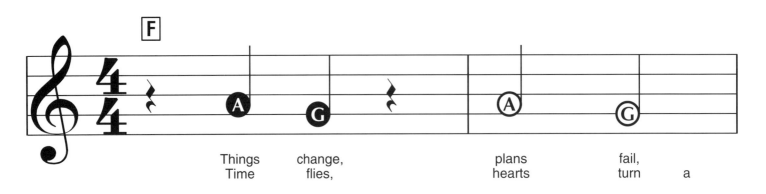

Things change, plans fail,
Time flies, hearts turn a

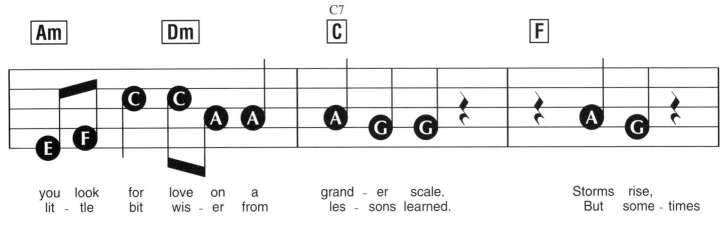

you look for love on a grand - er scale.
lit - tle bit wis - er from les - sons learned. Storms rise,
But some - times

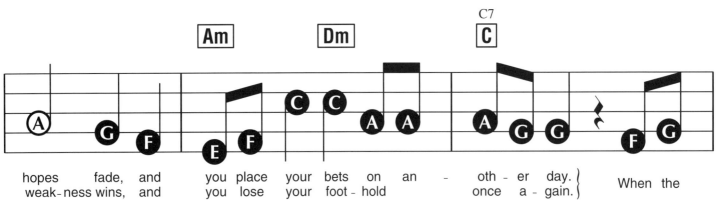

hopes fade, and you place your bets on an - oth - er day.
weak - ness wins, and you lose your foot - hold once a - gain.
When the

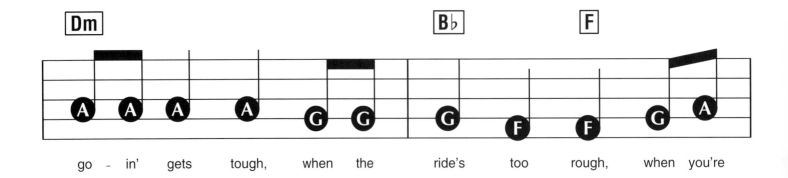

go - in' gets tough, when the ride's too rough, when you're

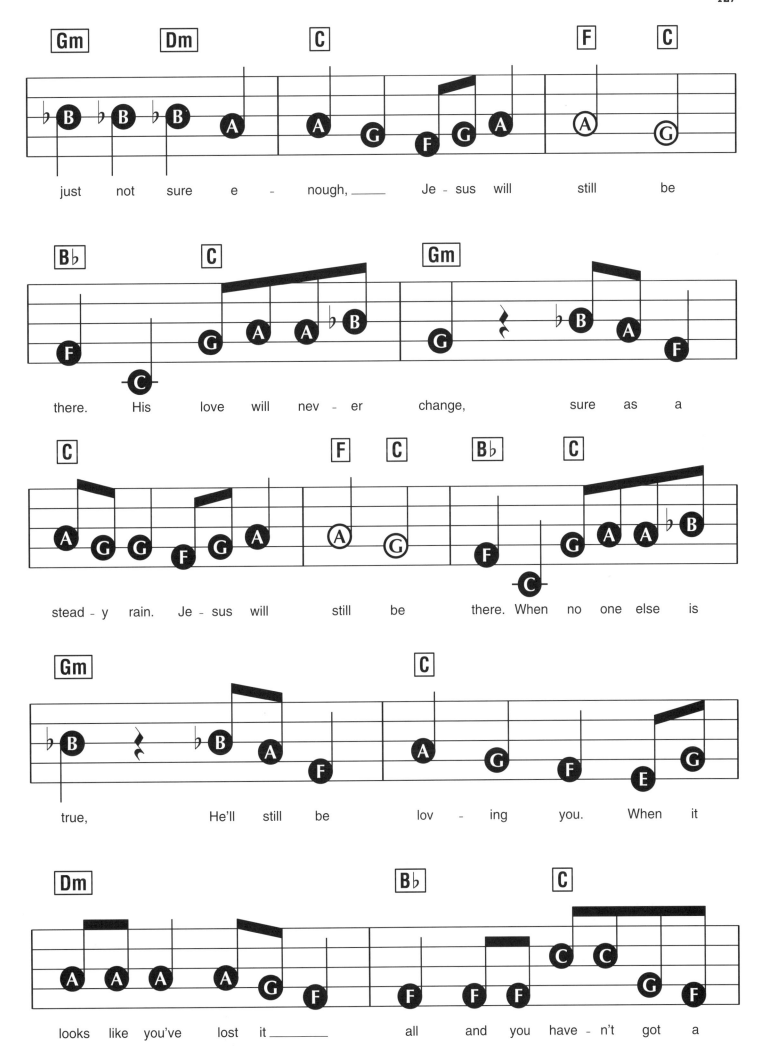

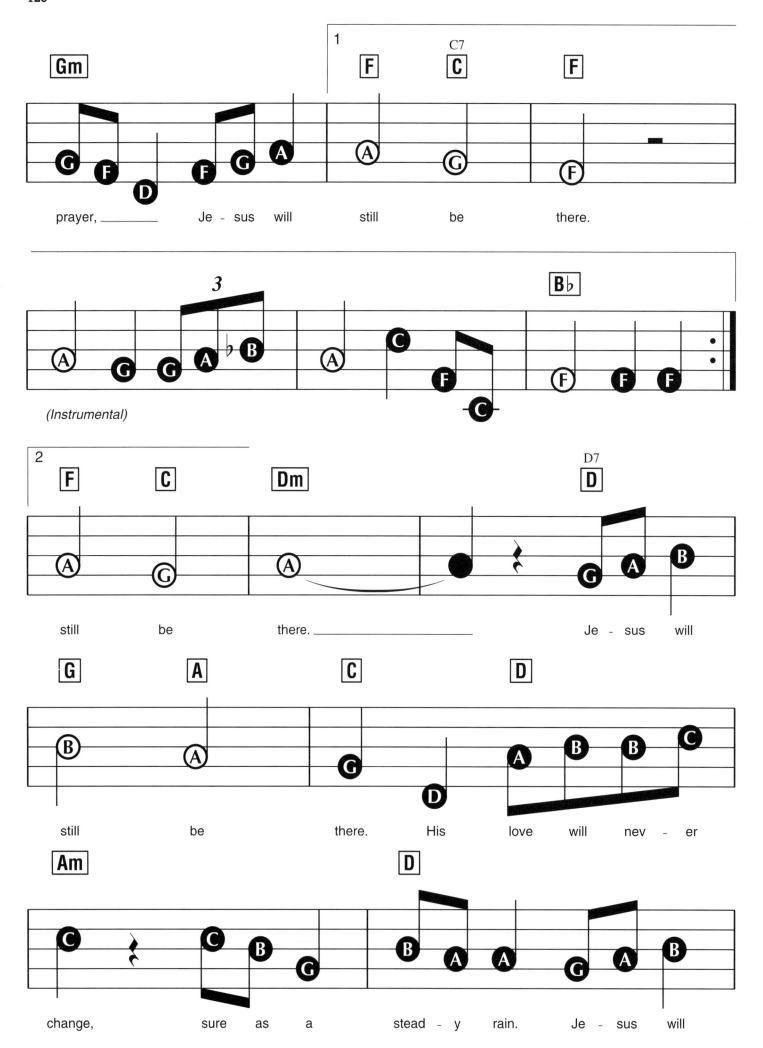

129

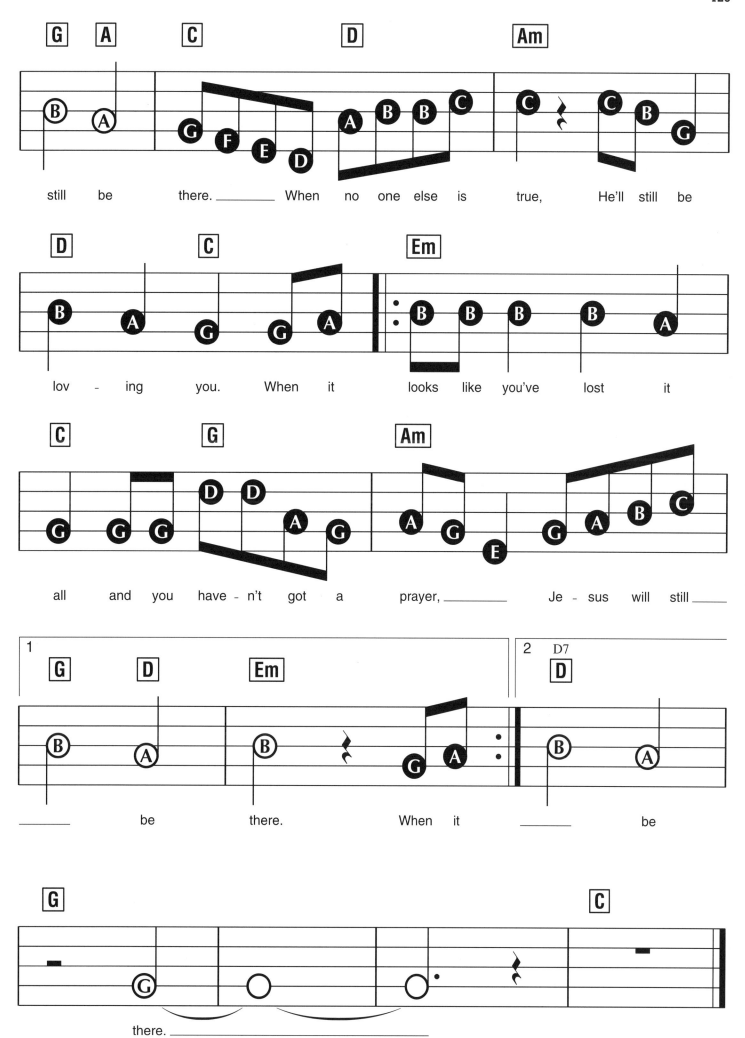

The Joy of the Lord

Registration 8
Rhythm: Pop

Words and Music by
Twila Paris

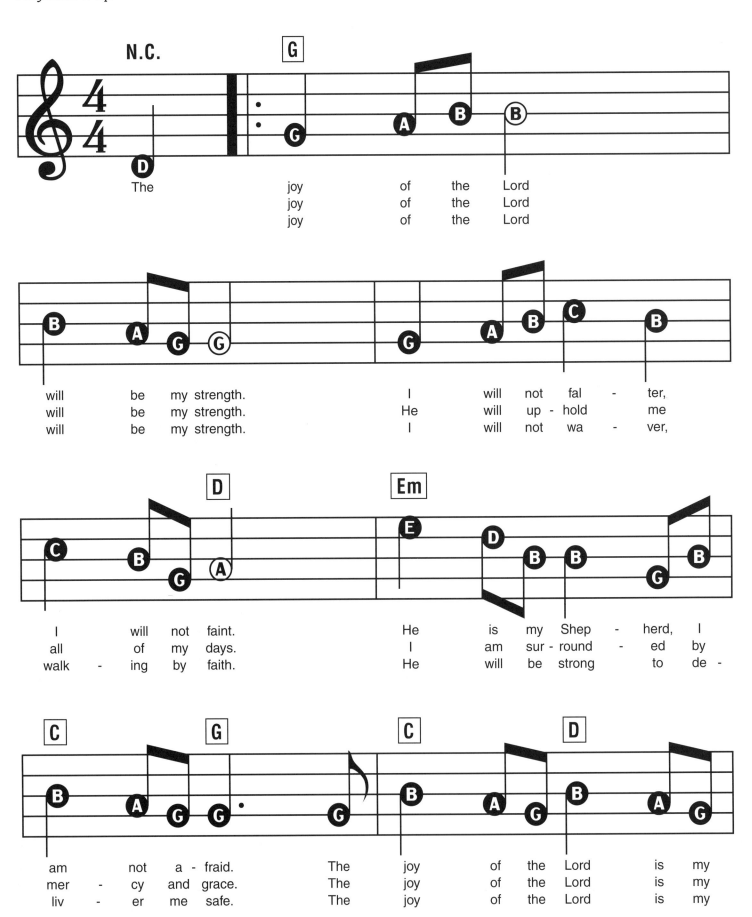

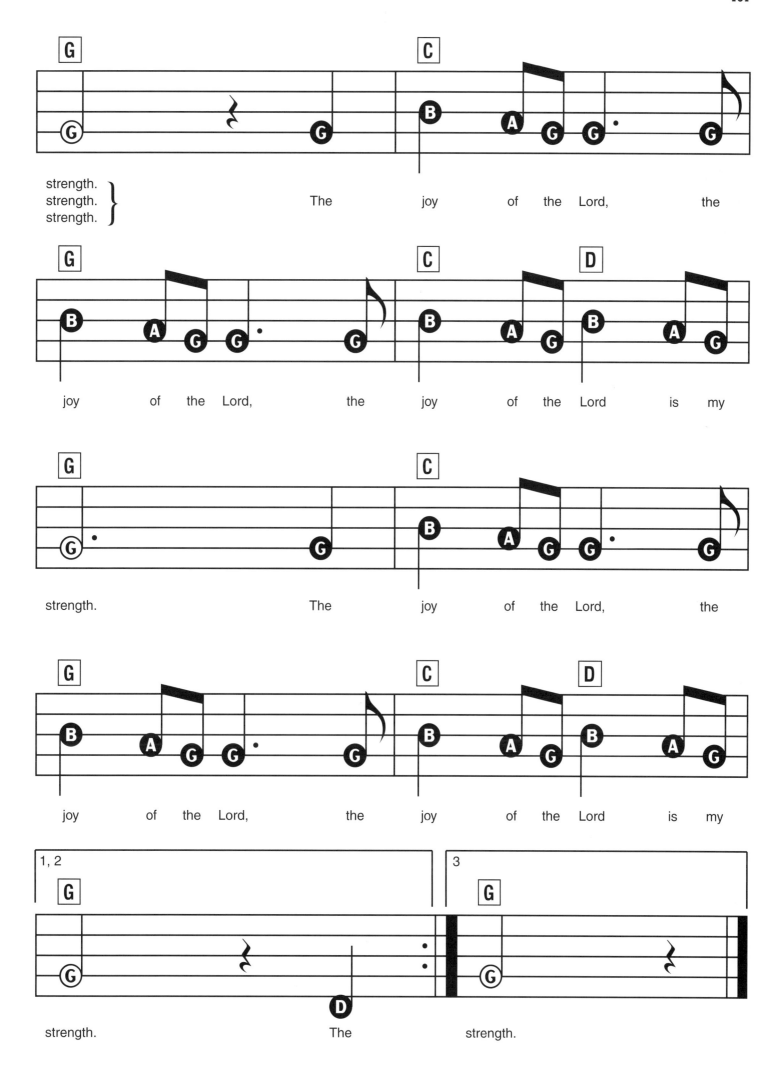

Just One

Registration 7
Rhythm: Rock or 8 Beat

Words and Music by Connie Harrington
and Jim Cooper

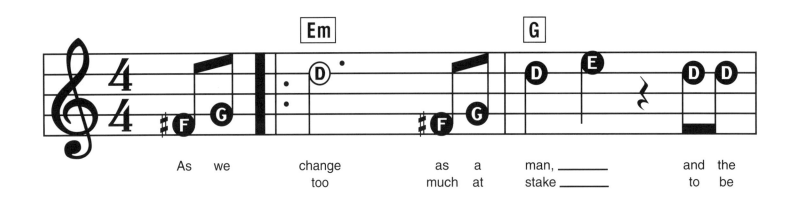

As we change as a man, _____ and the
too much at stake _____ to be

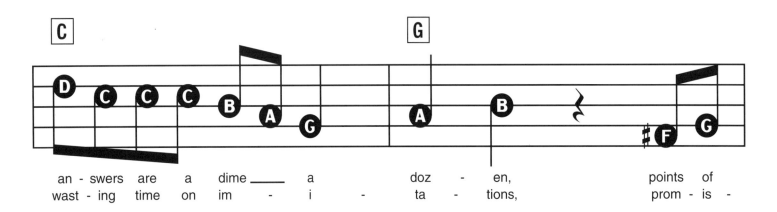

an - swers are a dime _____ a   doz - en,   points of
wast - ing time on im - i - ta - tions,   prom - is -

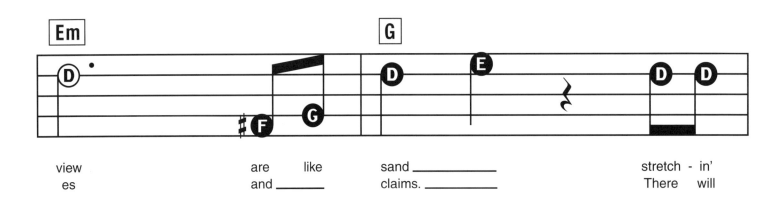

view   are like   sand _____   stretch - in'
es   and _____   claims. _____   There will

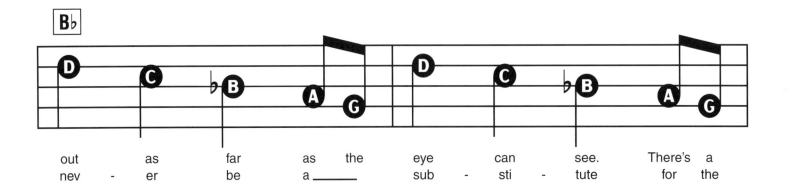

out as far as the eye can see. There's a
nev - er be a _____ sub - sti - tute for the

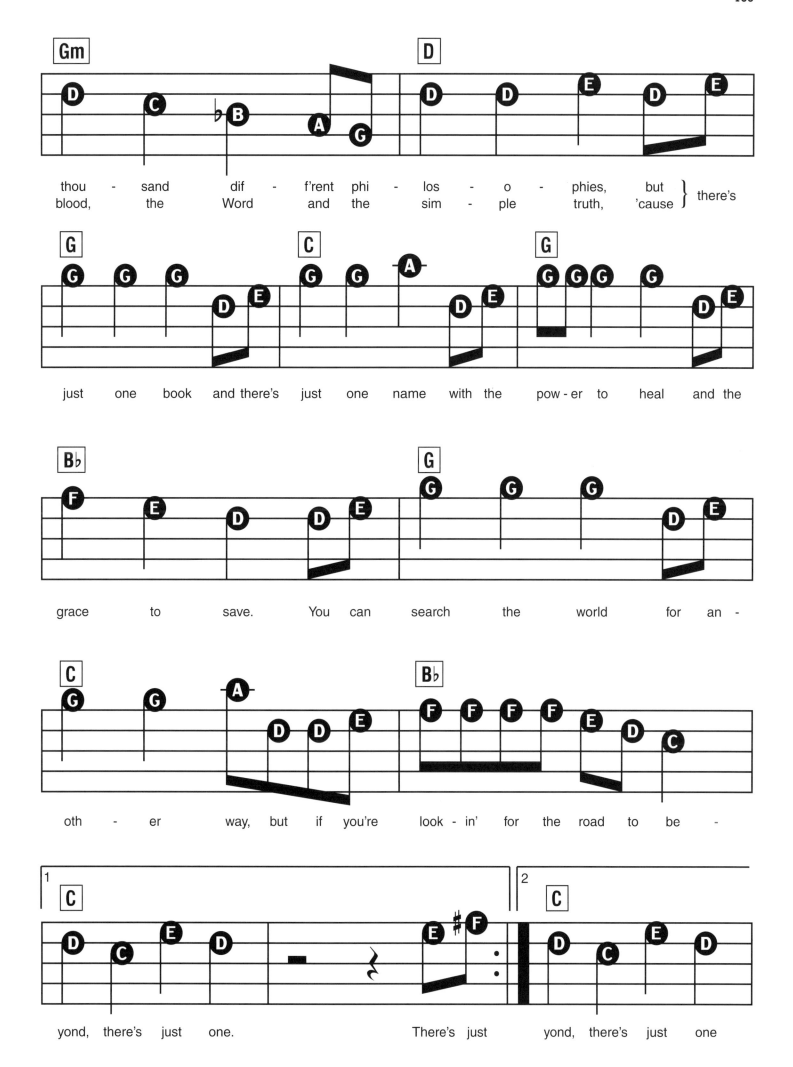

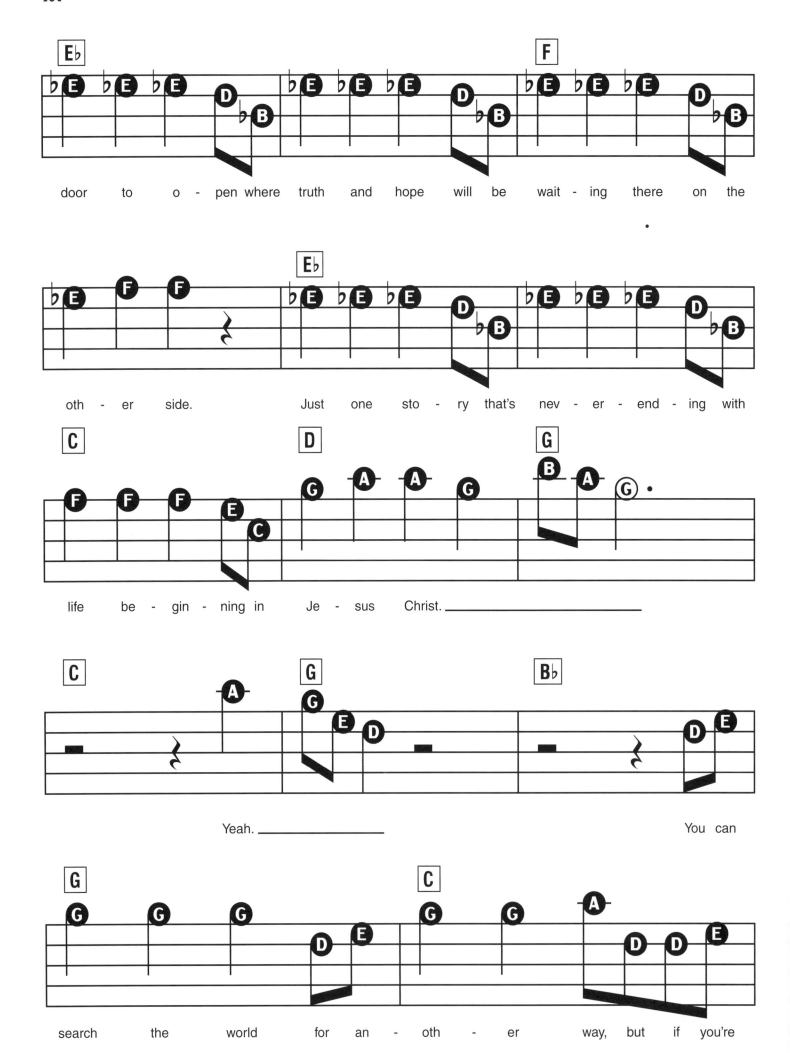

door   to   o - pen where   truth   and   hope   will   be   wait - ing   there   on   the

oth - er   side.   Just   one   sto - ry   that's   nev - er - end - ing   with

life   be - gin - ning   in   Je - sus   Christ. _____

Yeah. _____   You   can

search   the   world   for   an - oth - er   way,   but   if   you're

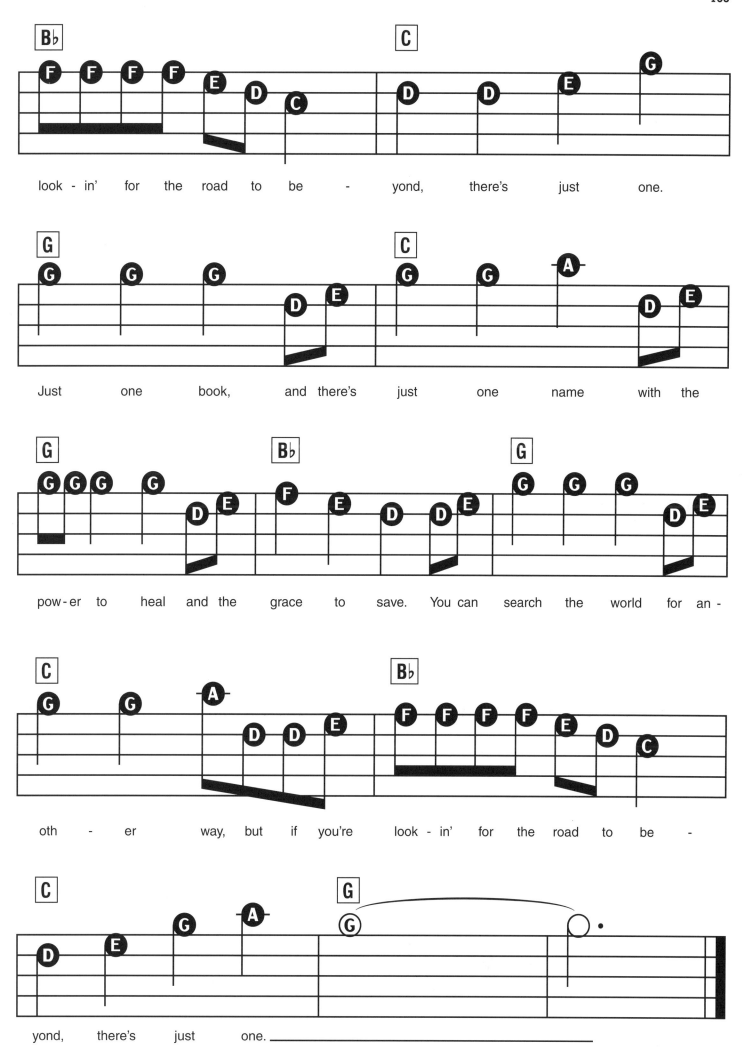

Lamb of God

Registration 1
Rhythm: Waltz

Words and Music by
Twila Paris

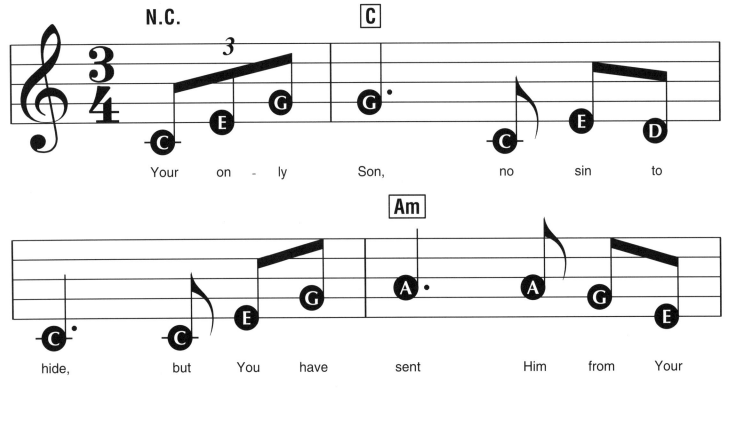

Your on - ly Son, no sin to hide, but You have sent Him from Your

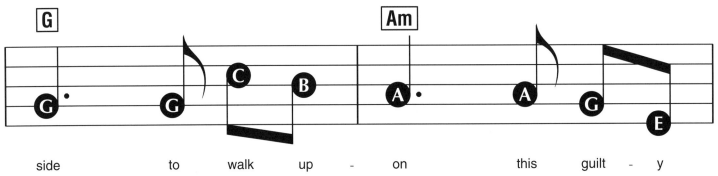

side to walk up - on this guilt - y

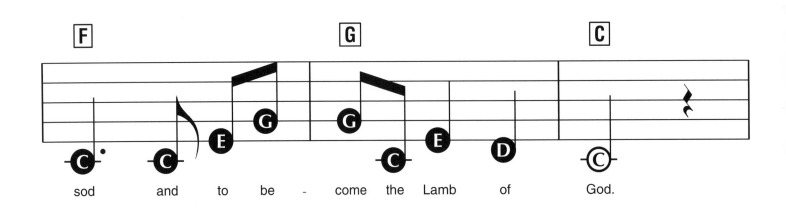

sod and to be - come the Lamb of God.

137

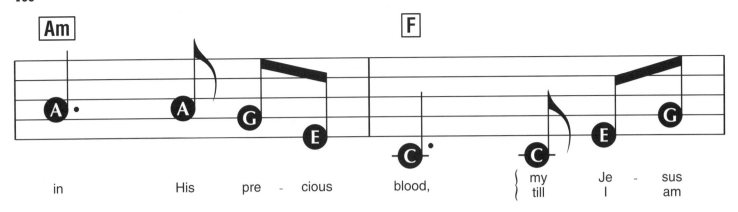

in His pre - cious blood, { my Je - sus
till I am

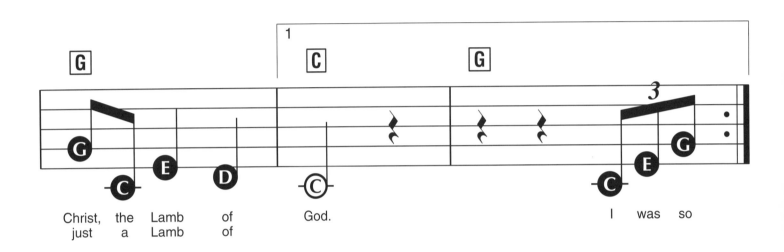

Christ, the Lamb of God. I was so
just a Lamb of

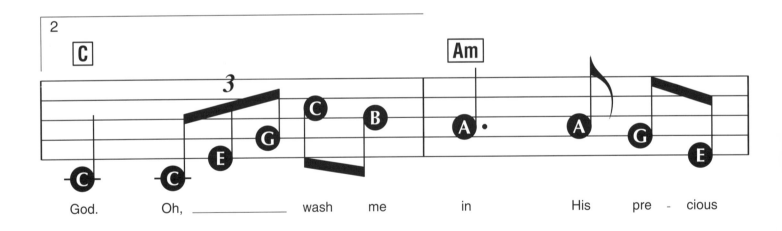

God. Oh, _____ wash me in His pre - cious

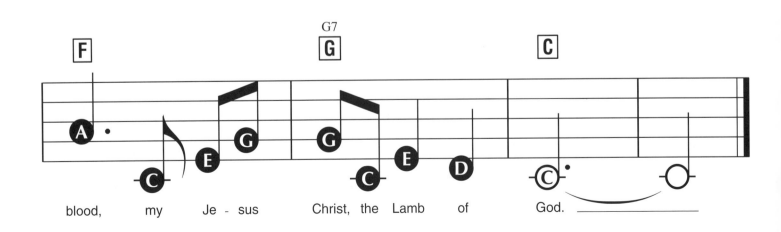

blood, my Je - sus Christ, the Lamb of God. _____

Love Will Be Our Home

Registration 2
Rhythm: Pop Rock or 8 Beat

Words and Music by
Steven Curtis Chapman

140

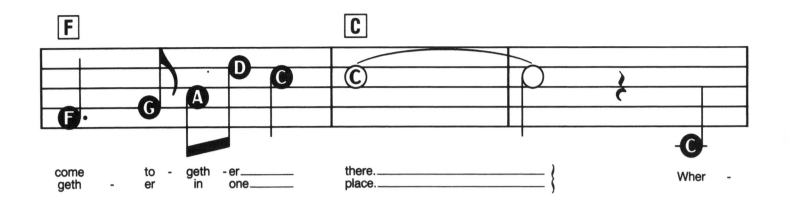

come to - geth -er_____ there._____
geth - er in one_____ place._____ } Wher -

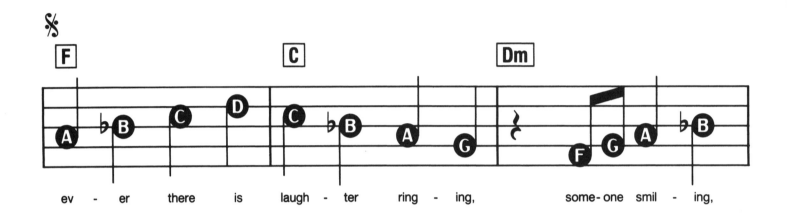

ev - er there is laugh - ter ring - ing, some- one smil - ing,

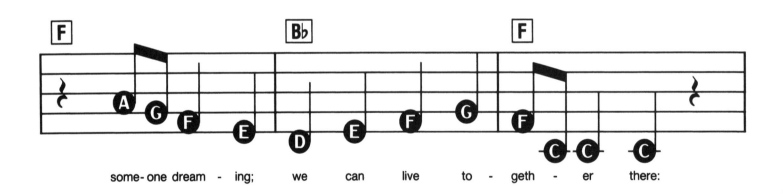

some- one dream - ing; we can live to - geth - er there:

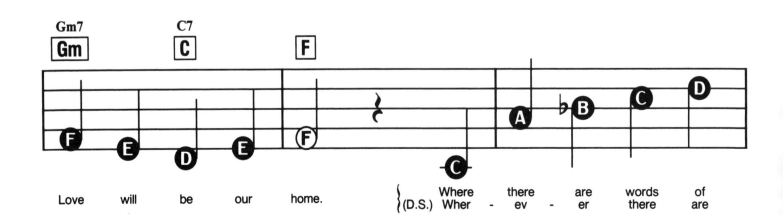

Love will be our home. {(D.S.) Where there are words of
Wher - ev - er there are

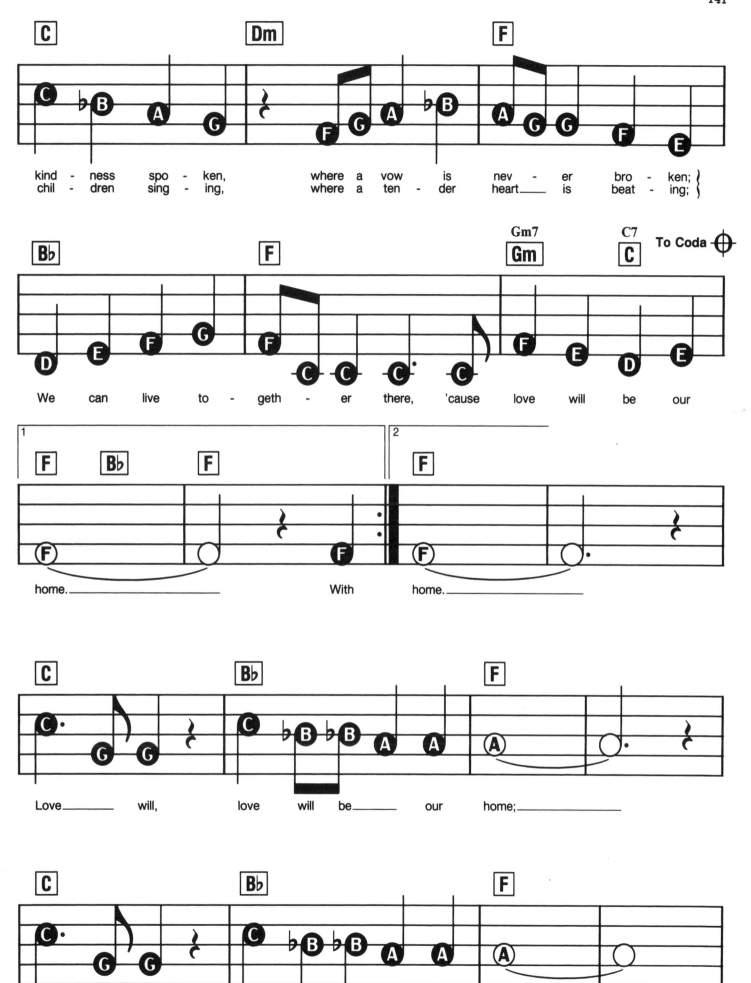

142

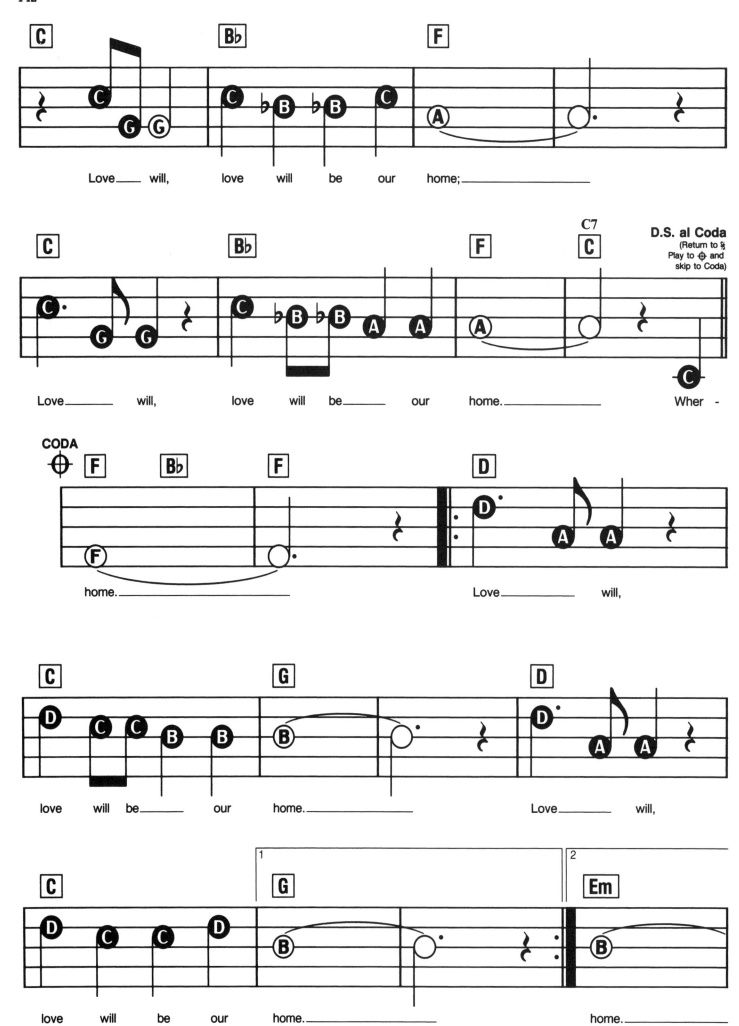

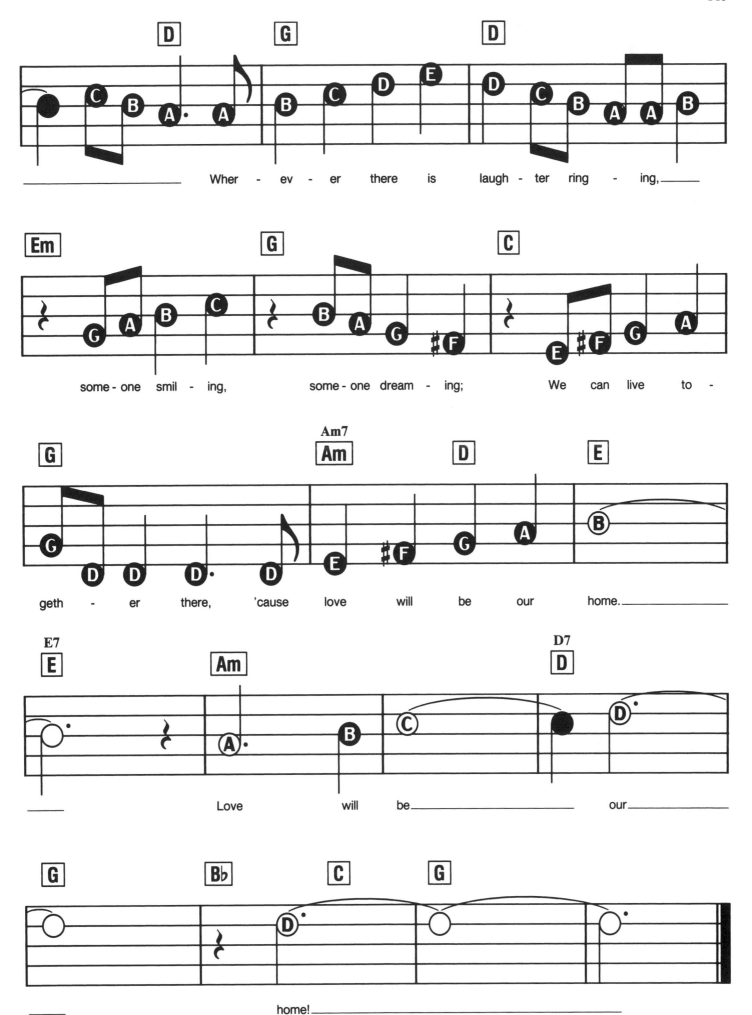

Love in Any Language

Registration 1
Rhythm: 8 Beat

Words and Music by John Mays
and Jon Mohr

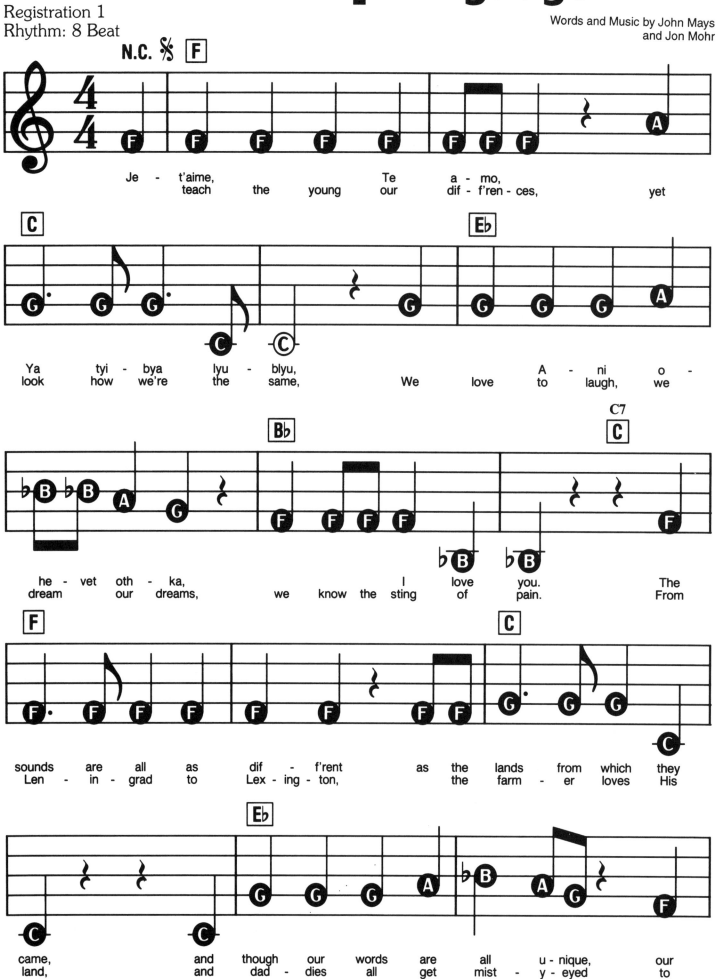

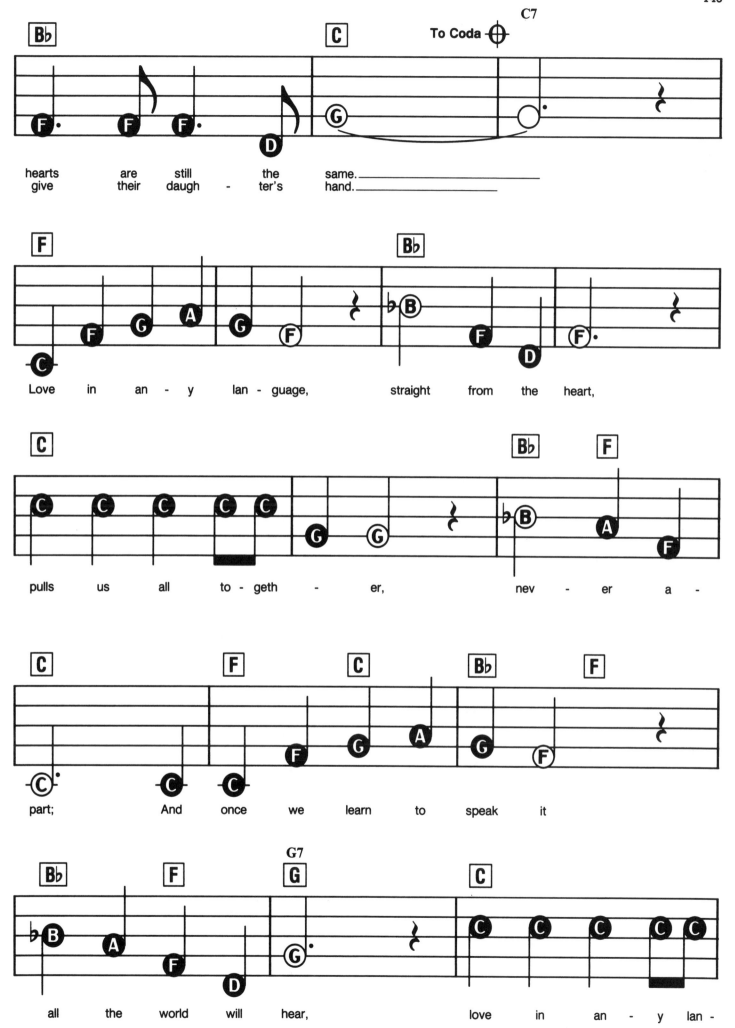

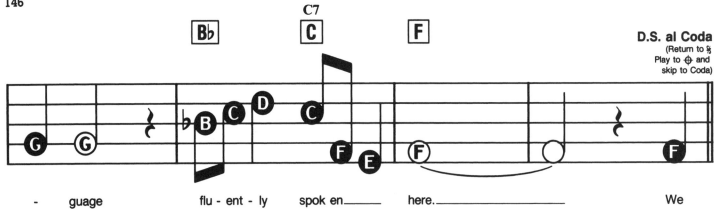

- guage   flu - ent - ly   spok en_____   here._____   We

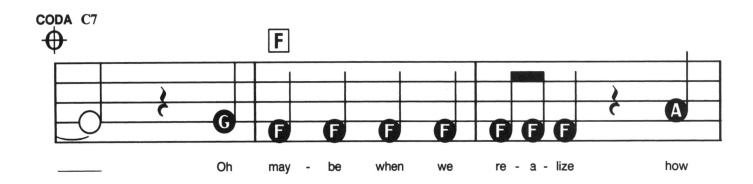

_____   Oh   may - be   when   we   re - a - lize   how

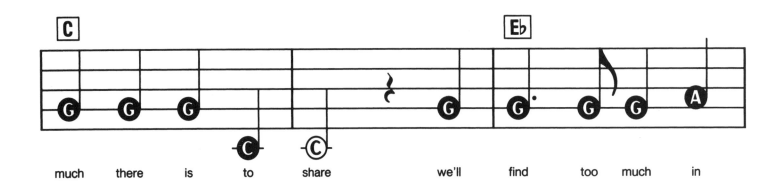

much   there   is   to   share   we'll   find   too   much   in

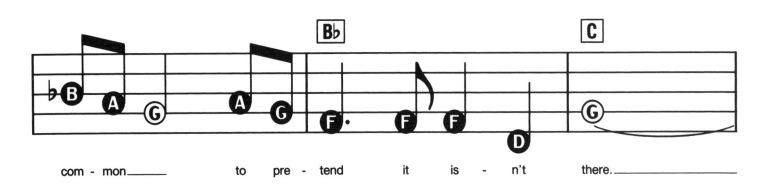

com - mon_____   to   pre - tend   it   is - n't   there._____

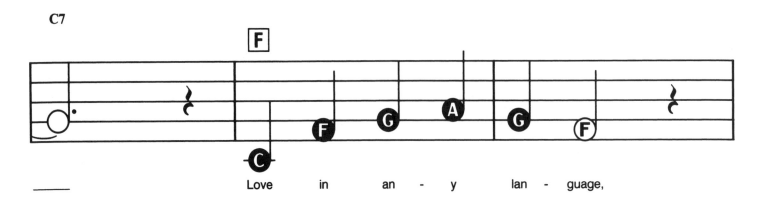

_____   Love   in   an - y   lan - guage,

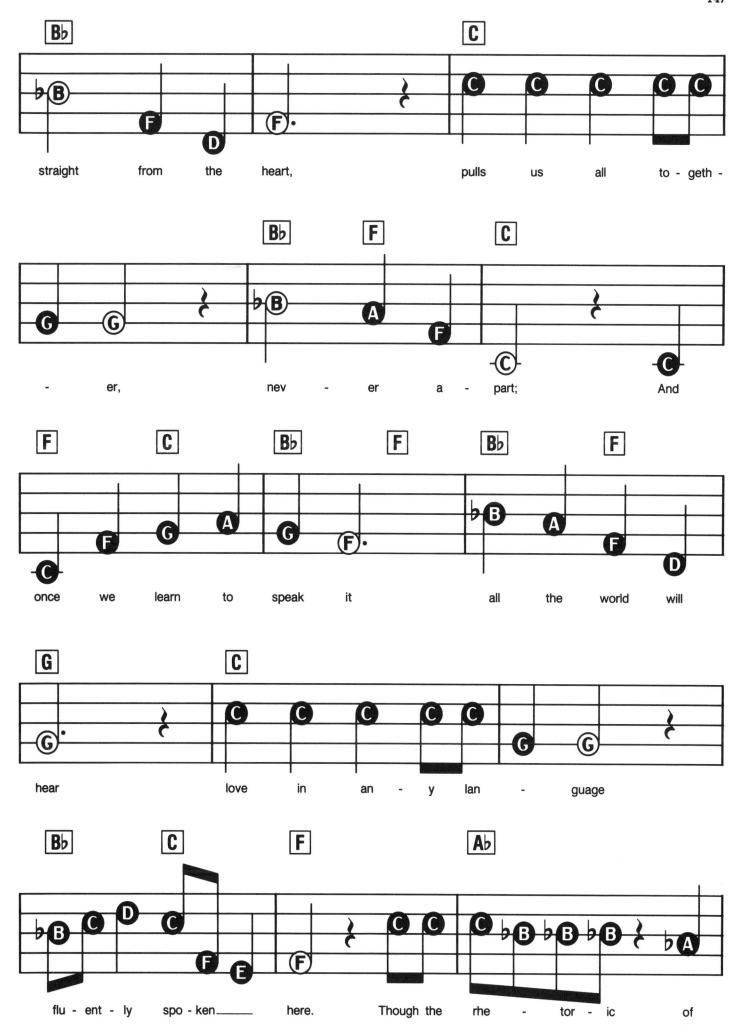

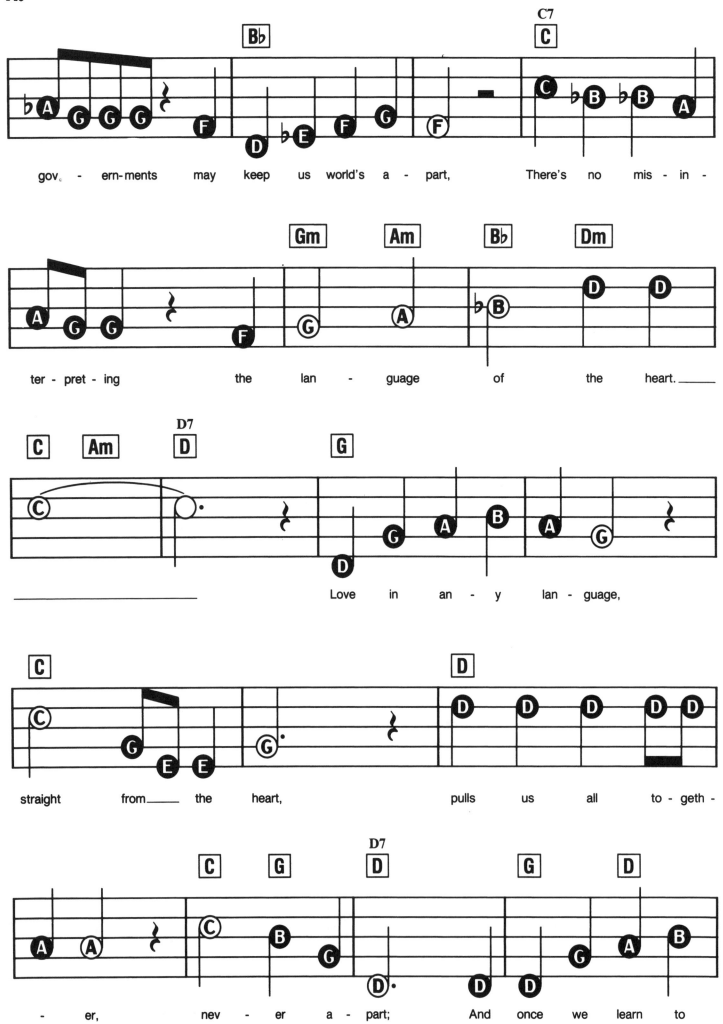

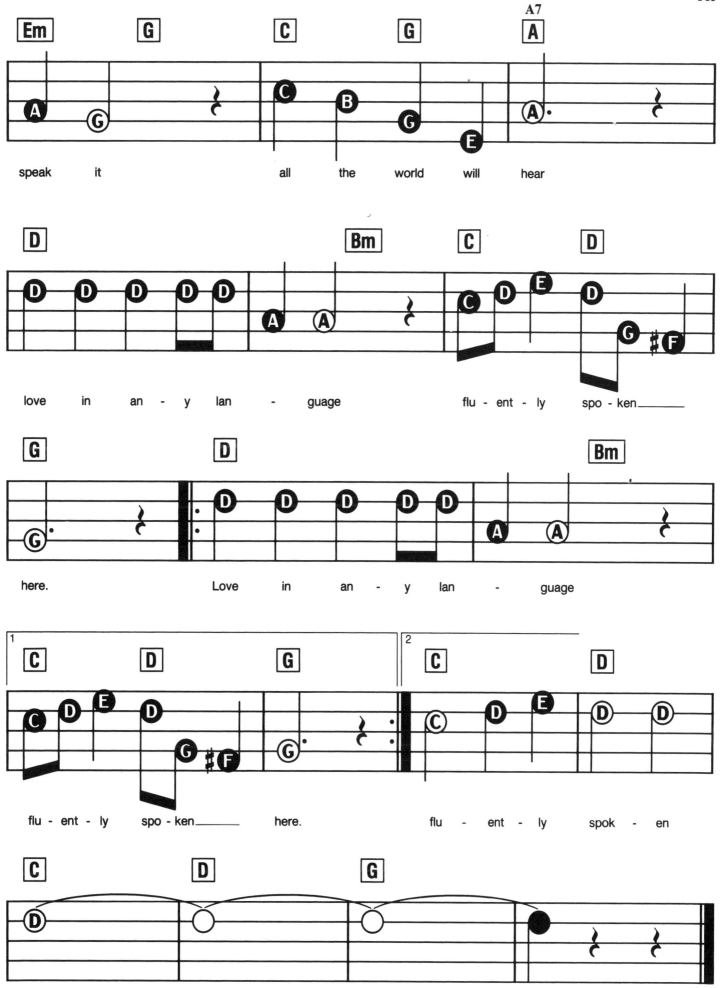

The Mission

Registration 3
Rhythm: Ballad or 8 Beat

Words and Music by Randall Dennis
and Jon Mohr

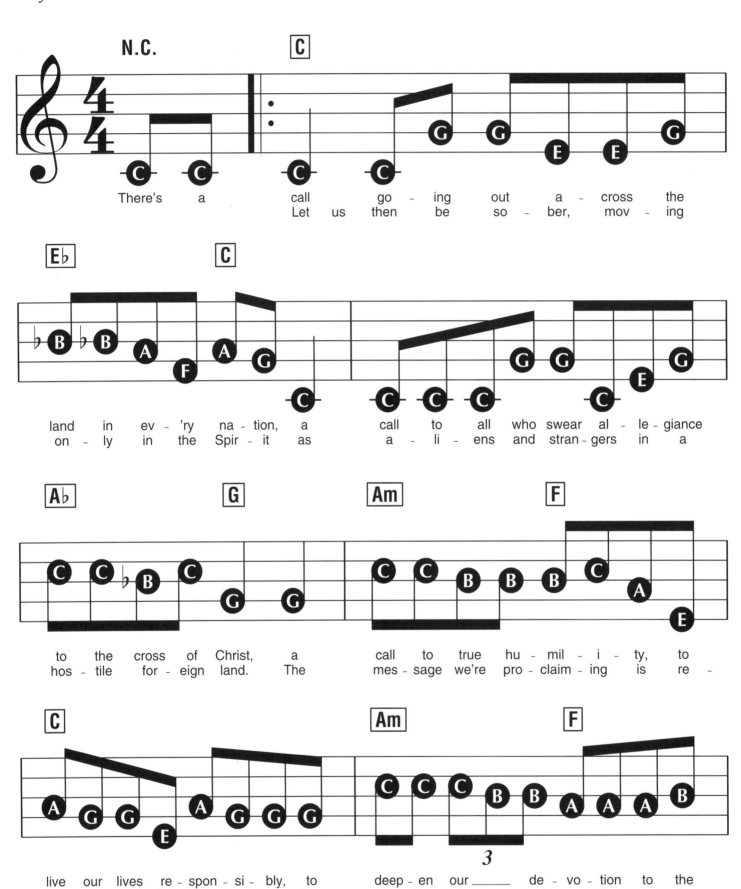

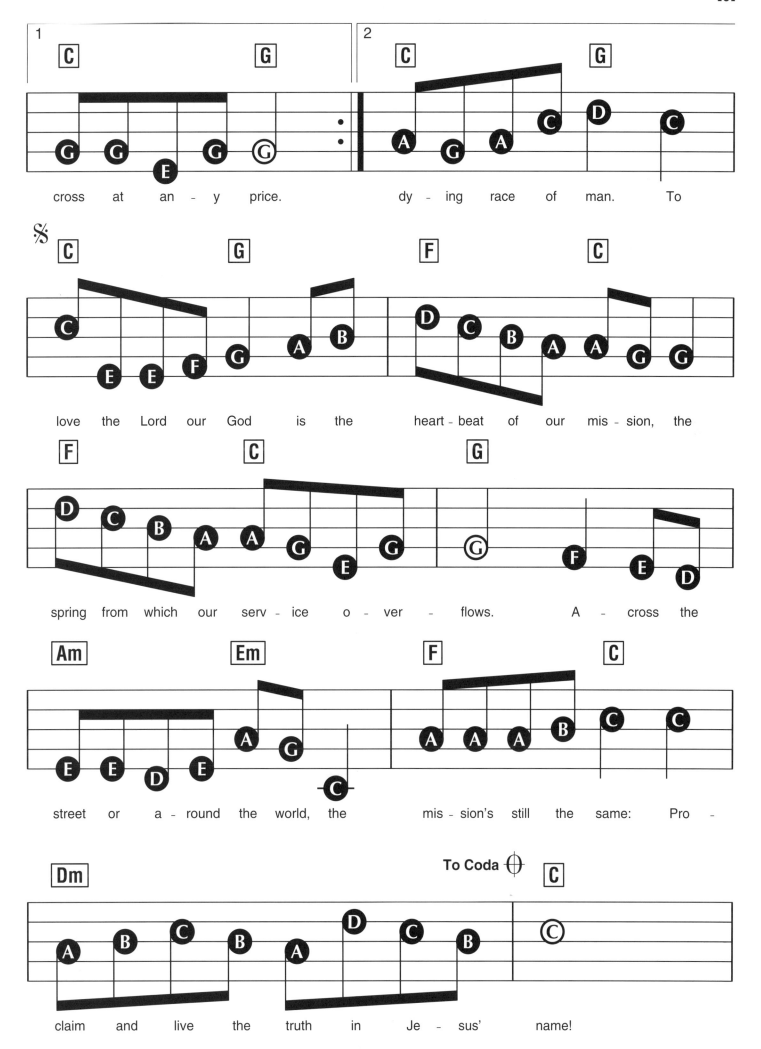

152

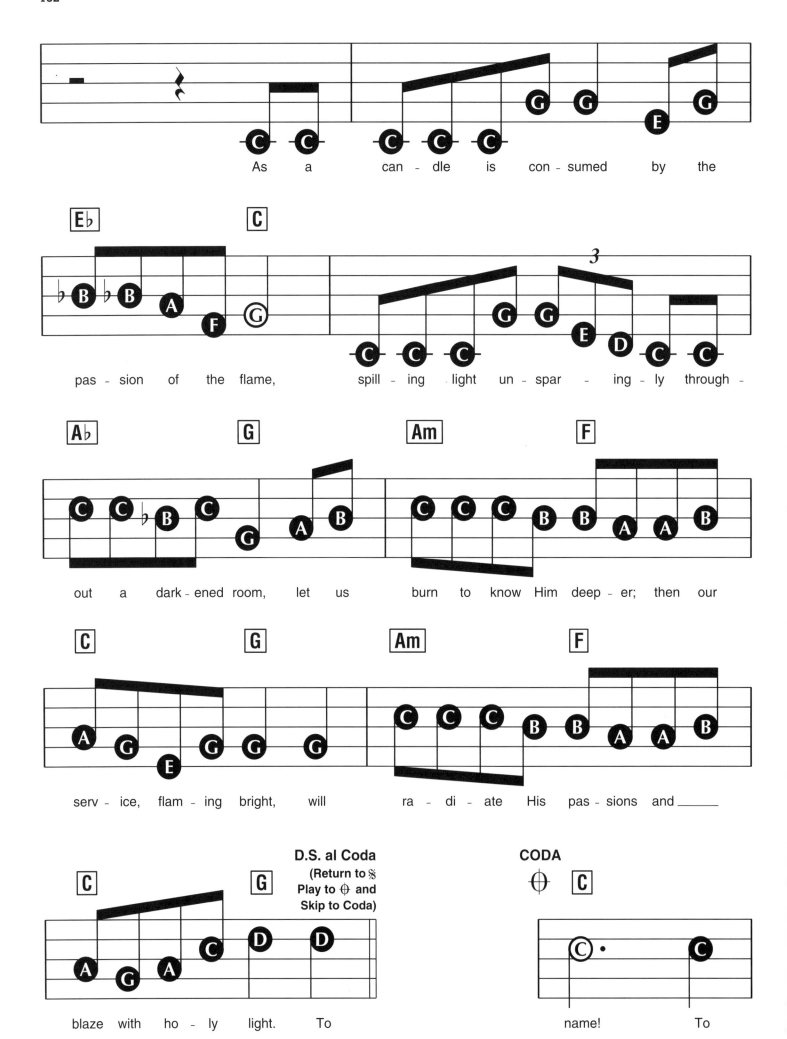

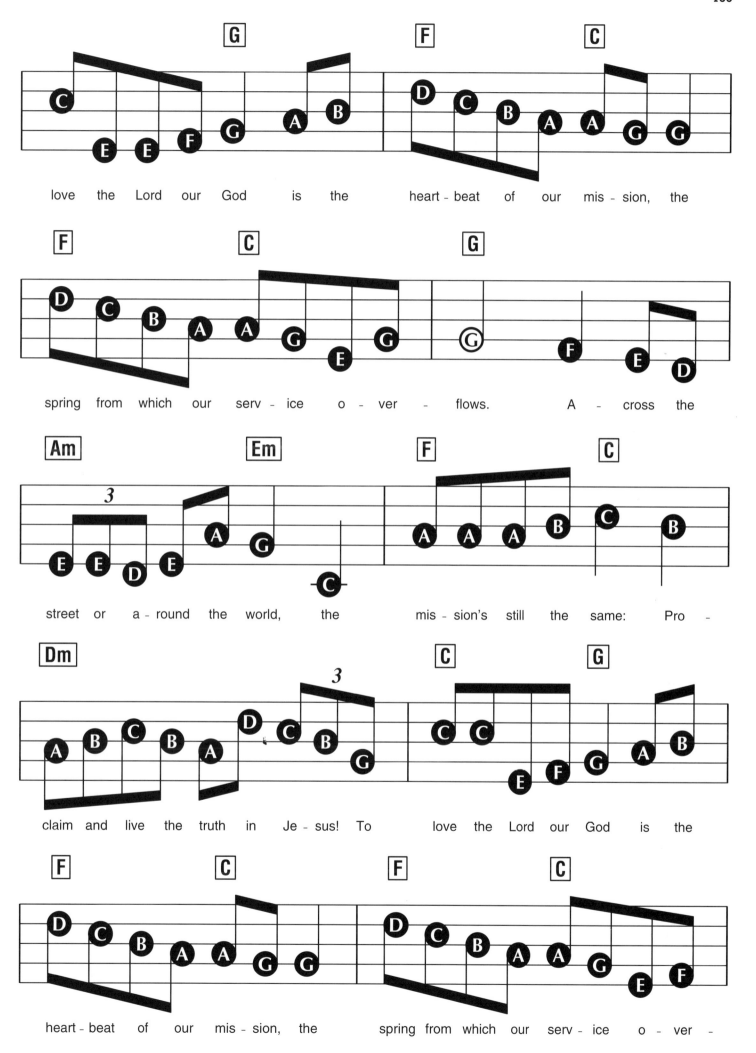

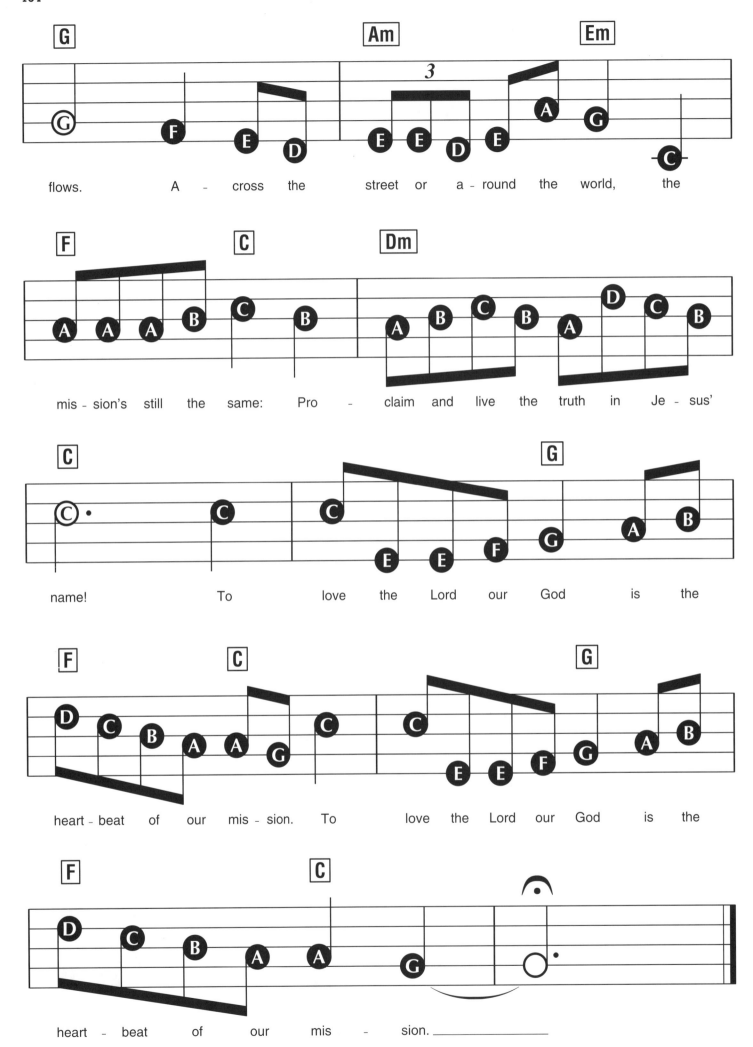

More to This Life

Registration 6
Rhythm: Rock or 16 Beat

Words and Music by Steven Curtis Chapman
and Phil Naish

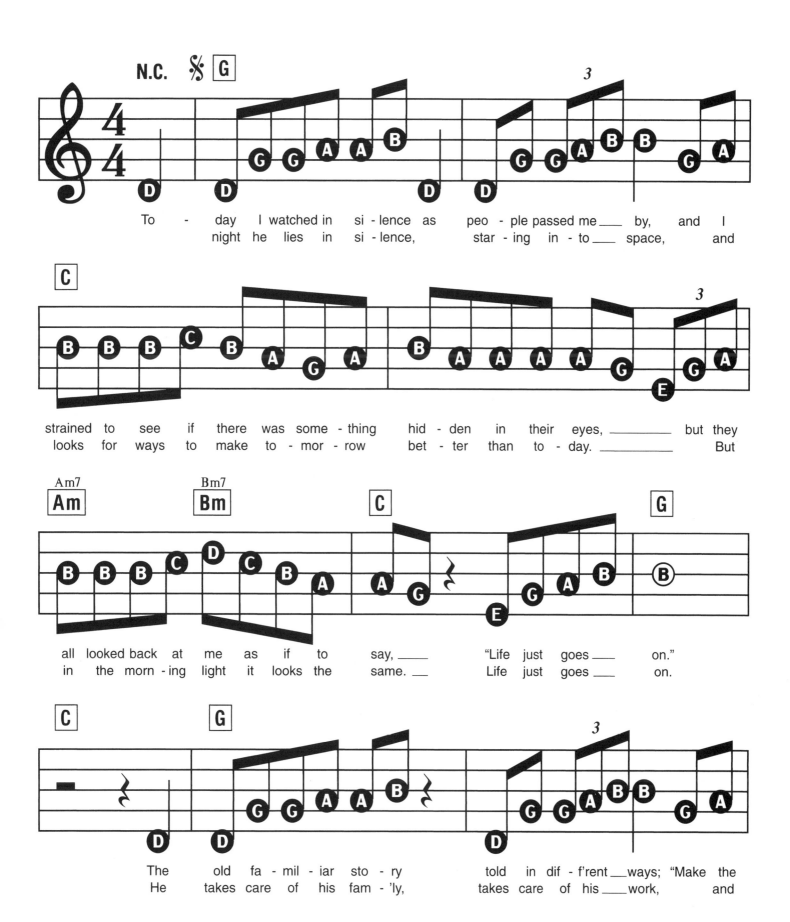

156

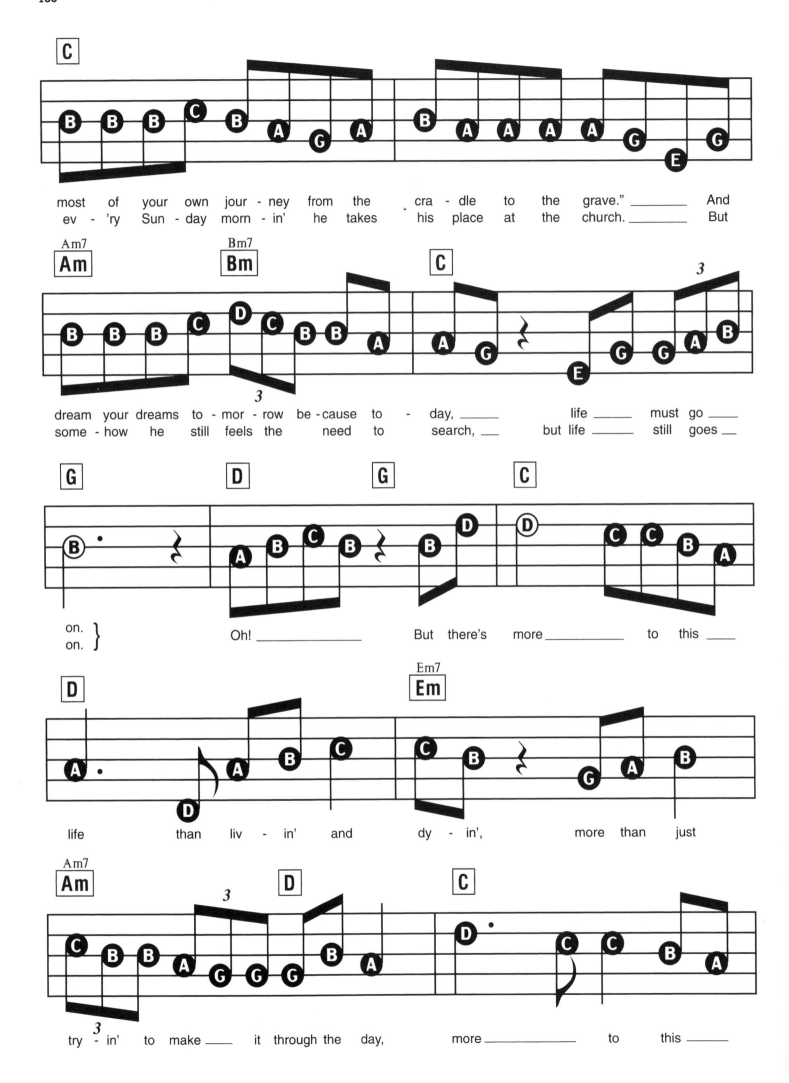

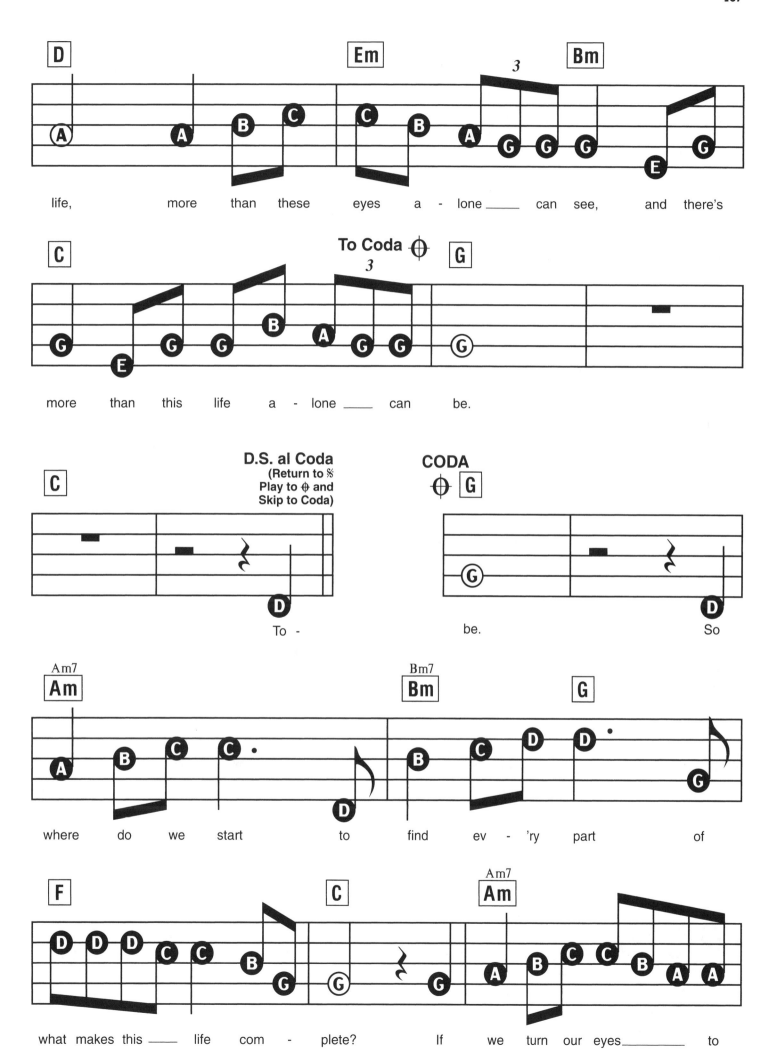

life, more than these eyes a - lone _____ can see, and there's

more than this life a - lone _____ can be.

To -

be. So

where do we start to find ev - 'ry part of

what makes this ___ life com - plete? If we turn our eyes_____ to

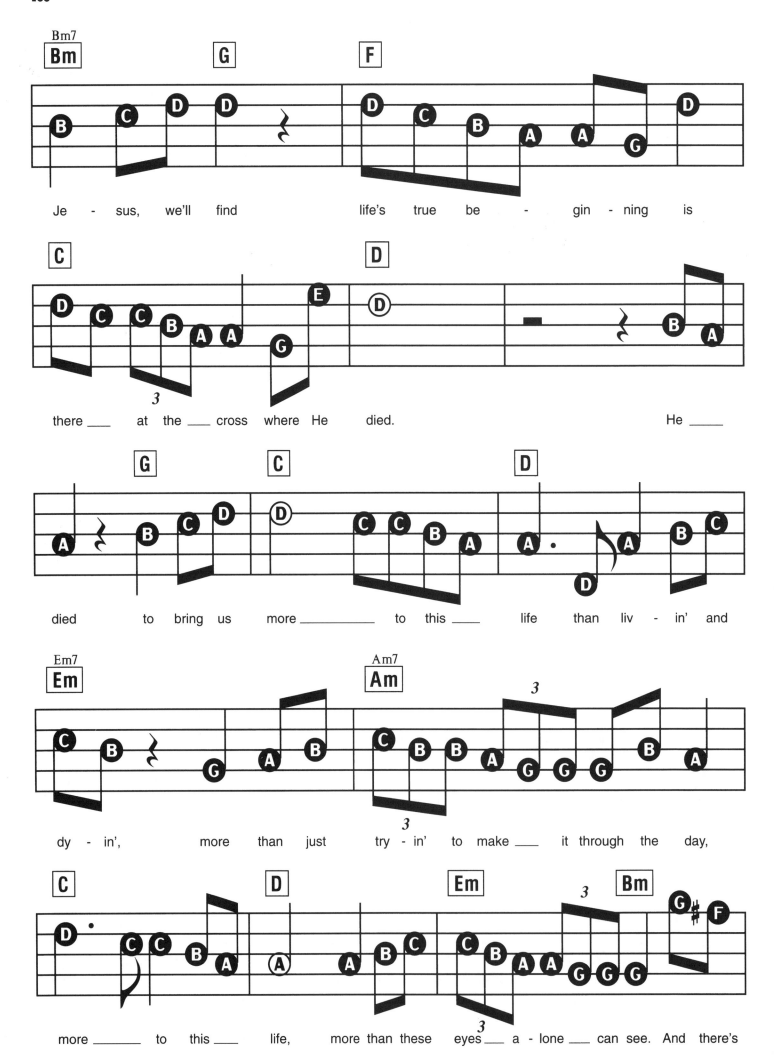

159

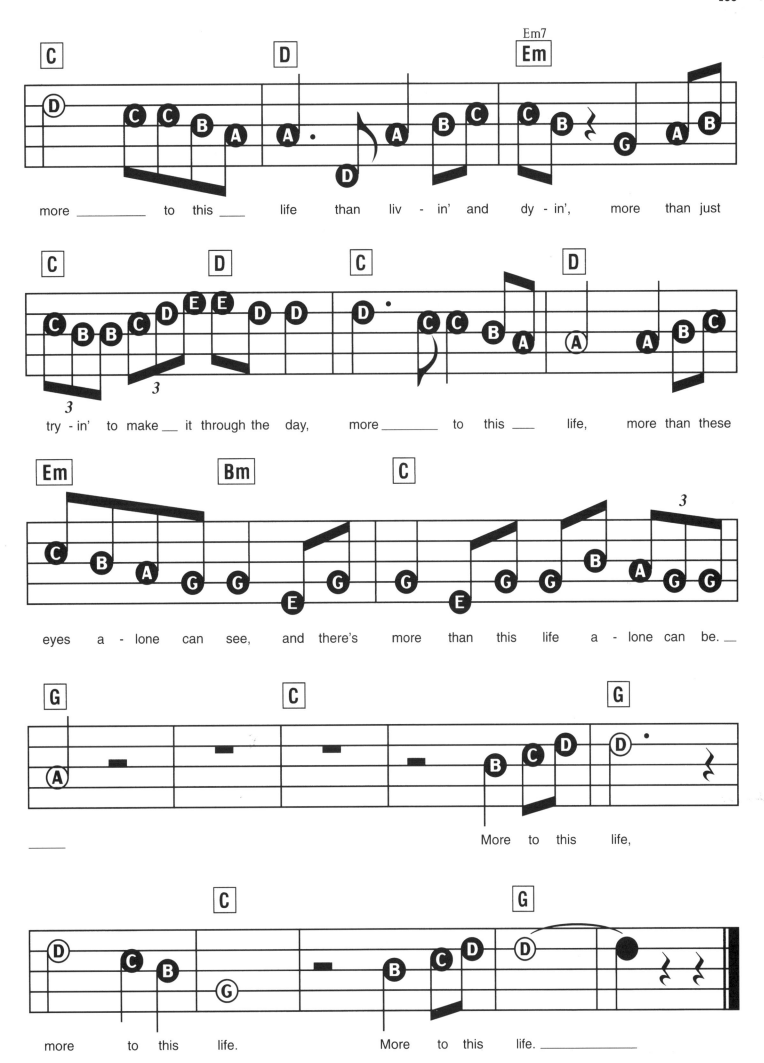

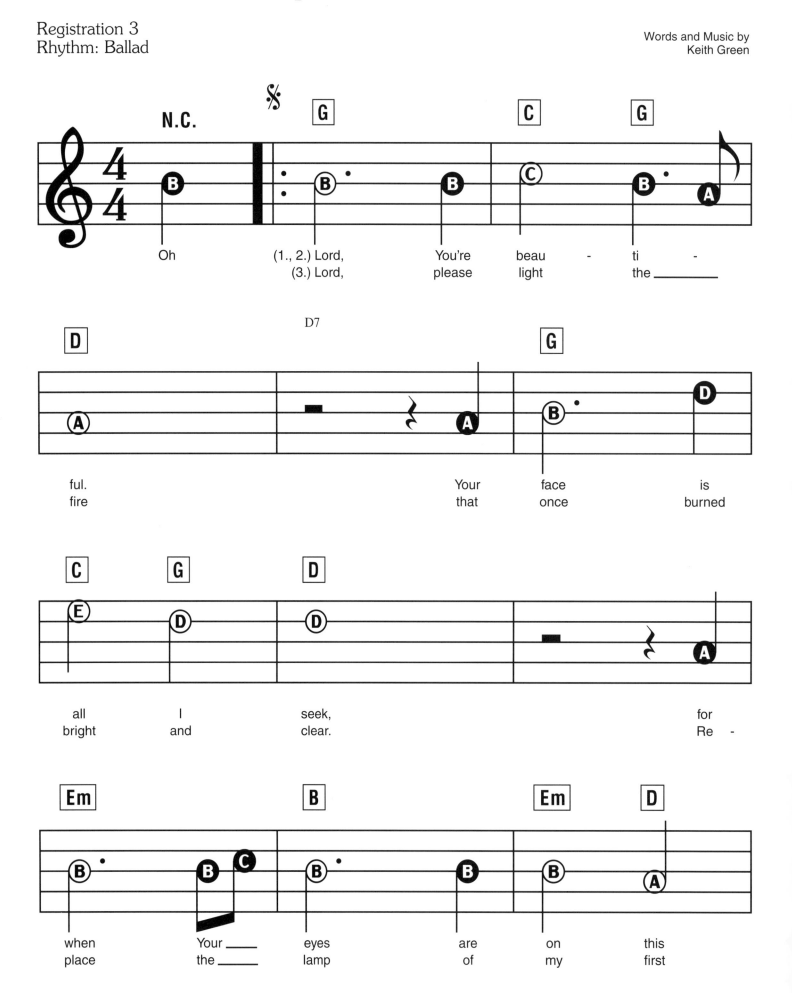

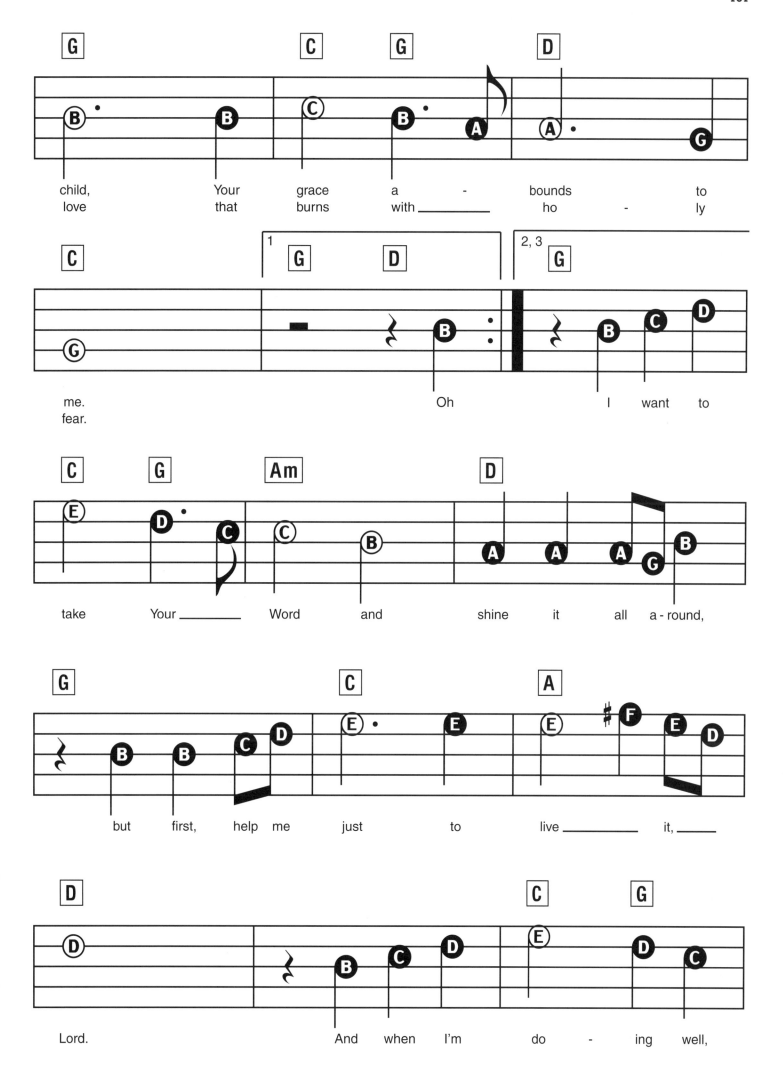

162

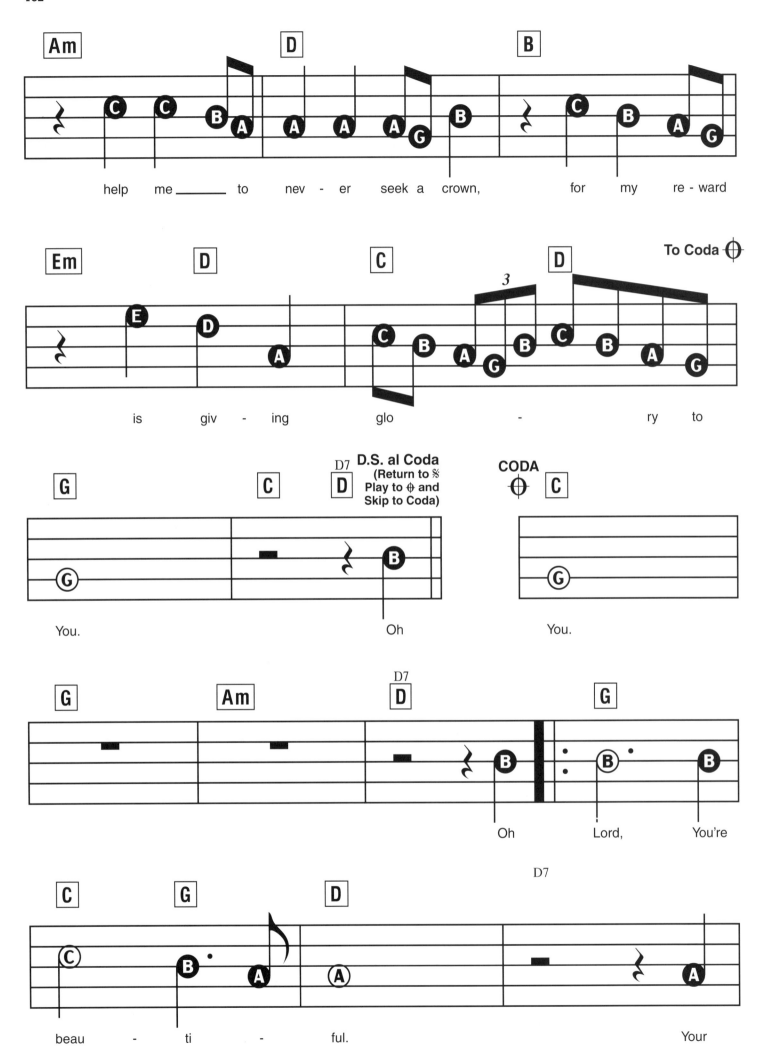

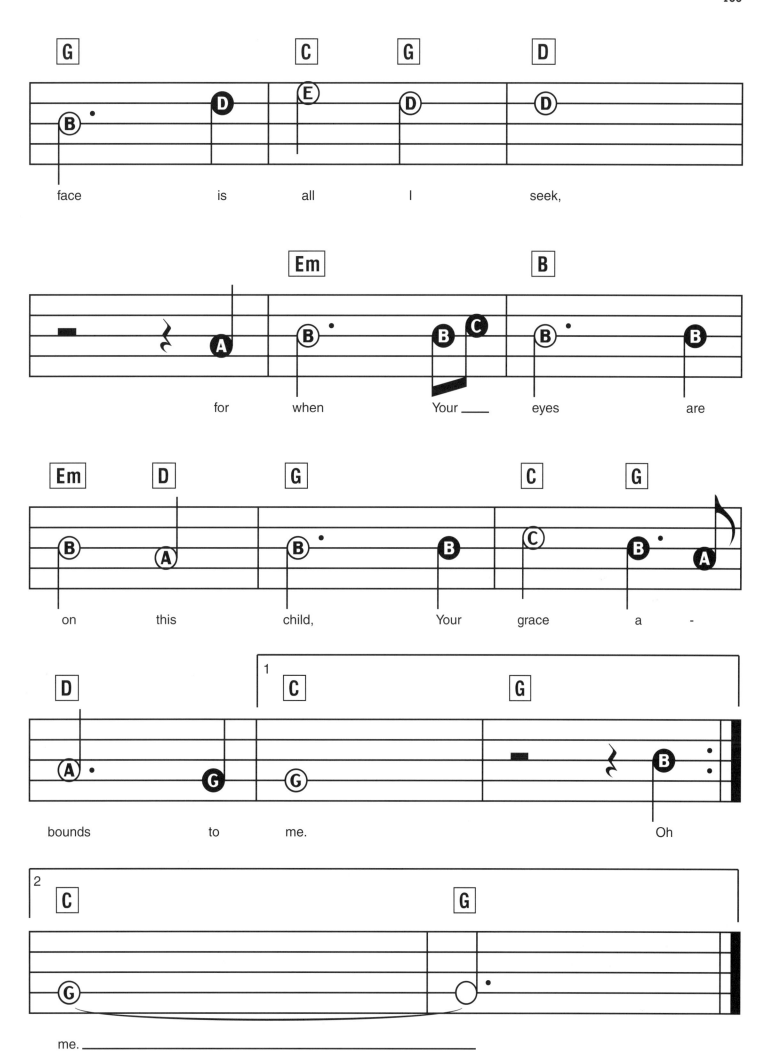

People Need the Lord

Registration 3
Rhythm: 8 Beat or Ballad

Words and Music by Phill McHugh
and Greg Nelson

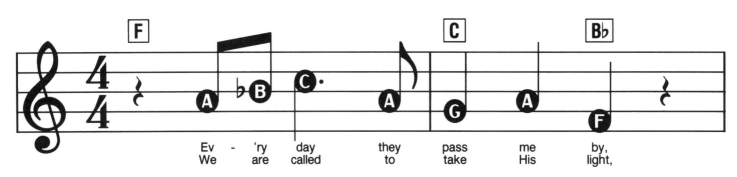

Ev - 'ry day they pass me by,
We are called to take His light,

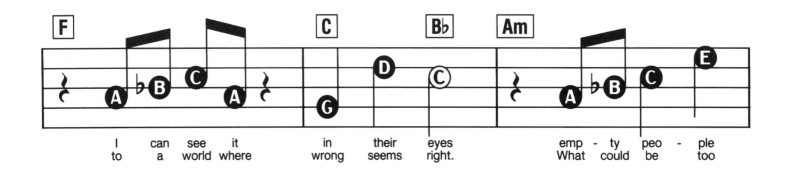

I can see it in their eyes
to a world where wrong seems right.

emp - ty peo - ple
What could be too

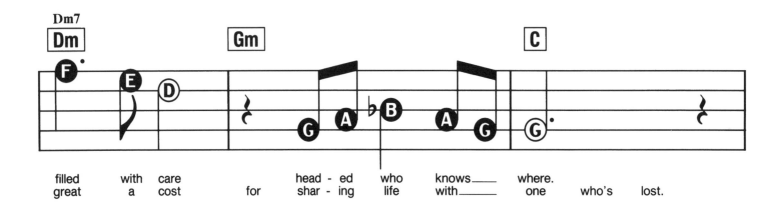

filled with care for head - ed who knows_____ where.
great a cost for shar - ing life with_____ one who's lost.

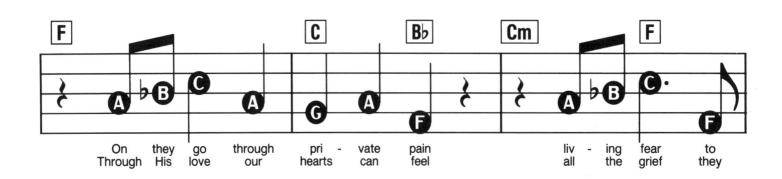

On they go through pri - vate pain
Through His love our hearts can feel

liv - ing fear to
all the grief to they

165

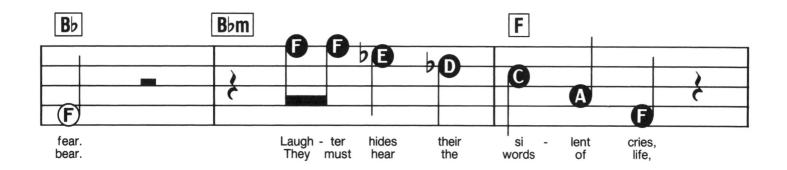

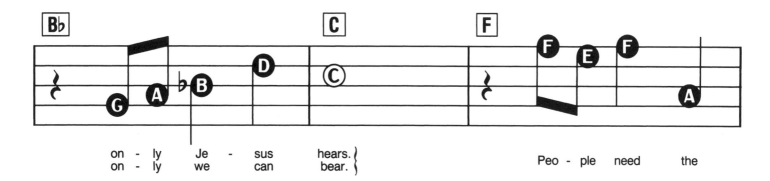

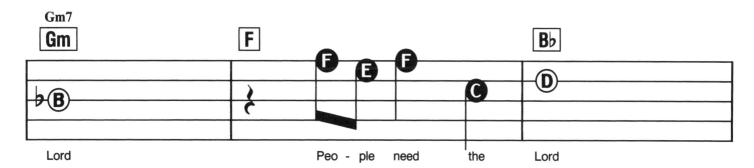

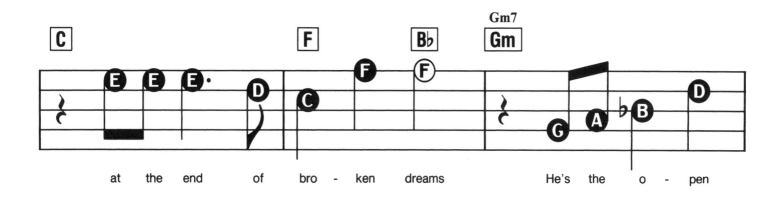

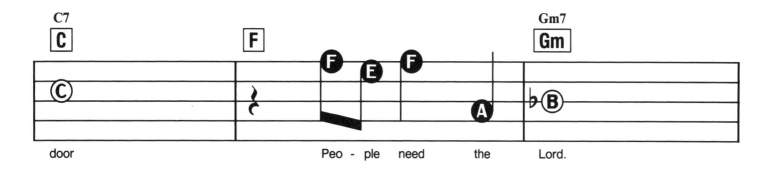

166

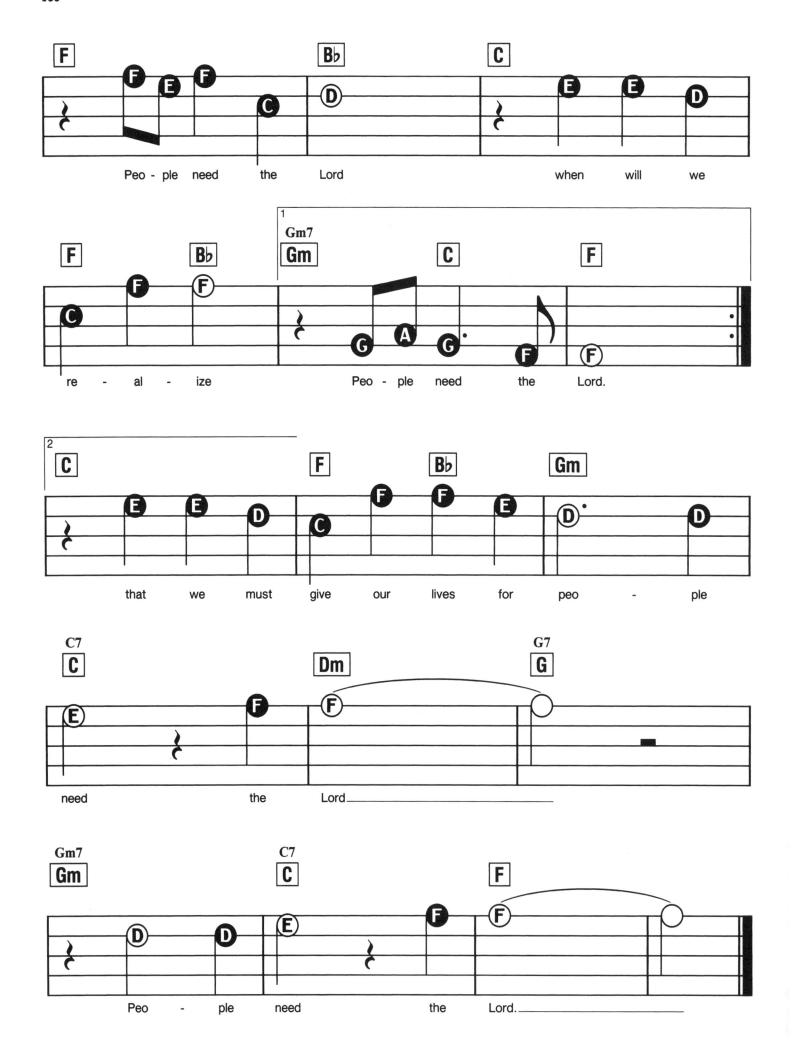

Signs of Life

Registration 5
Rhythm: Rock or Pops

Words and Music by
Steven Curtis Chapman

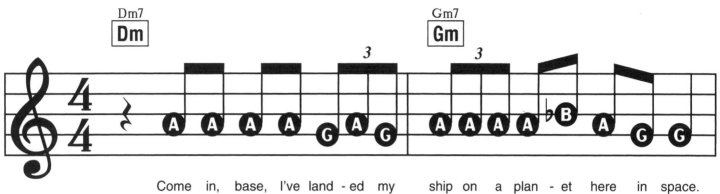

Come in, base, I've land-ed my ship on a plan-et here in space.

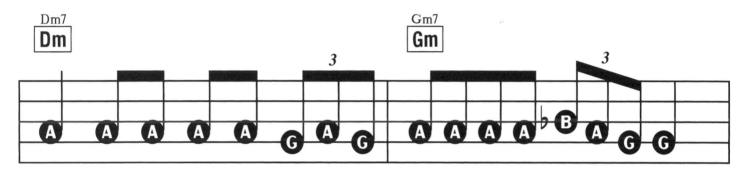

This is the one they say is in - hab - it - ed by the hu - man race.

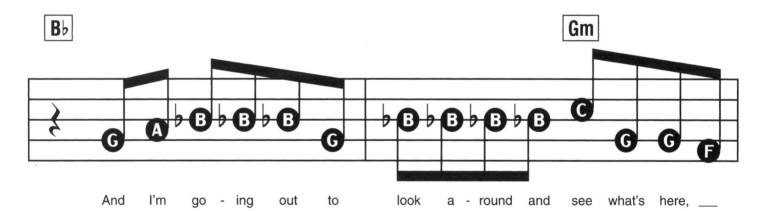

And I'm go - ing out to look a - round and see what's here, ___

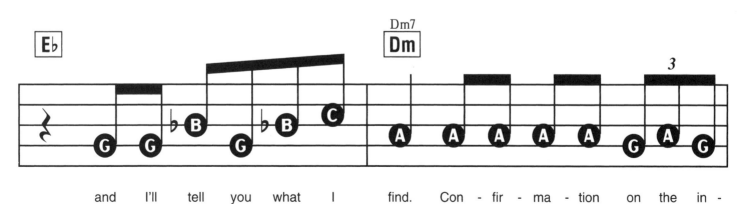

and I'll tell you what I find. Con - fir - ma - tion on the in -

168

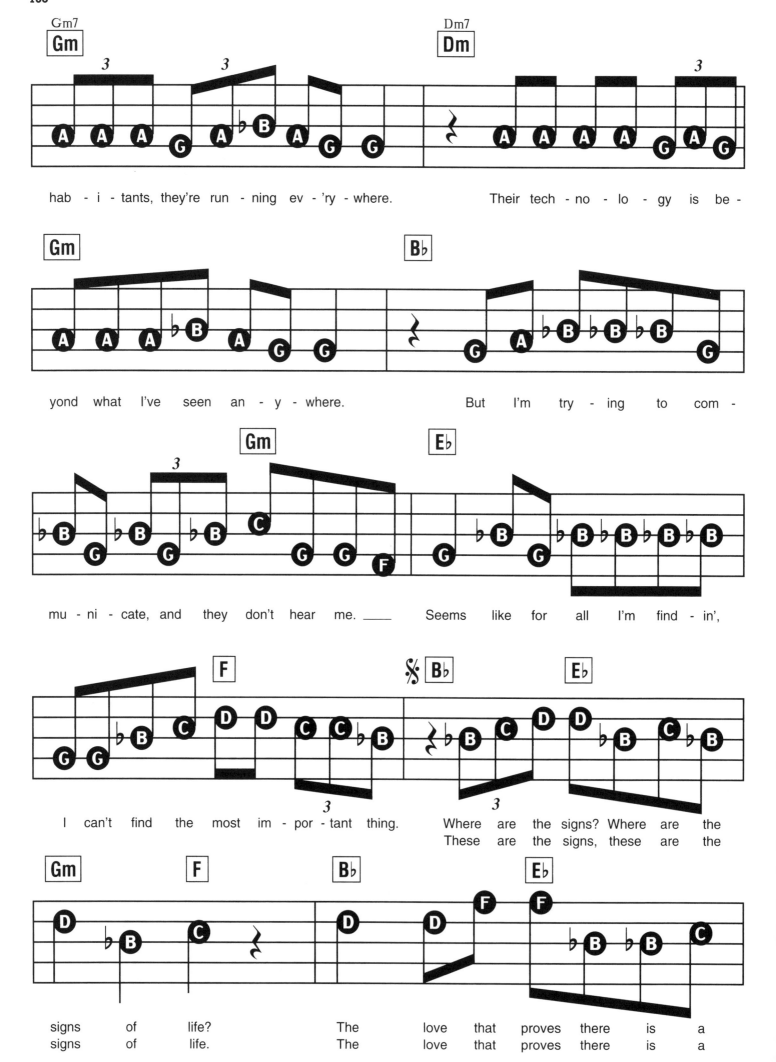

170

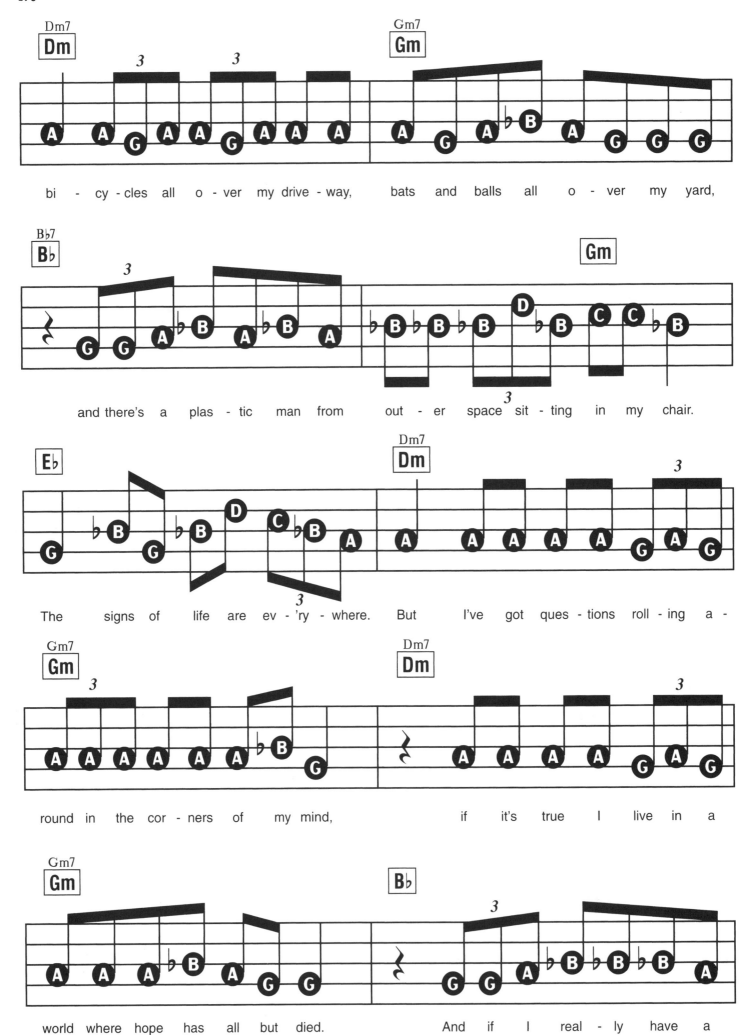

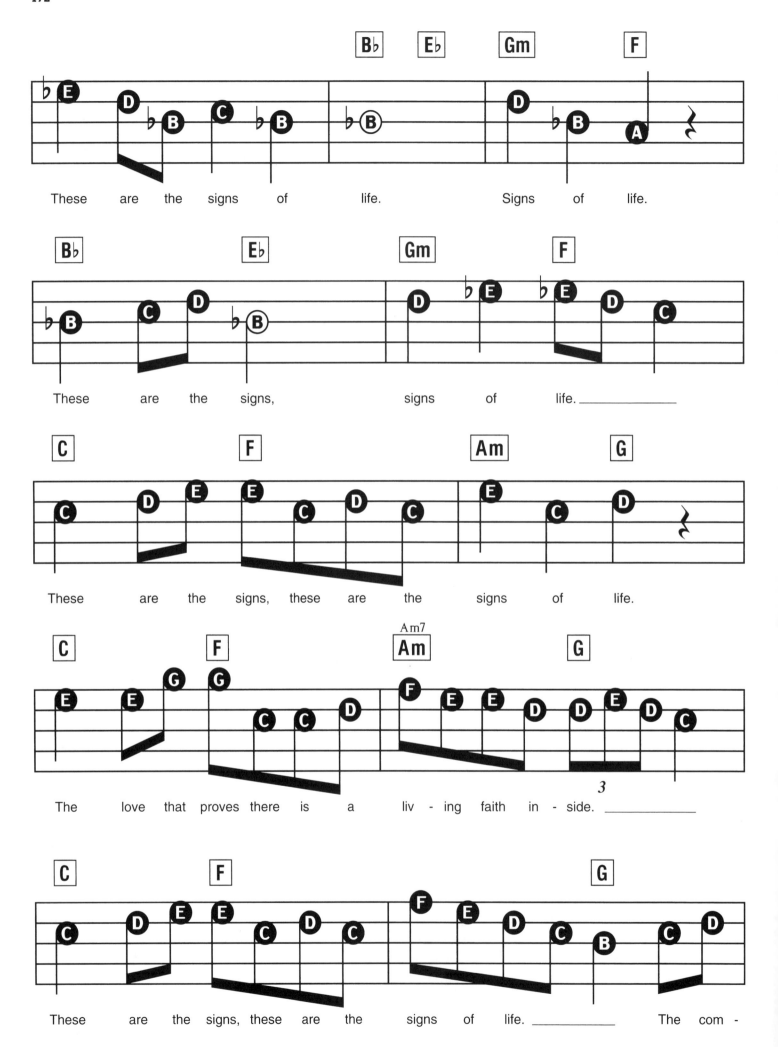

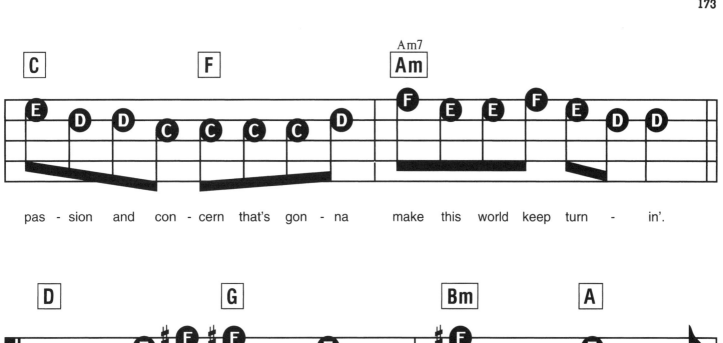

pas - sion and con - cern that's gon - na make this world keep turn - in'.

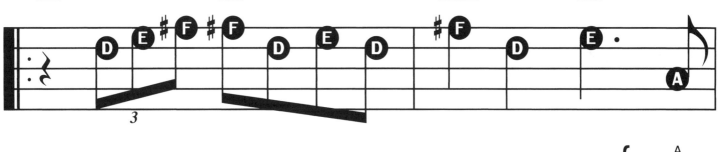

These are the signs, these are the signs of life. { A / The / This is

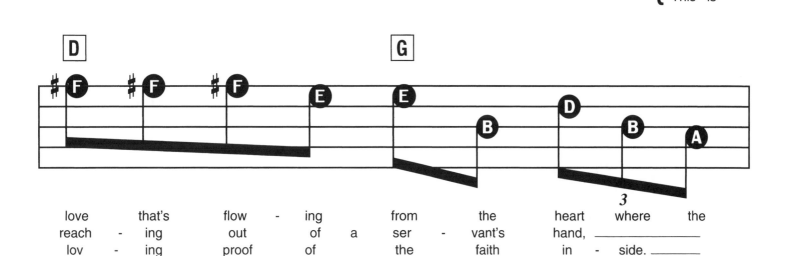

love that's flow - ing from the heart where the
reach - ing out of a ser - vant's hand, _____
lov - ing proof of the faith in - side. _____

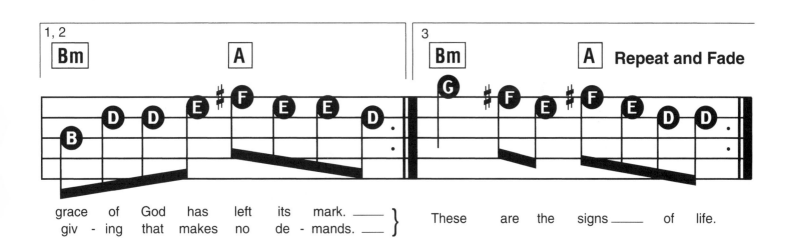

grace of God has left its mark. ___ }
giv - ing that makes no de - mands. ___ }
These are the signs ___ of life.

Place in This World

Registration 8
Rhythm: Rock or 8 Beat

Words by Wayne Kirkpatrick and Amy Grant
Music by Michael W. Smith

175

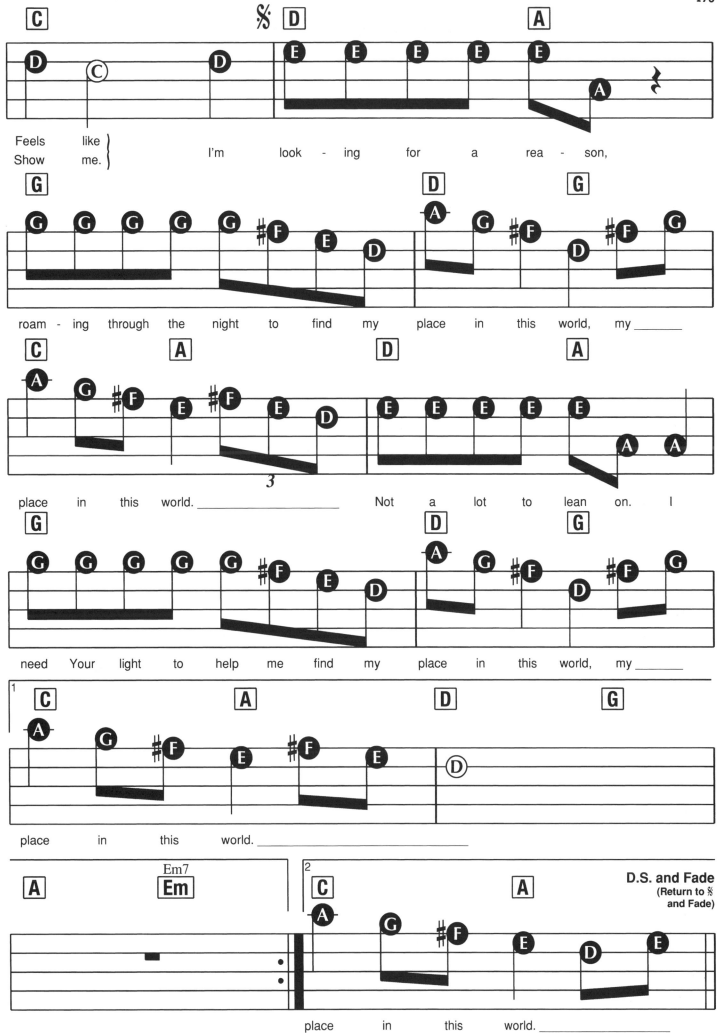

Shine on Us

Registration 3
Rhythm: Ballad

Words and Music by Michael W. Smith
and Debbie Smith

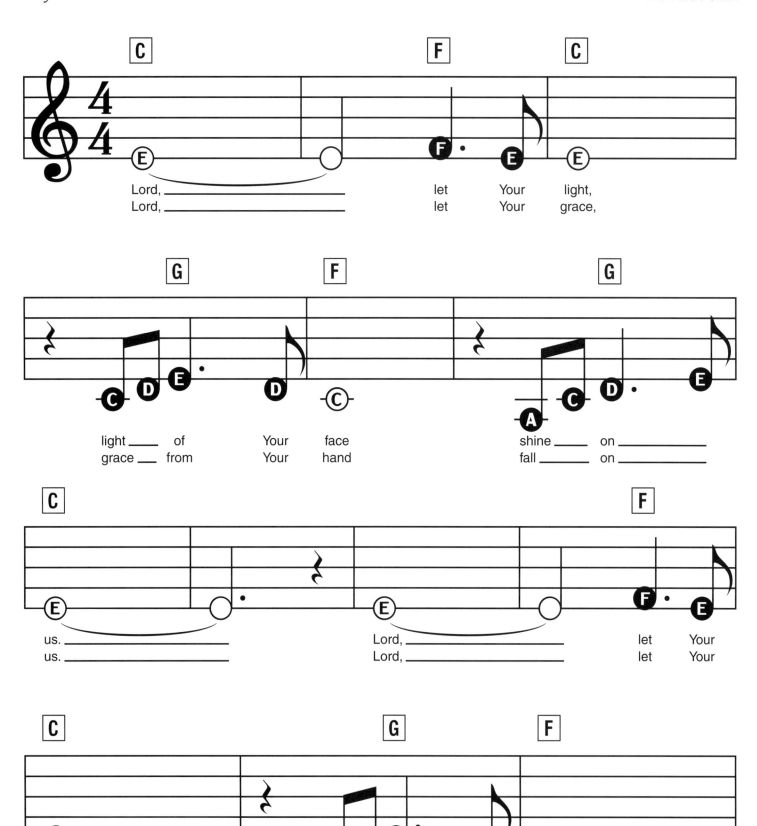

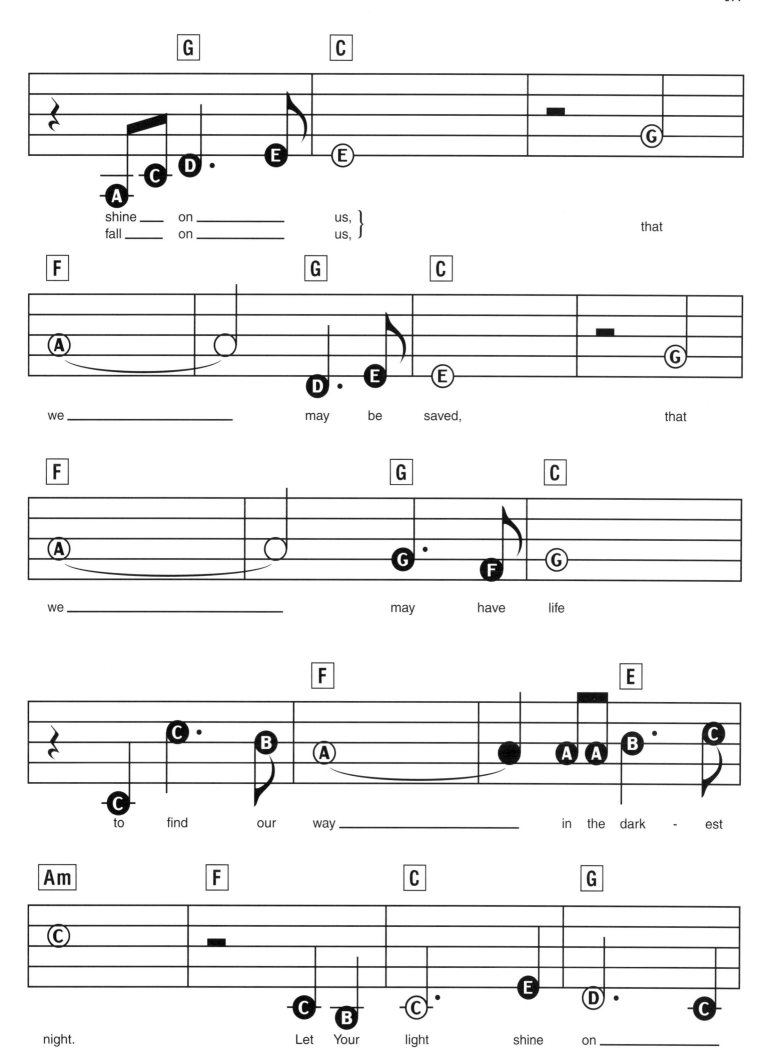

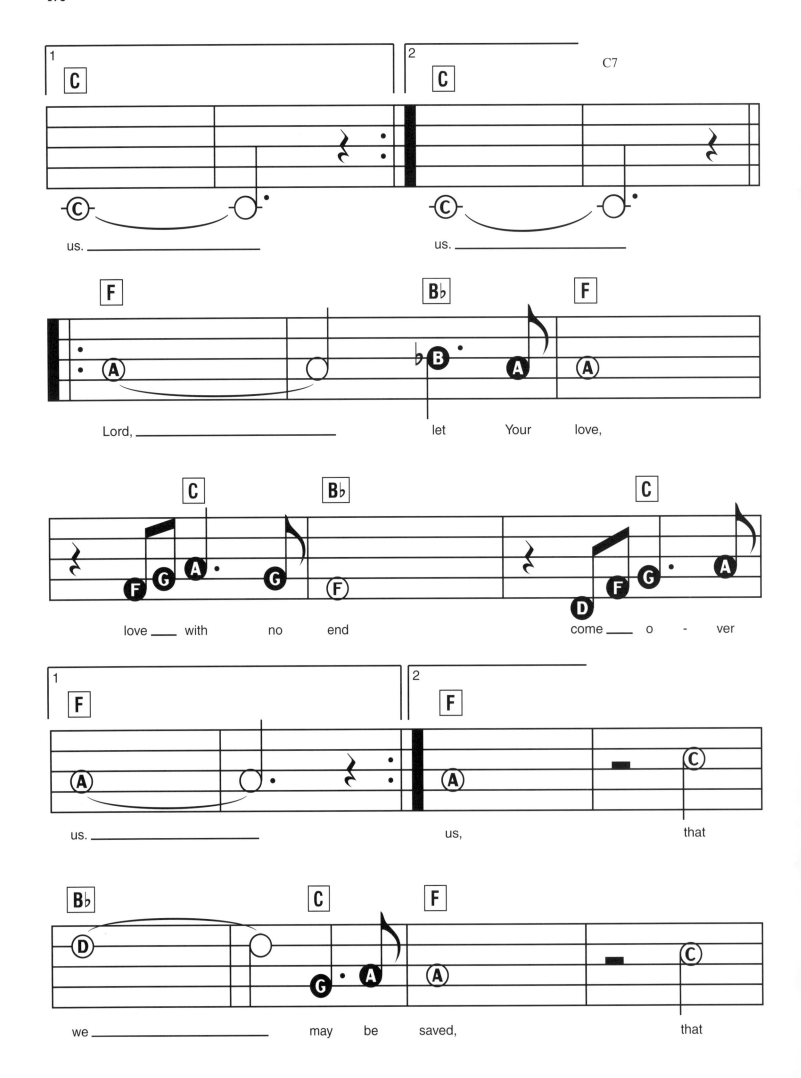

179

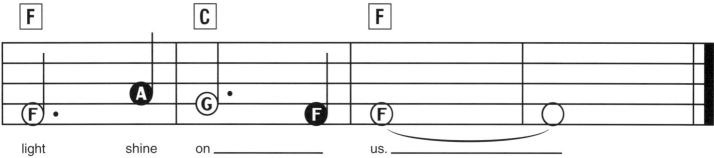

Steady On

Registration 8
Rhythm: Country Rock

Words and Music by Grant Cunningham
and Matt Huesmann

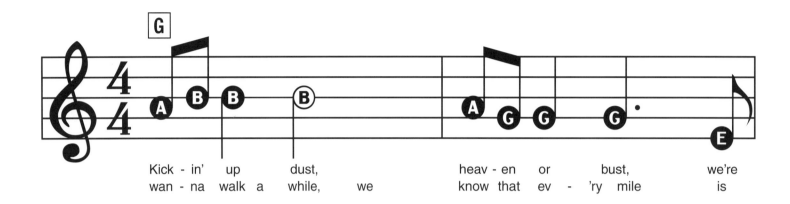

Kick - in' up   dust,   heav - en or   bust,   we're
wan - na walk a while, we know that ev - 'ry mile   is

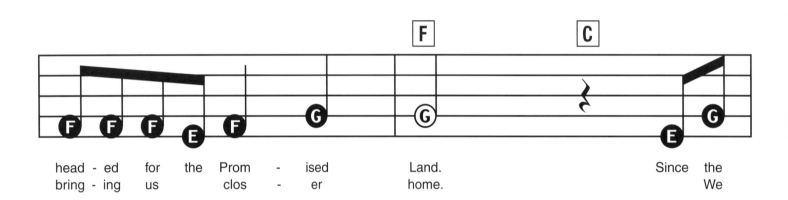

head - ed for the Prom - ised   Land.   Since the
bring - ing us clos - er   home.   We

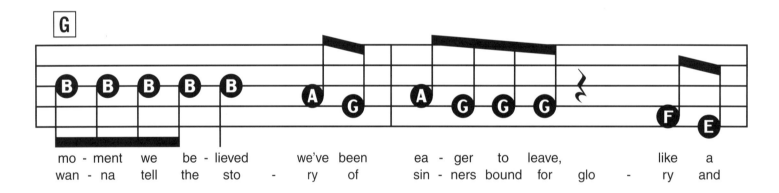

mo - ment we be - lieved   we've been   ea - ger to leave,   like a
wan - na tell the sto - ry of   sin - ners bound for glo - ry and

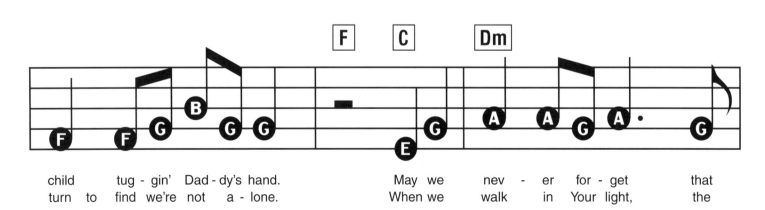

child   tug - gin' Dad - dy's hand.   May we nev - er for - get   that
turn to find we're not a - lone.   When we walk in Your light,   the

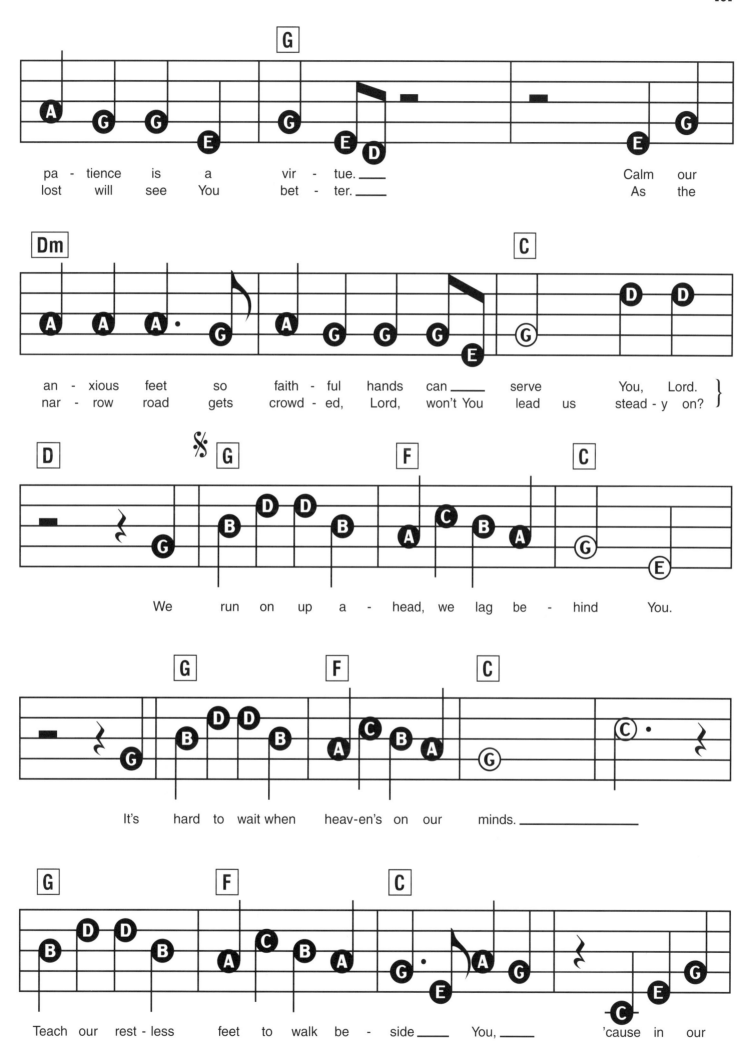

182

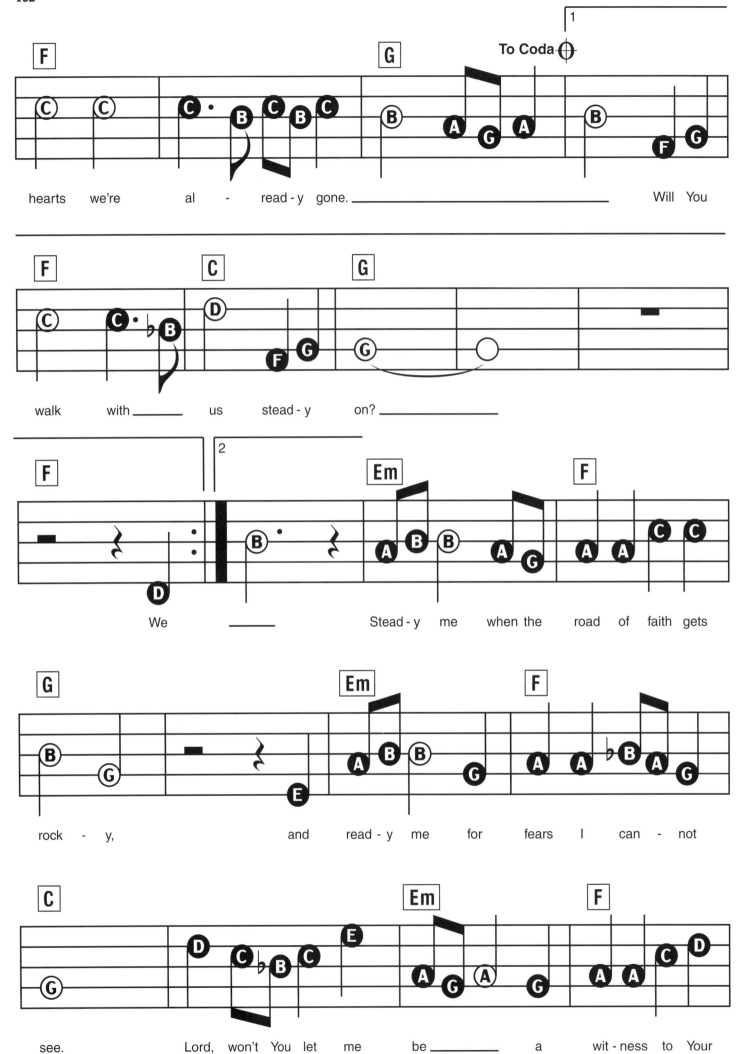

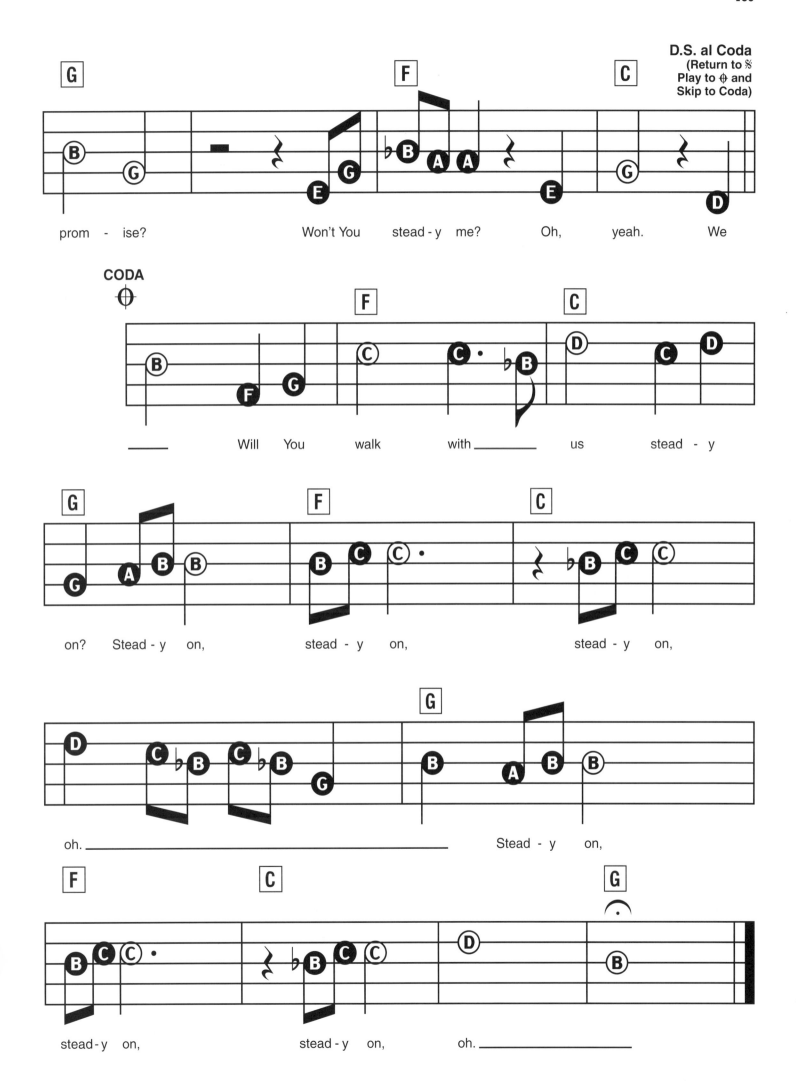

This Is Your Time

Registration 1
Rhythm: Waltz

Words and Music by Michael W. Smith
and Wes King

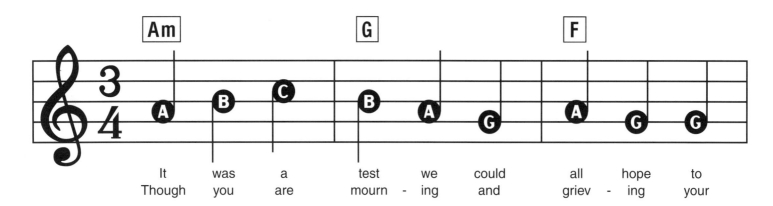

It was a test we could all hope to
Though you are mourn - ing and griev - ing to your

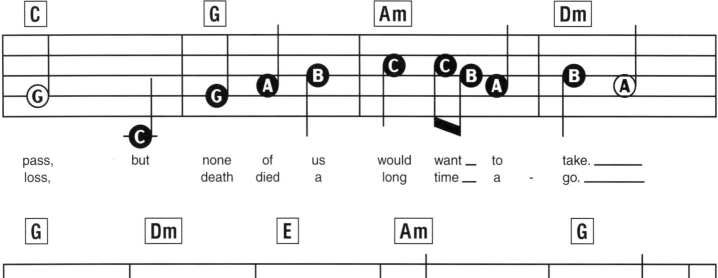

pass, but none of us would want __ to take. _____
loss, death died a long time __ a - go. _____

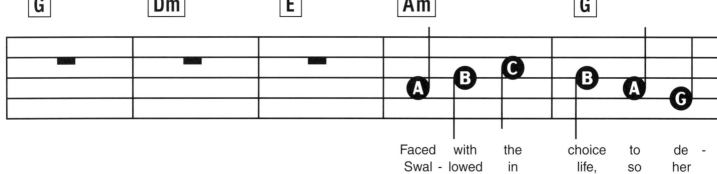

Faced with the choice to de -
Swal - lowed in life, so her

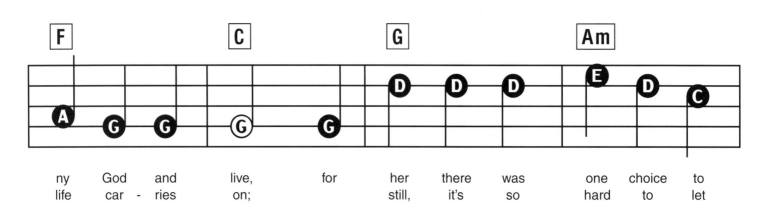

ny God and live, for her there was one choice to
life car - ries on; still, it's so hard to let

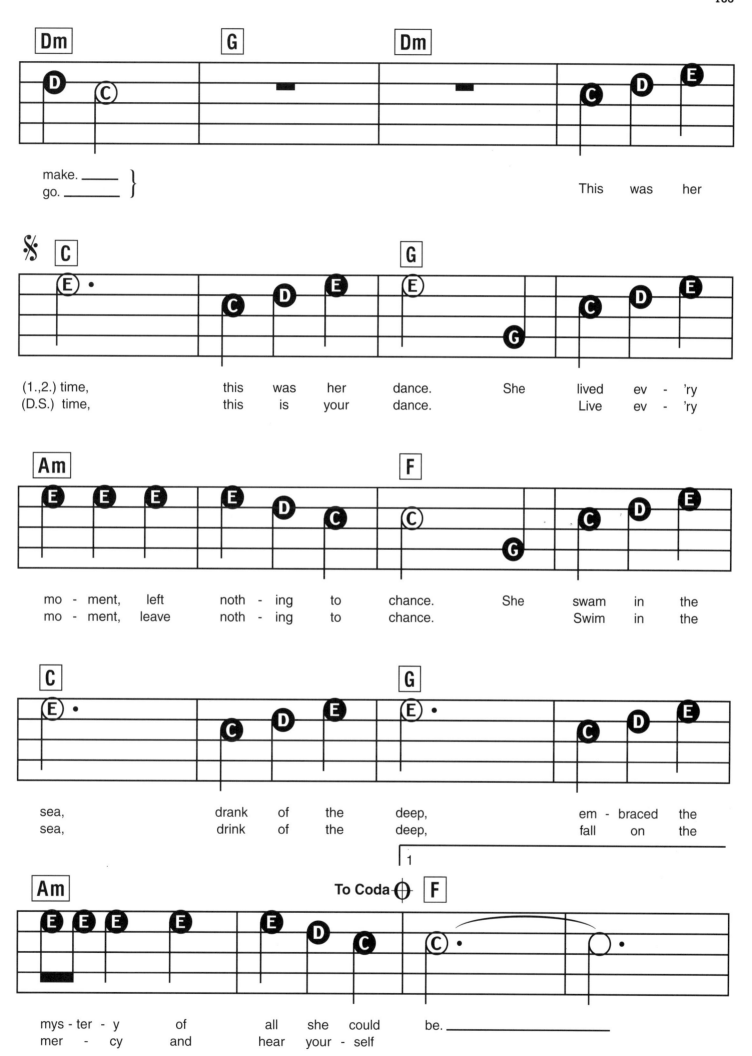

make. _____ }
go. _____

This was her

(1.,2.) time,   this was her dance.   She lived ev - 'ry
(D.S.) time,   this is your dance.   Live ev - 'ry

mo - ment, left noth - ing to chance.   She swam in the
mo - ment, leave noth - ing to chance.   Swim in the

sea,   drank of the deep,   em - braced the
sea,   drink of the deep,   fall on the

mys - ter - y of   all she could   be. _____
mer - cy and   hear your - self

186

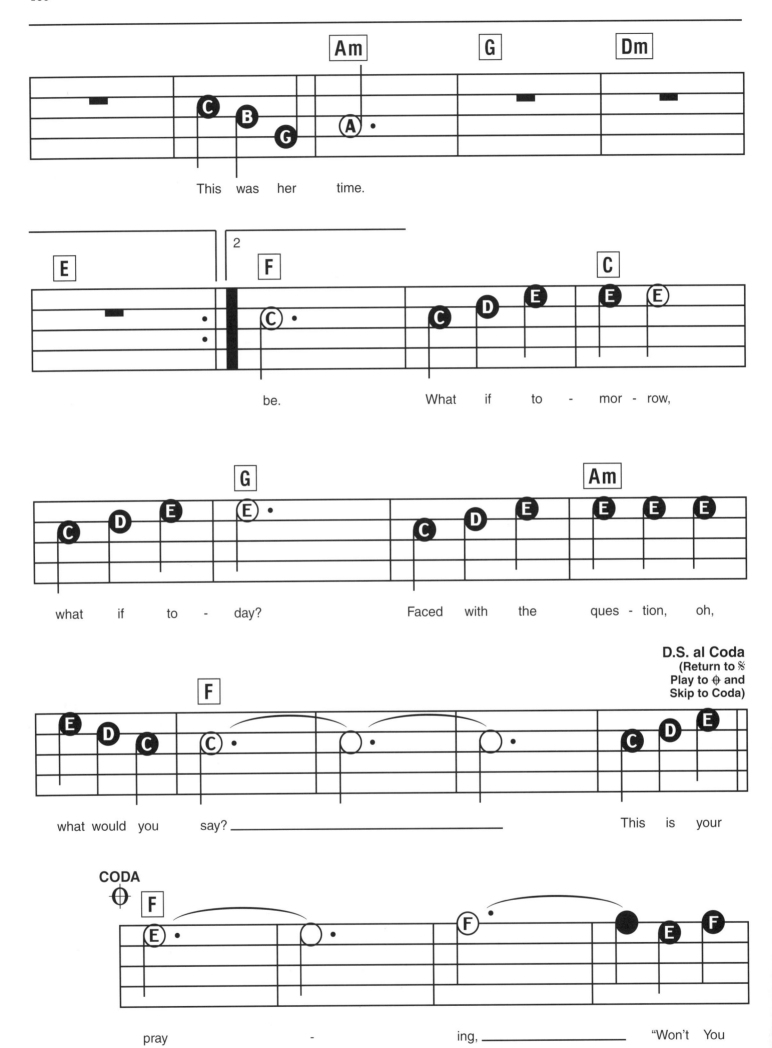

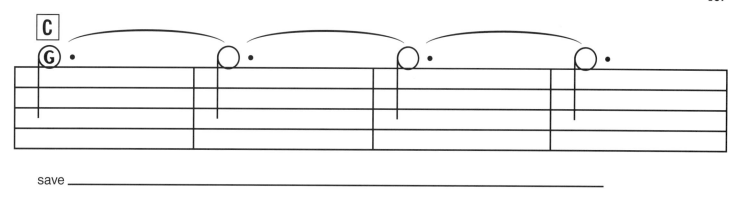

save _____

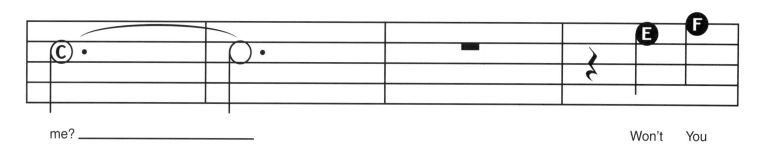

me? _____ Won't You

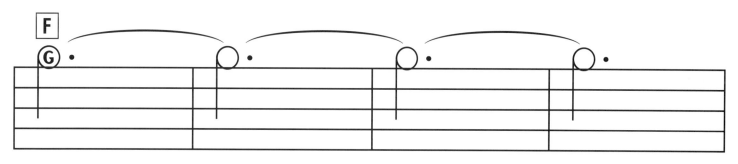

save _____

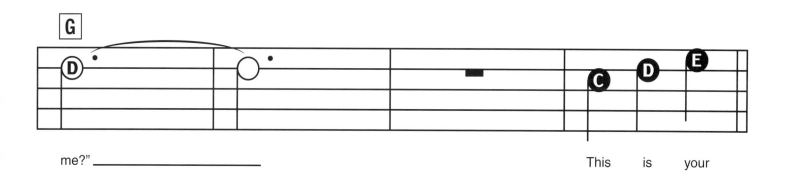

me?" _____ This is your

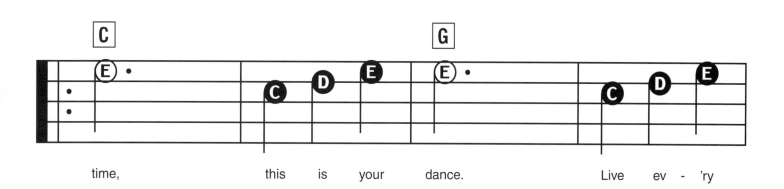

time, this is your dance. Live ev - 'ry

188

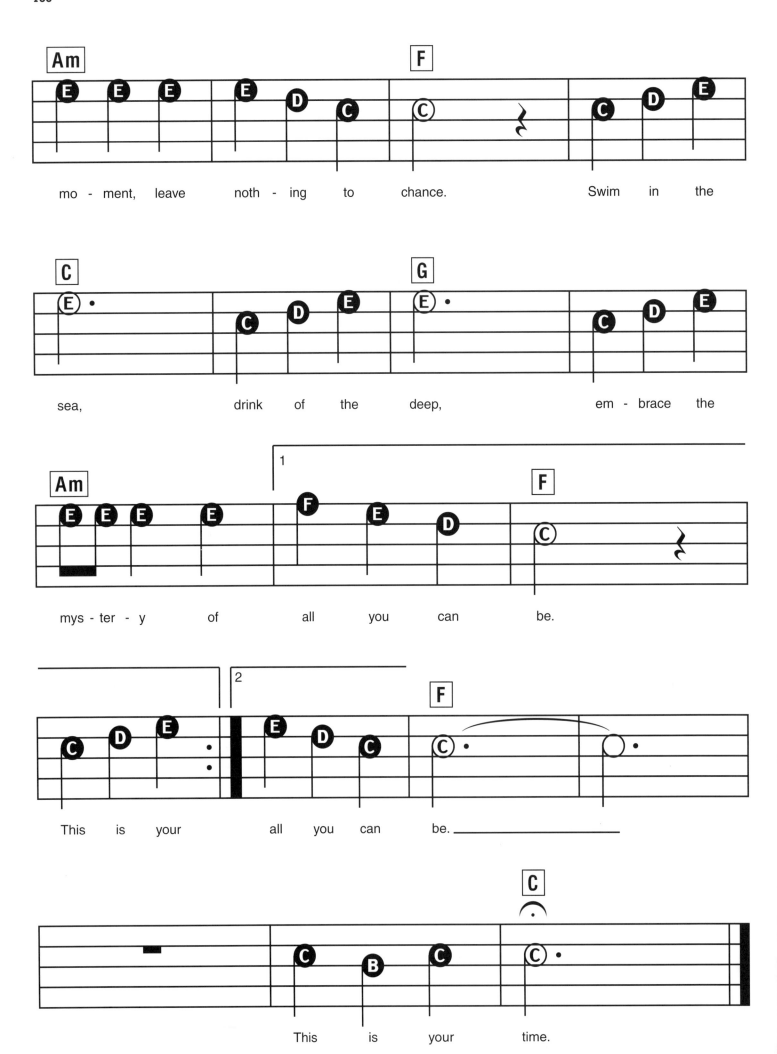

We Can Make a Difference

Registration 7
Rhythm: Pop or Funk

Words and Music by Mark Heimermann
and David Mullen

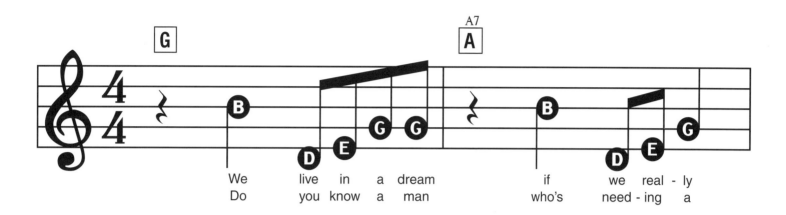

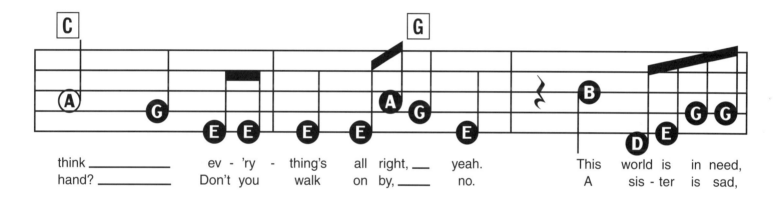

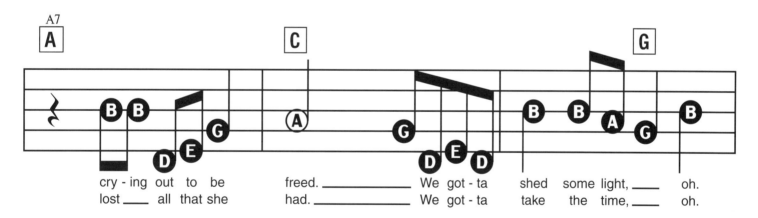

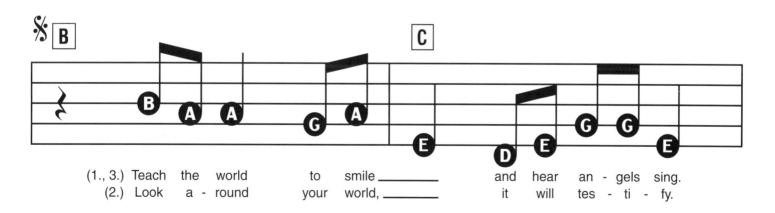

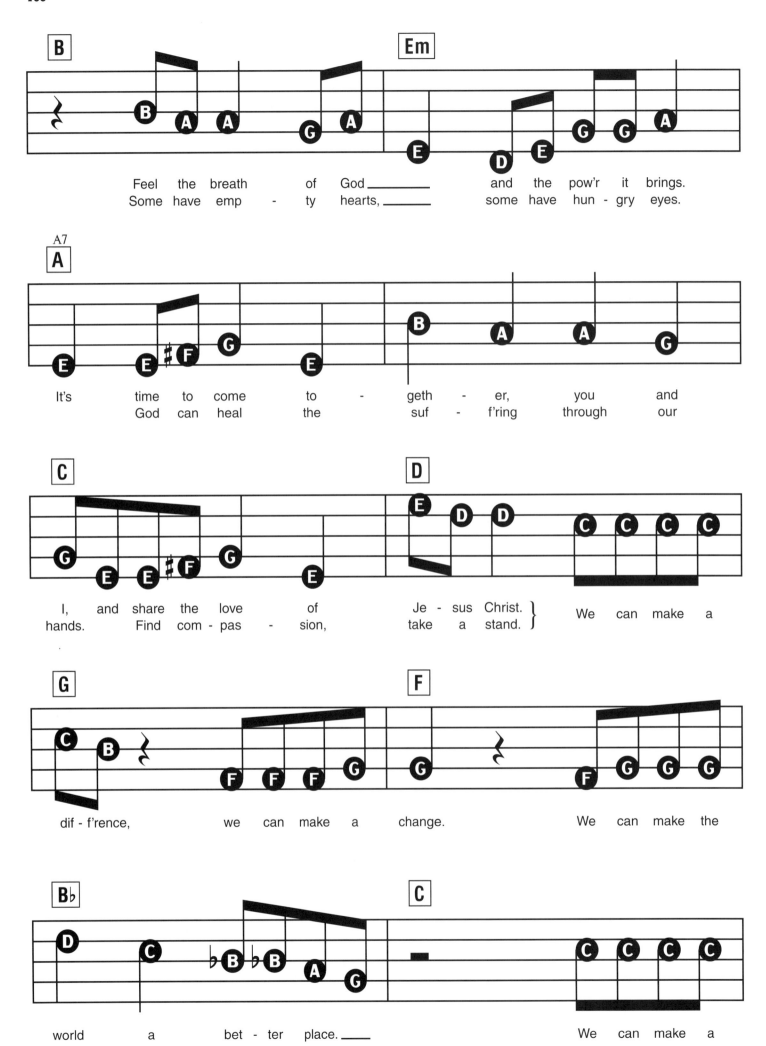

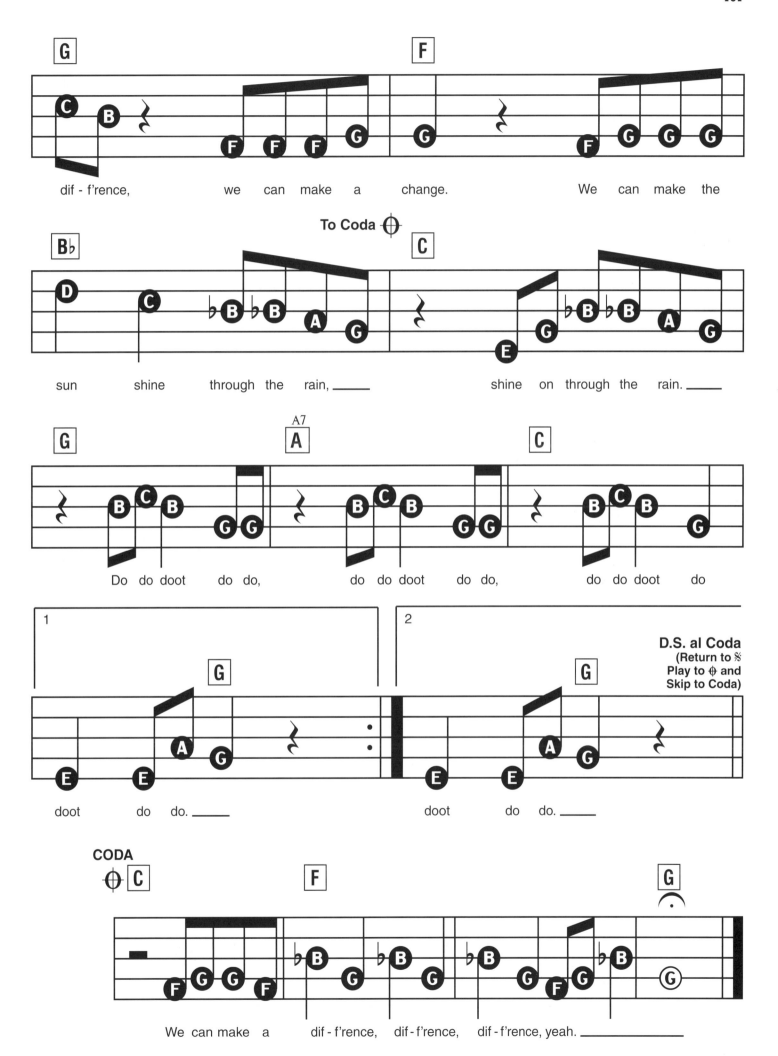

This Mystery

Registration 8
Rhythm: 8 Beat

Words and Music by
Nichole Nordeman

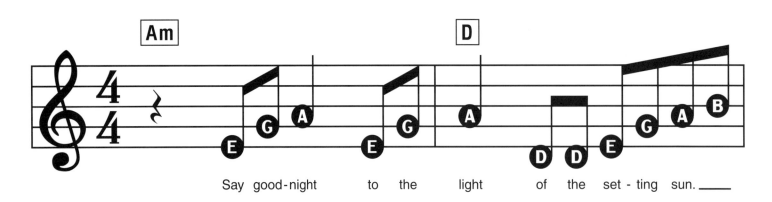

Say good-night to the light of the set-ting sun. _____

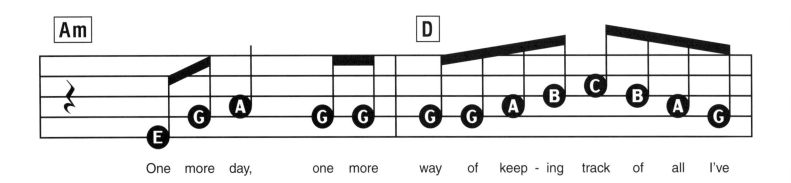

One more day, one more way of keep-ing track of all I've

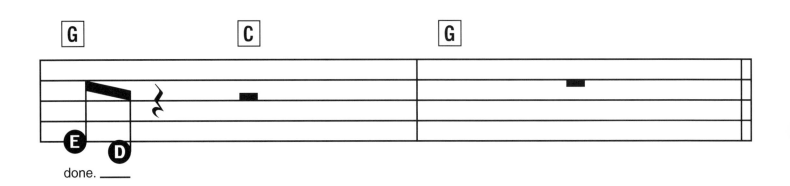

done. _____

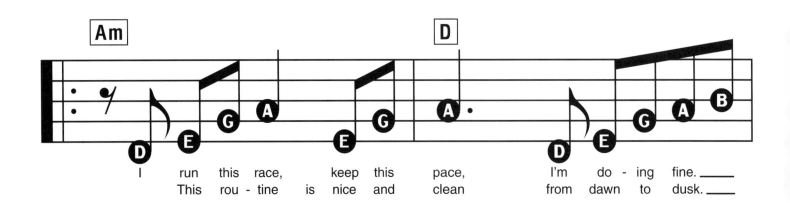

I run this race, keep this pace, I'm do-ing fine. _____
This rou-tine is nice and clean from dawn to dusk. _____

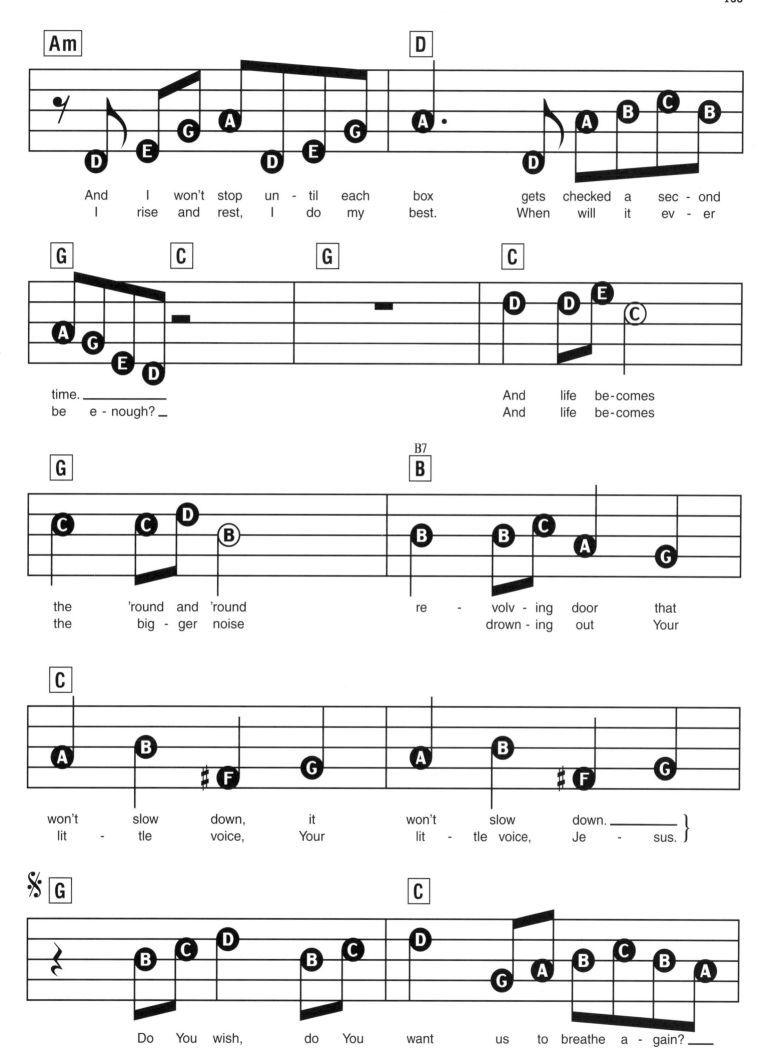

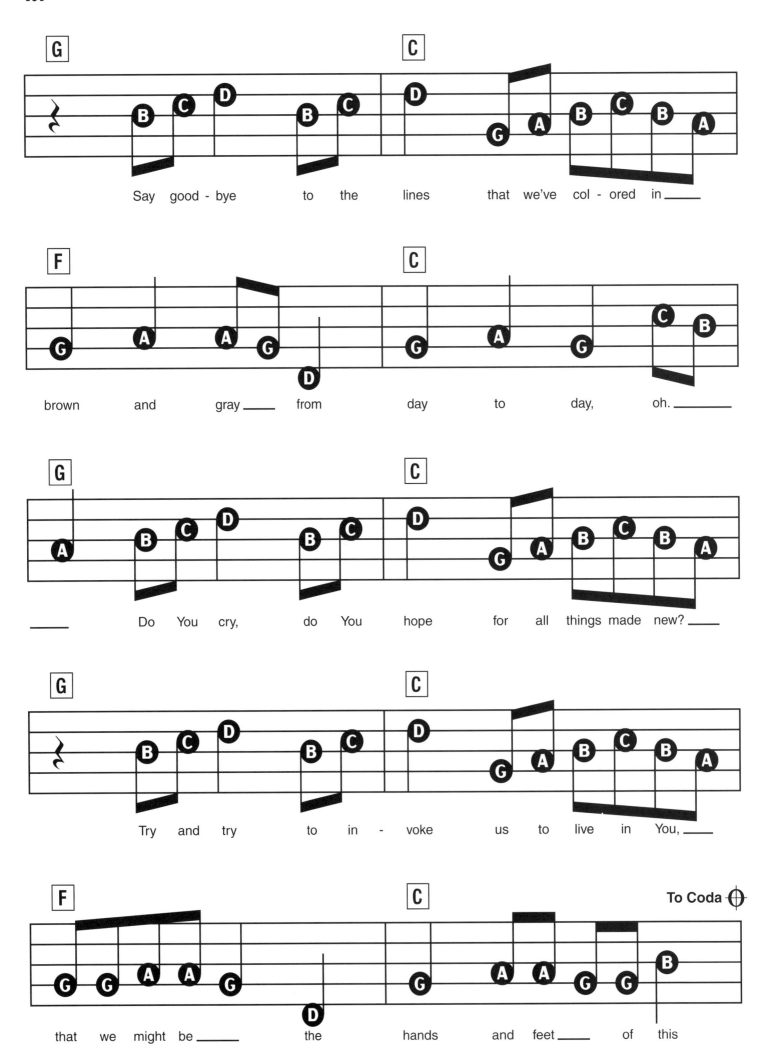

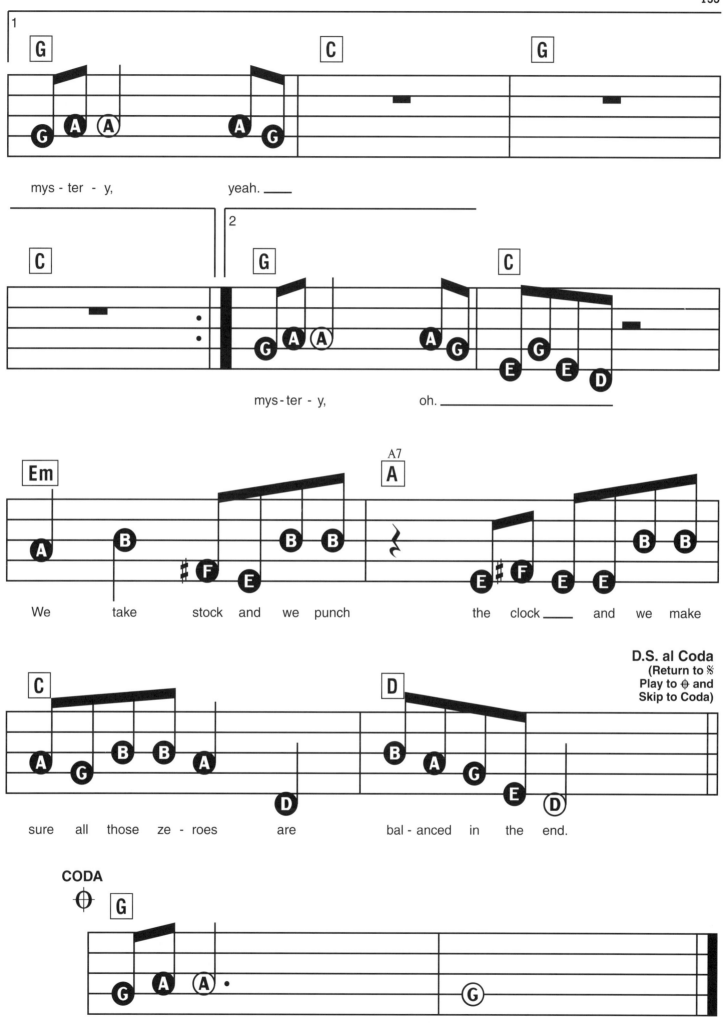

mys - ter - y,   yeah. ____

mys - ter - y,   oh. _____

We   take   stock   and   we   punch   the   clock ____ and   we   make

D.S. al Coda
(Return to %
Play to ⊕ and
Skip to Coda)

sure   all   those   ze - roes   are   bal - anced   in   the   end.

CODA

mys - ter - y. _____

Thy Word

Registration 5
Rhythm: Ballad

Words and Music by Michael W. Smith
and Amy Grant

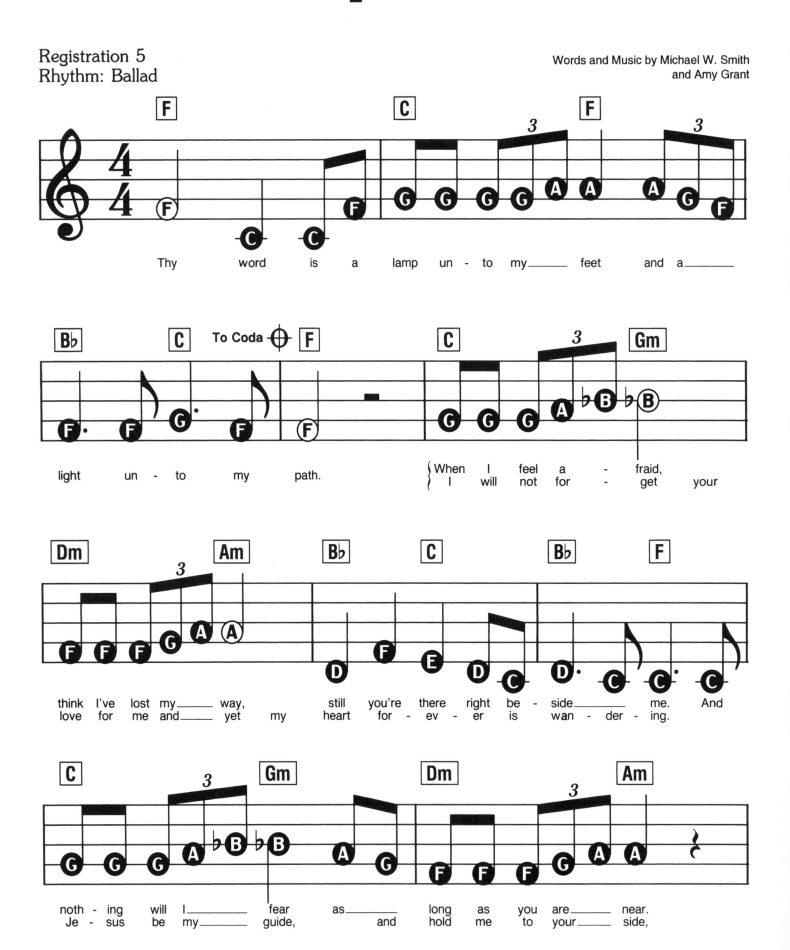

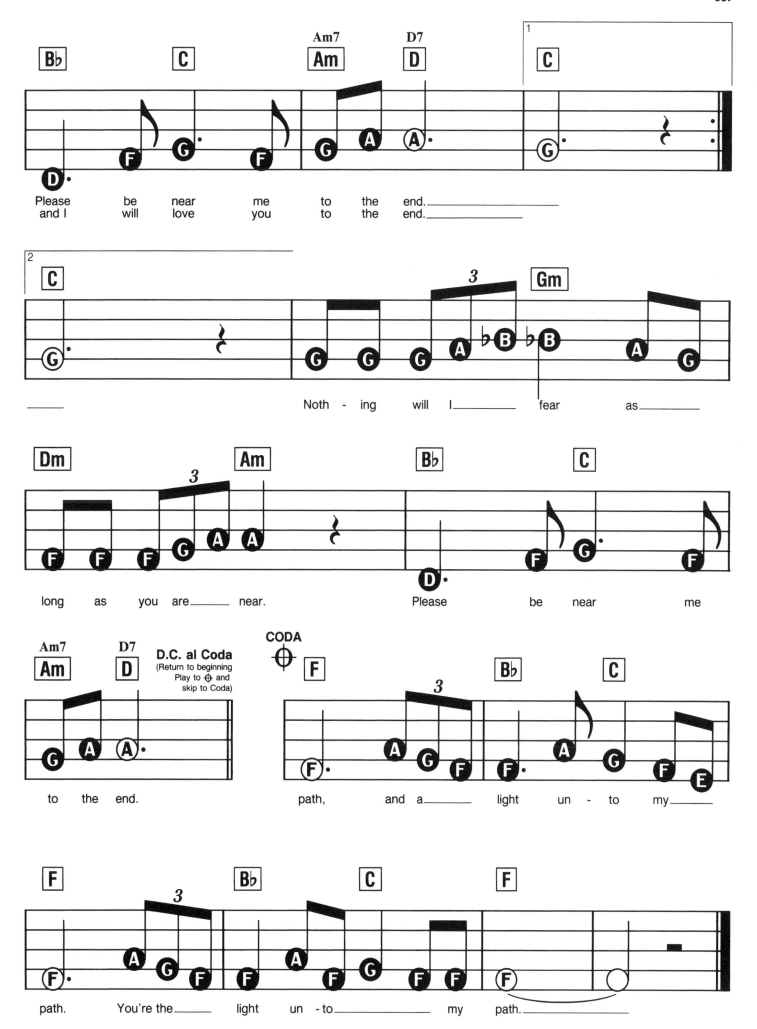

Via Dolorosa

Registration 3
Rhythm: 8 Beat or Ballad

Words and Music by Billy Sprague
and Niles Borop

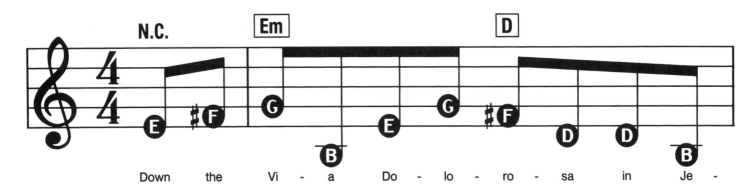

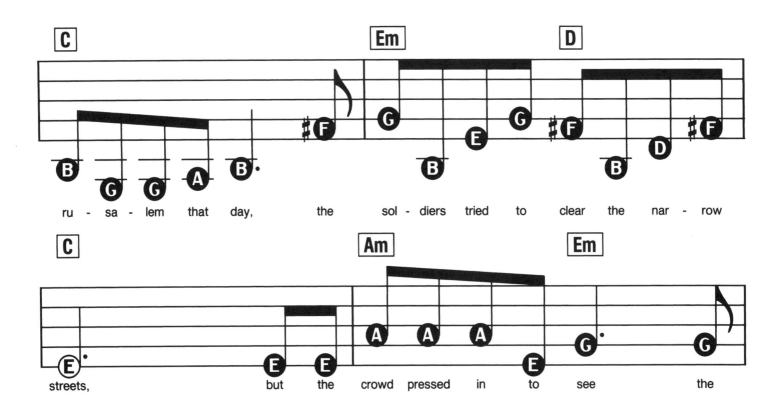

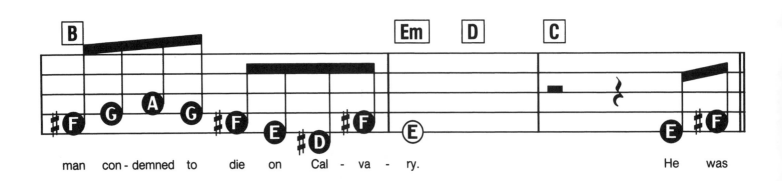

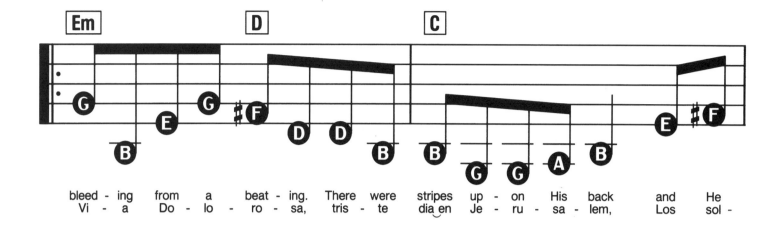

bleed - ing from a beat - ing. There were stripes up - on His back, and He
Vi - a Do - lo - ro - sa, tris - te dia en Je - ru - sa - lem, Los sol -

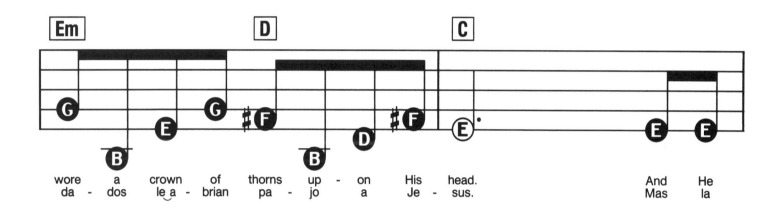

wore a crown of thorns up - on His head. And He
da - dos le a - brian pa - jo a Je - sus. Mas la

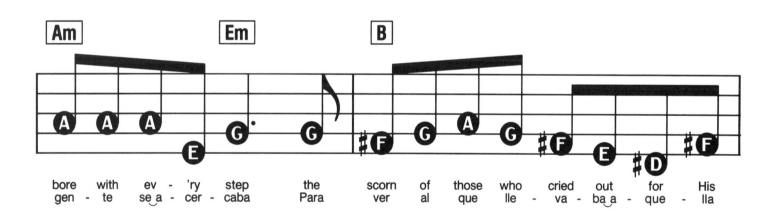

bore with ev - 'ry step the scorn of those who cried out for His
gen - te se a - cer - caba Para ver al que lle - va - ba a - que lla

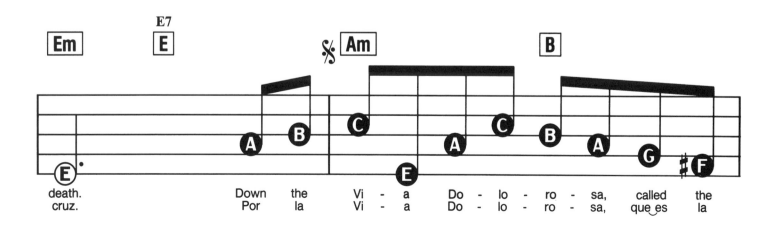

death. Down the Vi - a Do - lo - ro - sa, called the
cruz. Por la Vi - a Do - lo - ro - sa, que es la

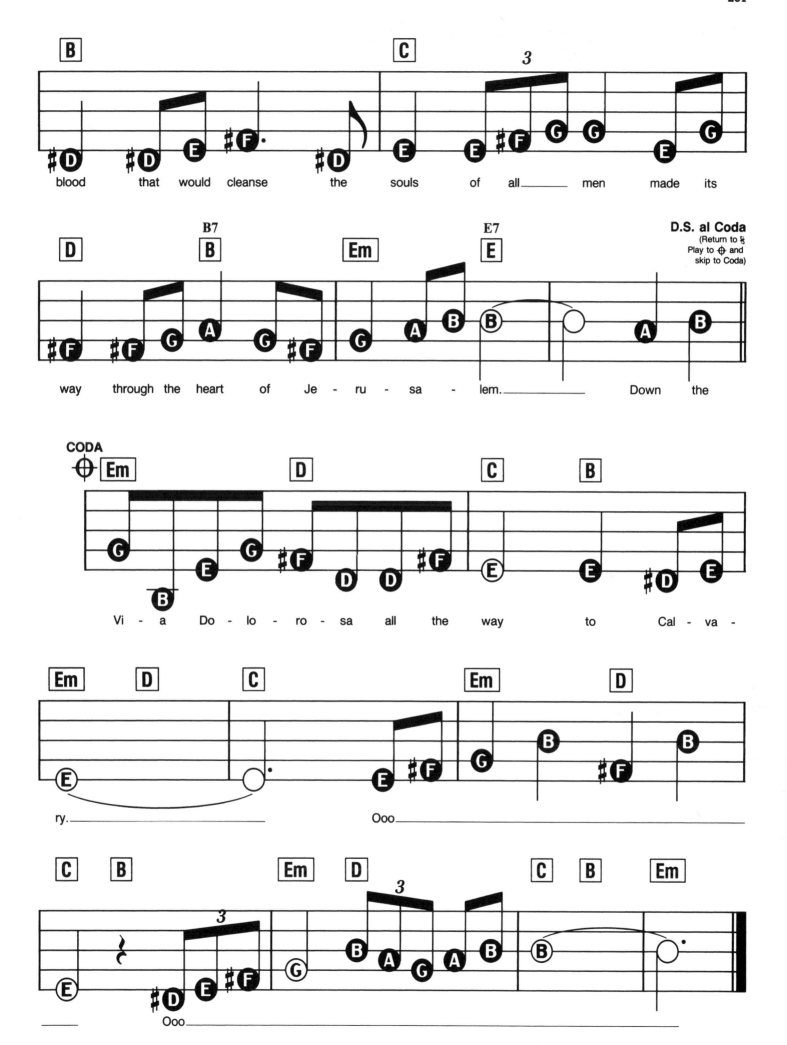

The Warrior Is a Child

Registration 4
Rhythm: Rock

Words and Music by
Twila Paris

C   **F**

B   C   D   C   B   C   B   A   A   A   A

Late - ly I've____ been win - ning bat - tles left and right.
Un - a - fraid____ be - cause His ar - mor is the best.

G   **C**

G   B   C   D   C   B   C

But e - ven win - ners can get
But e - ven sol - diers need a

F   **Dm7 / Dm**

B   A   A   A   A   A   G   G   E

wound - ed in the fight. Peo - ple say that
qui - et place to rest. Peo - ple say that

C   *3*   **F**

A   G   G   E   D   C   A   G   G   E   G

I'm a - maz - ing,____ strong be - yond my years.____
I'm a - maz - ing,____ nev - er face re - treat.____

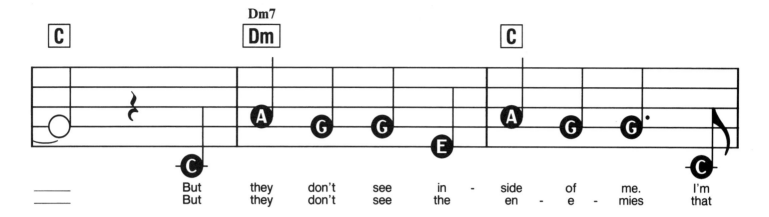
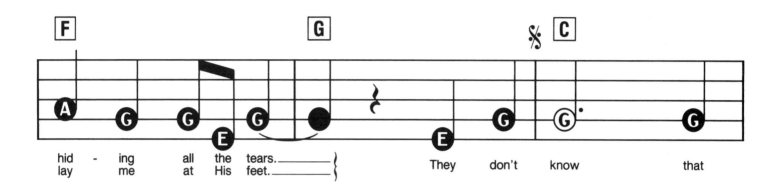
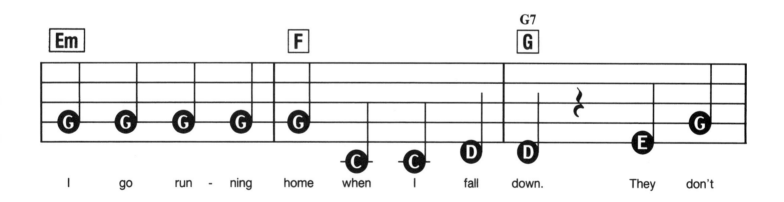
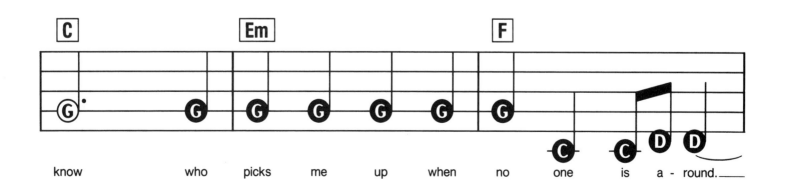

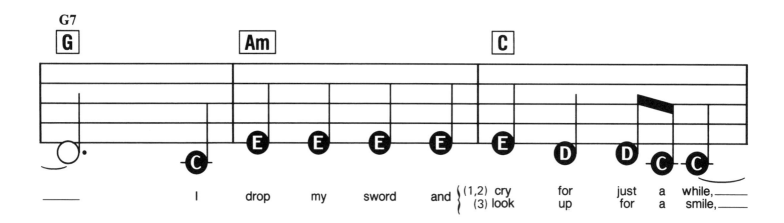

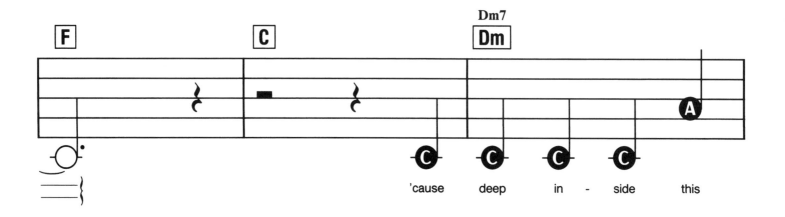

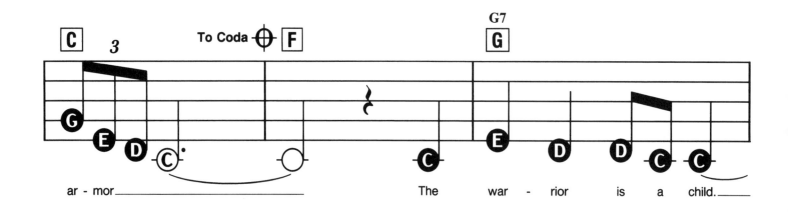

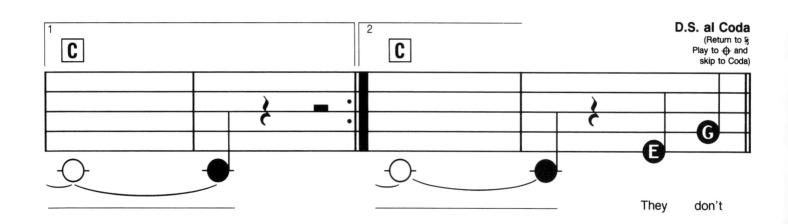

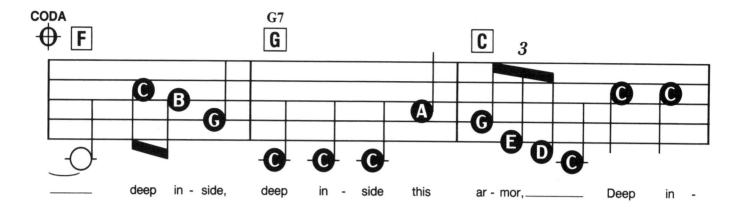

deep in - side, deep in - side this ar - mor,_____ Deep in -

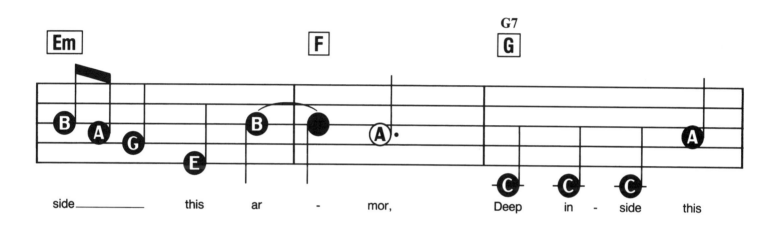

side_____ this ar - mor, Deep in - side this

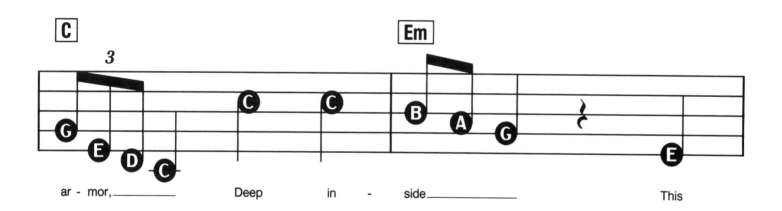

ar - mor,_____ Deep in - side_____ This

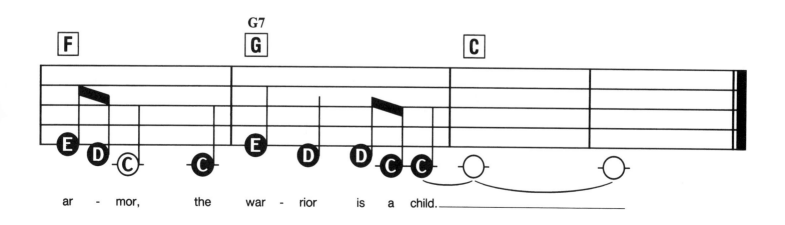

ar - mor, the war - rior is a child._____

Where There Is Faith

Registration 3
Rhythm: Ballad or 8 Beat

Words and Music by
Billy Simon

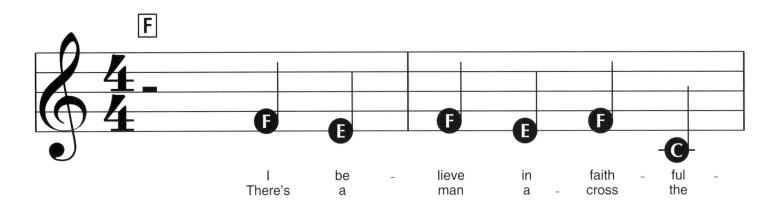

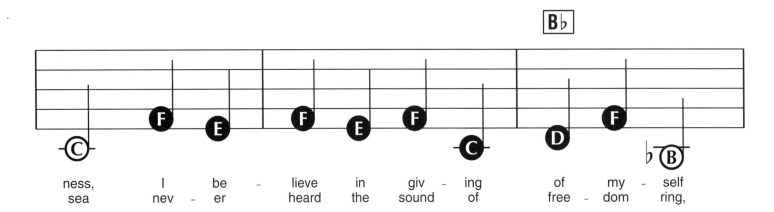

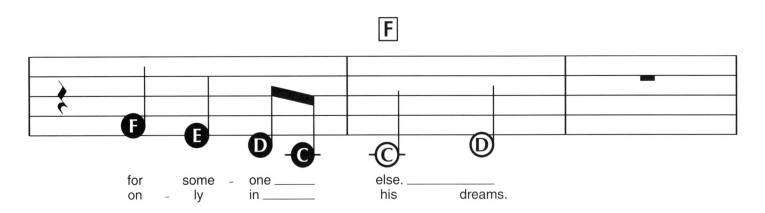

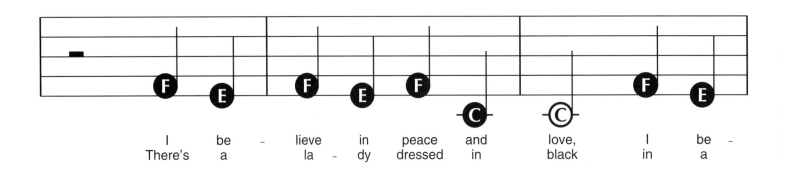

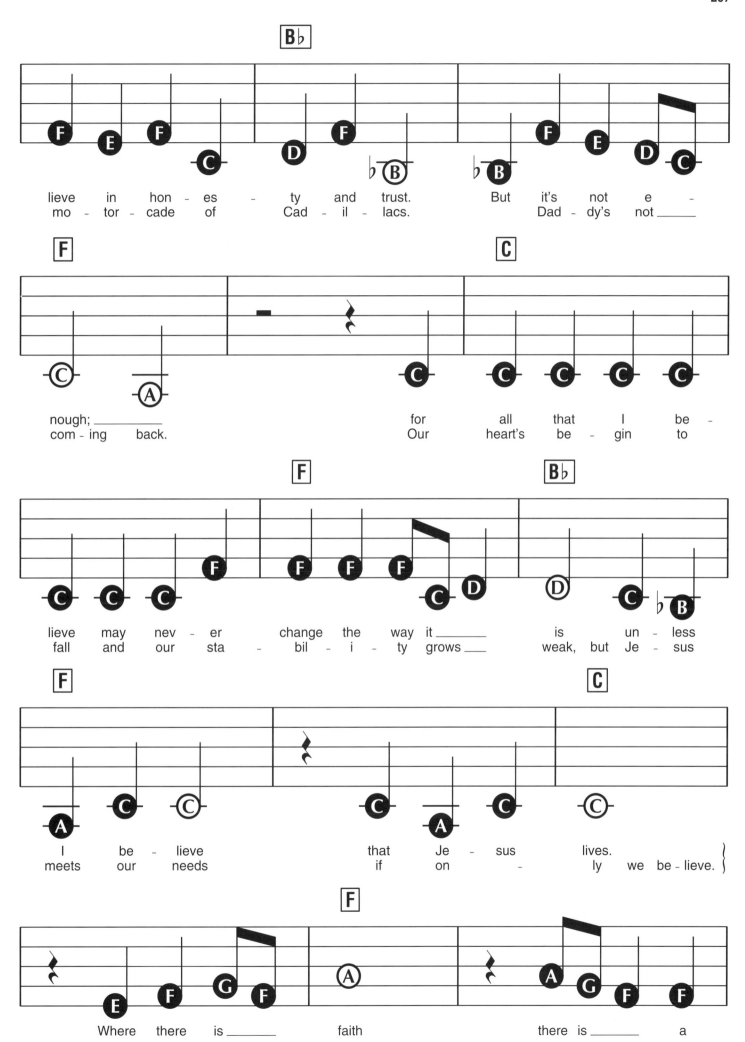

208

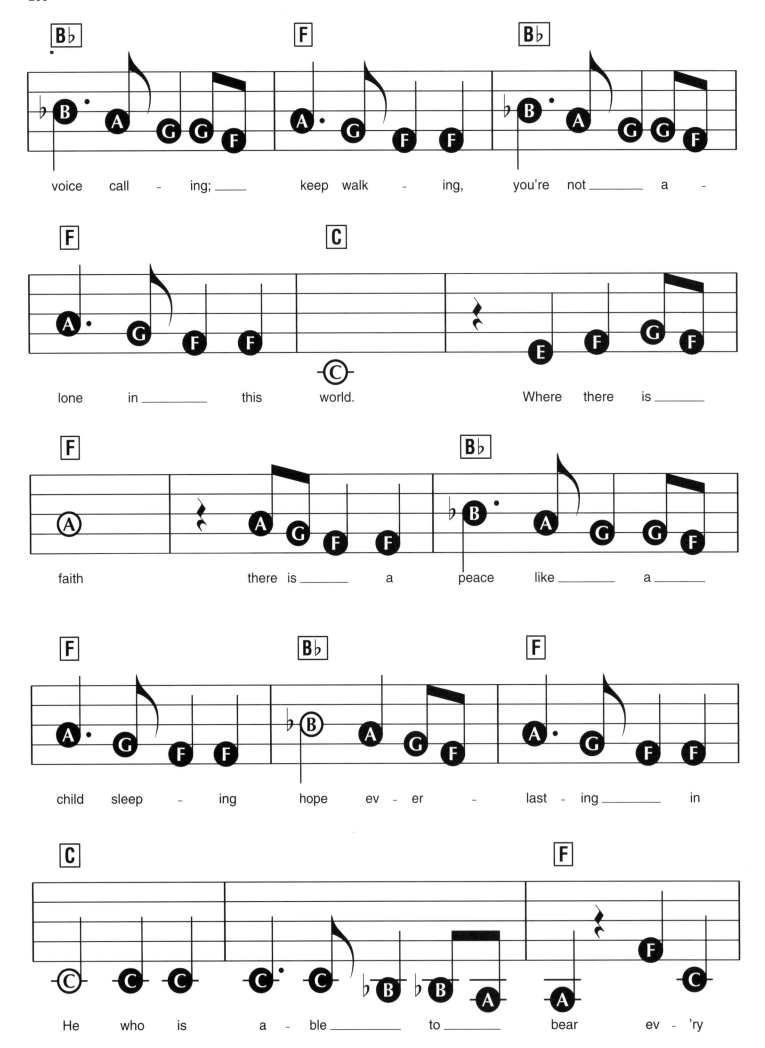

209

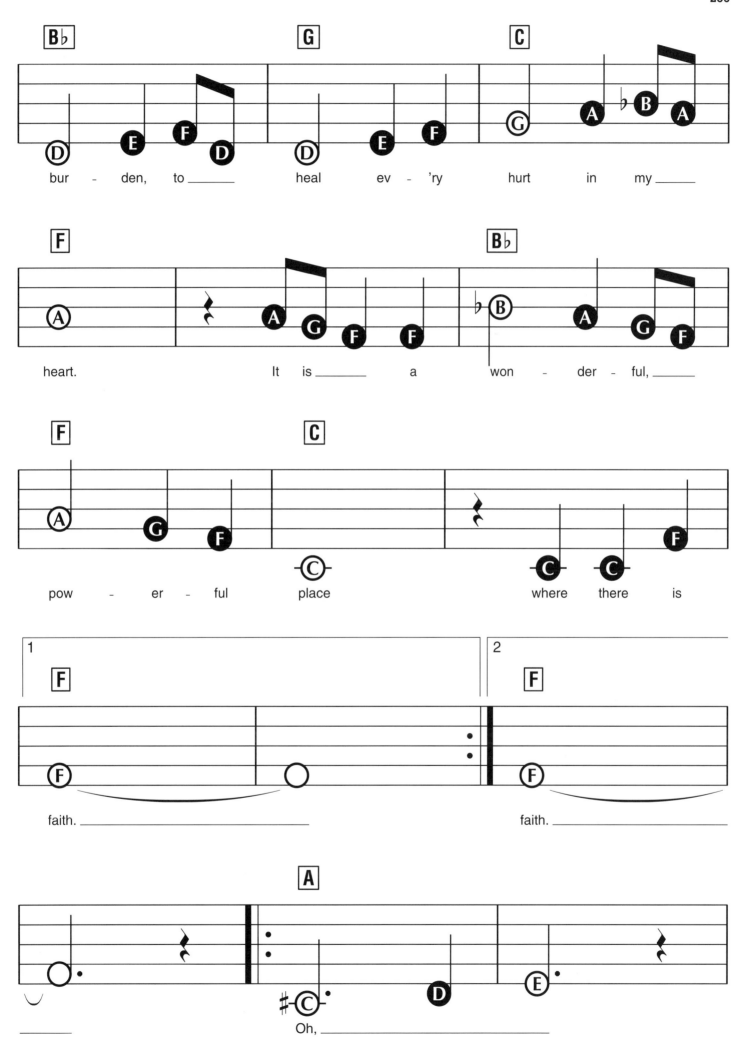

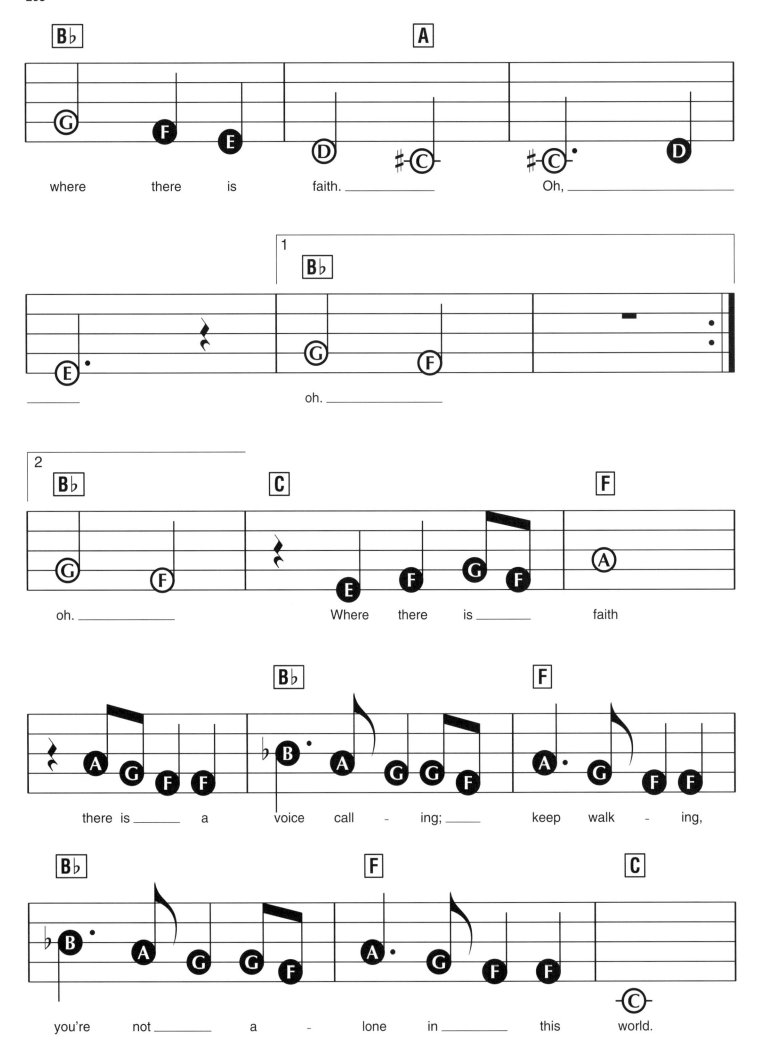

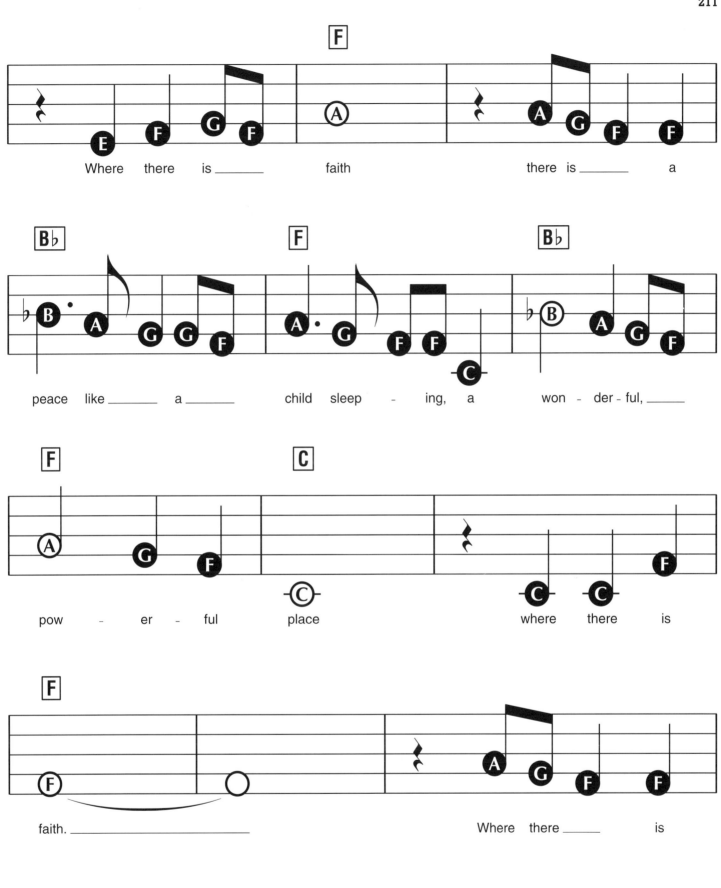

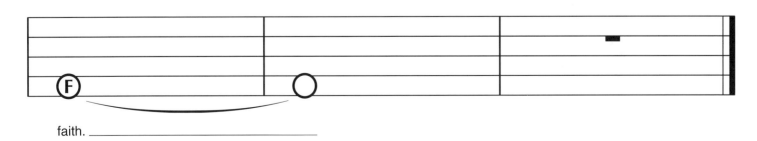

Wisdom

Registration 8
Rhythm: Pop

Words and Music by
Twila Paris

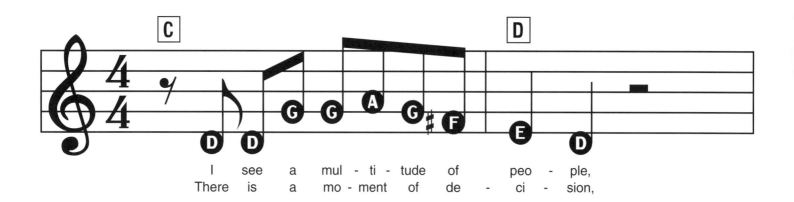

I see a mul - ti - tude of peo - ple,
There is a mo - ment of de - ci - sion,

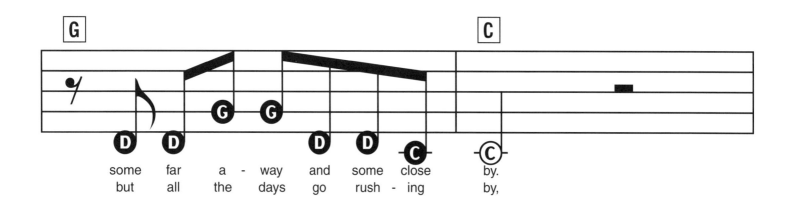

some far a - way and some close by.
but all the days go rush - ing by,

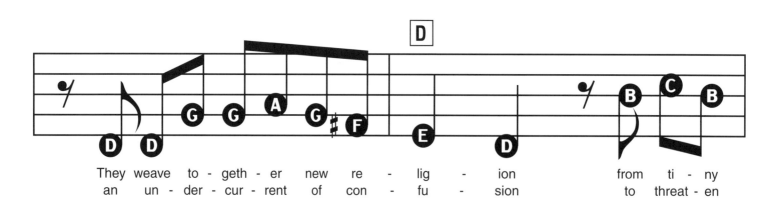

They weave to - geth - er new re - lig - ion from ti - ny
an un - der - cur - rent of con - fu - sion to threat - en

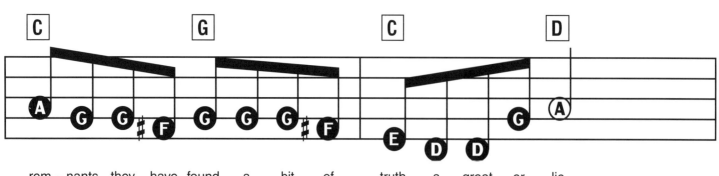

rem - nants they have found, a bit of truth, a great - er lie.
all that we be - lieve, with lit - tle time to won - der why.

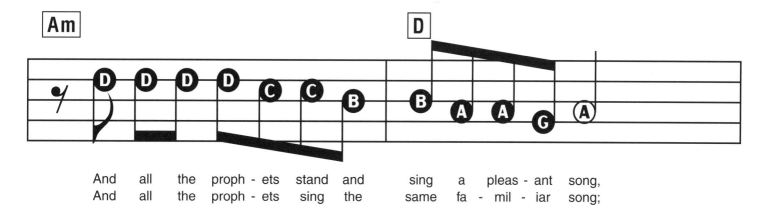

And all the proph - ets stand and sing a pleas - ant song,
And all the proph - ets sing the same fa - mil - iar song;

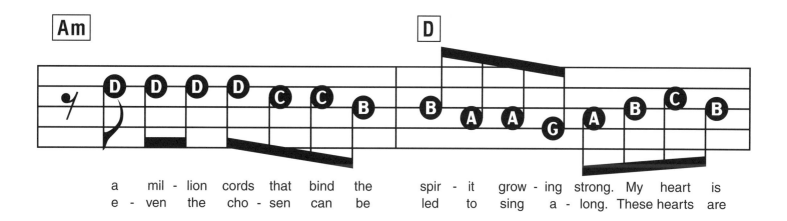

a mil - lion cords that bind the spir - it grow - ing strong. My heart is
e - ven the cho - sen can be led to sing a - long. These hearts are

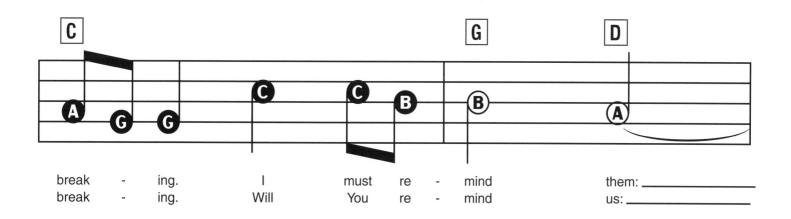

break - ing. I must re - mind them: _____
break - ing. Will You re - mind us: _____

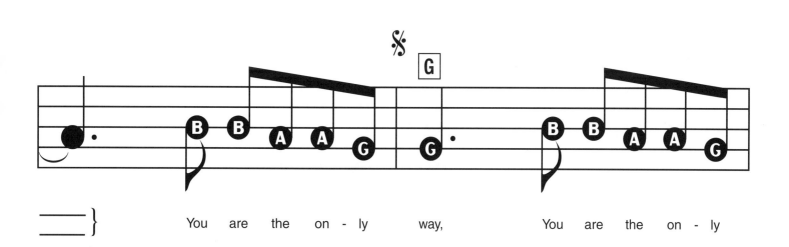

_____ } You are the on - ly way, You are the on - ly

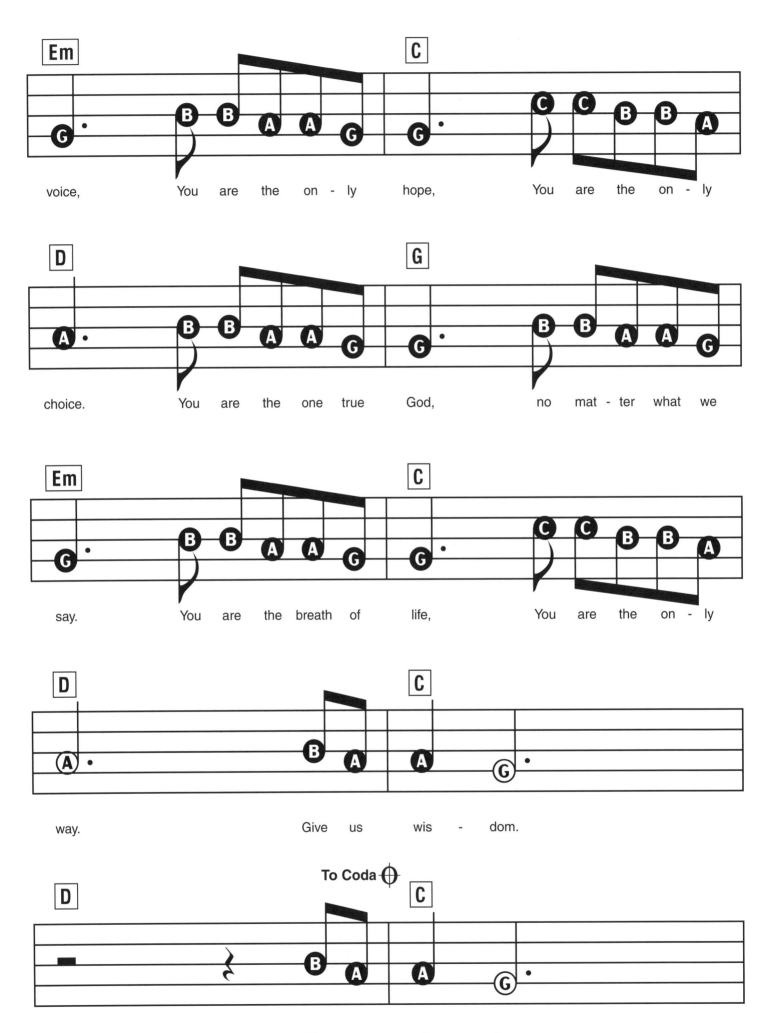

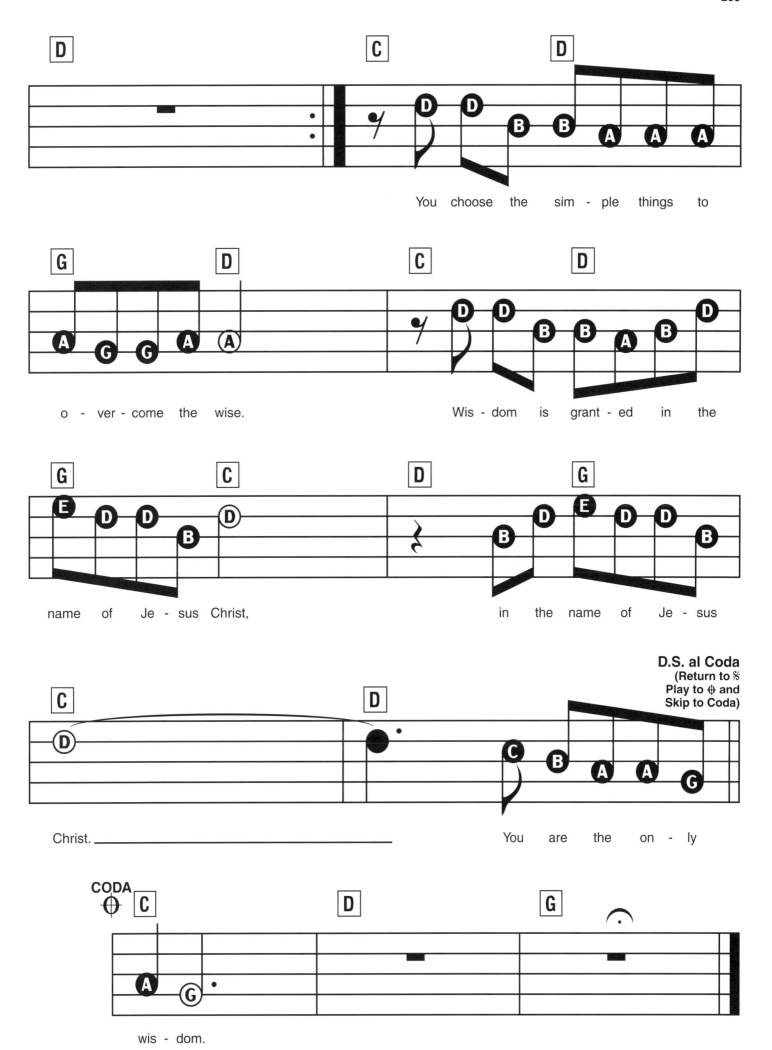

Registration Guide

- Match the Registration number on the song to the corresponding numbered category below. Select and activate an instrumental sound available on your instrument.

- Choose an automatic rhythm appropriate to the mood and style of the song. (Consult your Owner's Guide for proper operation of automatic rhythm features.)

- Adjust the tempo and volume controls to comfortable settings.

Registration

1	Mellow	Flutes, Clarinet, Oboe, Flugel Horn, Trombone, French Horn, Organ Flutes
2	Ensemble	Brass Section, Sax Section, Wind Ensemble, Full Organ, Theater Organ
3	Strings	Violin, Viola, Cello, Fiddle, String Ensemble, Pizzicato, Organ Strings
4	Guitars	Acoustic/Electric Guitars, Banjo, Mandolin, Dulcimer, Ukulele, Hawaiian Guitar
5	Mallets	Vibraphone, Marimba, Xylophone, Steel Drums, Bells, Celesta, Chimes
6	Liturgical	Pipe Organ, Hand Bells, Vocal Ensemble, Choir, Organ Flutes
7	Bright	Saxophones, Trumpet, Mute Trumpet, Synth Leads, Jazz/Gospel Organs
8	Piano	Piano, Electric Piano, Honky Tonk Piano, Harpsichord, Clavi
9	Novelty	Melodic Percussion, Wah Trumpet, Synth, Whistle, Kazoo, Perc. Organ
10	Bellows	Accordion, French Accordion, Mussette, Harmonica, Pump Organ, Bagpipes